Learning and Teaching Mathematics 0-8

Learning and Teaching Mathematics 0-8

Edited by
Helen Taylor
and Andrew Harris

Los Angeles | London | New Delhi
Singapore | Washington DC

Los Angeles | London | New Delhi
Singapore | Washington DC

SAGE Publications Ltd
1 Oliver's Yard
55 City Road
London EC1Y 1SP

SAGE Publications Inc.
2455 Teller Road
Thousand Oaks, California 91320

SAGE Publications India Pvt Ltd
B 1/I 1 Mohan Cooperative Industrial Area
Mathura Road
New Delhi 110 044

SAGE Publications Asia-Pacific Pte Ltd
3 Church Street
#10-04 Samsung Hub
Singapore 049483

Commissioning editor: Jude Bowen
Associate editor: Miriam Davey
Production editor: Nicola Marshall
Copyeditor: Rosemary Campbell
Proofreader: Fabienne Pedroletti Gray
Indexer: Martin Hargreaves
Marketing manager: Catherine Slinn
Cover design: Wendy Scott
Typeset by: C&M Digitals (P) Ltd, Chennai, India
Printed and bound in Great Britain by Ashford
Colour Press Ltd

First edition published 2014

Library of Congress Control Number: 2013935225

British Library Cataloguing in Publication data

A catalogue record for this book is available from
the British Library

ISBN 978-1-4462-5331-1
ISBN 978-1-4462-5332-8 (pbk)

Contents

List of Figures

Acknowledgements

We would like to thank family members, friends and colleagues of the authors, including Maria Elsam. Special thanks go to the children, staff and parents of the following Kent primary schools: Godinton Primary (especially Rachel Taylor), Ightham Primary, Wingham Primary, Lunsford Primary, Capel Primary, Slade Primary and Hadlow Primary. All have kindly given their permission to include photographs, our observations and their work.

About the Editors and Contributors

Helen Taylor is the Primary Lead Tutor for Teach First at Canterbury Christ Church University. Her work also involves teaching primary mathematics to student teachers and mentor training for experienced teachers supporting students during their professional placements. She has taught across the age range in primary schools in Kent and was a deputy head teacher.

Andrew Harris is a Senior Lecturer at Canterbury Christ Church University, teaching primary mathematics on undergraduate and postgraduate programmes. Previously, he was the Joint Programme Leader for the PGCE Part-time/Modular programme at University College of St Martin and taught in primary schools in Derbyshire and Gloucestershire. His research focuses on mathematical knowledge for teaching, the selection, sequencing and use of examples in teaching mathematics and progression in calculation strategies.

The contributors

Gina Donaldson was a primary classroom teacher for 11 years, teaching across the primary phase. She is now a Senior Lecturer at Canterbury Christ Church University, teaching primary mathematics to student teachers. She leads a Mathematics programme at Masters level, working with practising teachers across Kent, Medway and Essex seeking the status of Primary Mathematics Specialist Teacher.

Jill Matthews has recently retired from her Senior Lecturer post at Canterbury Christ Church University, where she coordinated the Year 3 BA (Hons) in Primary Education. She taught primary mathematics to undergraduate student teachers. She held the role of BA Year 3 Partnership Placement Tutor for many years, supporting students on their professional placements. Her research interests relate to language development and 'talk for learning', particularly within the context of mathematics, and she is currently completing her PhD.

Louise O'Sullivan is Head of School Partnership at Canterbury Christ Church University. She is particularly involved in supporting student teachers on their professional placements. Louise is interested in supporting teachers, both qualified and unqualified, in improving their mathematics teaching. She also teaches mathematics on PGCE and undergraduate programmes and is particularly interested in children's approaches to number, calculation and measures.

Bridie Price is a Senior Lecturer at Canterbury Christ Church University teaching both primary mathematics and primary art. She also has a special interest in the use of display in primary schools. Bridie has taught in primary schools in London and Kent and has been a deputy head teacher and acting head teacher.

Paula Stone is a Senior Lecturer in Primary Education. She teaches professional studies and primary mathematics on undergraduate and postgraduate programmes, and employment-based routes into teaching. Paula specialises in teaching enhanced primary mathematics courses and encourages her students to contribute to the mathematics community through publication in subject association magazines. She has made regular contributions to the NCETM Primary Magazine.

Karen Vincent worked as a teacher in early years, primary and secondary education for 17 years before taking up a post as a Senior Lecturer in the Department of Primary Education at Canterbury Christ Church University in 2010. She teaches across a range of primary teacher training programmes specialising in Early Years education. Her research interests include young children's perceptions of learning and the transition between Year R and Year 1. She is Programme Director for the Primary Education Progression Route.

Jon Wild has worked in the primary education sector for over 25 years, co-ordinating mathematics, science and ICT, before moving successfully into leadership and management as a deputy head teacher and head teacher. His interest in initial teacher education and continuing professional development led him to Canterbury Christ Church University where he teaches in the primary mathematics team. Jon has a special interest in mathematics and ICT, particularly in using ICT to enhance effective teaching and management within schools.

Clare Wiseman is a Senior Lecturer in the Department of Childhood Studies at Canterbury Christ Church University. She previously lectured on both the undergraduate and postgraduate initial teacher education programmes. Prior to joining Canterbury Christ Church University, Clare was a Primary Mathematics Consultant for Kent Local Authority. Previously, she had taught across Foundation Stage, Key Stage 1 and Key Stage 2 in Kent primary schools for 12 years.

Introduction

Children encounter mathematical ideas in everyday life from birth onwards. Babies quickly learn to distinguish differences in numerical quantities and begin to explore the shapes of the objects and spaces around them. As children develop, mathematics increasingly provides skills, models and ways of thinking which can be used to interpret and describe the contexts and objects they experience and to solve problems. Developing a good understanding of early mathematical ideas provides a foundation for success in everyday tasks and in increased employment and education prospects when reaching adulthood.

To fully understand the mathematical teaching and learning for the 0–8 age group, we need both a secure personal knowledge of the mathematics involved and an understanding of how children learn mathematics and of the range of teaching approaches (pedagogy) which will best support their learning. This book is written to help you to develop your understanding of teaching and learning of mathematics for the 0–8 age group. As you read the book, you will also encounter a range of effective, interesting and engaging approaches to promote mathematical learning for young children. Fostering an enthusiasm for mathematics and mathematical confidence in young children is a vital part of supporting their mathematical development.

The book is divided into two main parts. Part 1 addresses specific issues associated with the learning and teaching of mathematics from birth to age 8. In Part 2 we explore the progression in learning about different areas of mathematics encountered by young children and discuss possible approaches to teaching and suggested activities to support learning. Throughout Parts 1 and 2 of the book we have discussed the role of problem solving as a central aspect of mathematical learning.

Each chapter begins with an overview of the chapter material. Case studies provide illustrations of particular aspects of learning or teaching which are then analysed in order to offer insights about key principles for effective practice. Significant research is highlighted in each chapter to help you apply the findings to your own professional context and practice. In each chapter, prompts are provided to encourage you to reflect about the practice you have experienced and to consider ways in which practice may be enhanced. Each chapter ends with a summary and suggestions for further reading which you can explore to extend your understanding. You can find a glossary of mathematical terms used in each chapter at the end of the book.

Part 1

Issues in Mathematical Learning and Teaching

How Children Learn Mathematics and the Implications for Teaching

Helen Taylor

 Chapter Overview

In this chapter you can read about:

- Why and how young children learn mathematics
- The importance of practical activities
- Starting with children's interests
- Children solving problems
- The progression of children's mathematical ideas from birth to 8 years old.

The nature of mathematics and young children learning

- What do you think mathematics is?
- Is it appropriate and important for very young children?
- At what age do you think children should start learning mathematical ideas?
- How can adults help?

Mathematics is defined as 'the abstract science of number, quantity and space' by *The Concise Oxford Dictionary* (Allen, 1990: 732). It can be seen as a way of organising ideas in order to develop concepts. Skemp (1971) identified that having a concept involves more than knowing its name; it involves being able to use the understanding developed from recognition of similarities between particular examples of the concept. Freudenthal (1973) argued that children develop concepts as a result of experiences and thinking about those experiences. This may seem remote from children aged from birth to 8, however babies and young children are naturally curious and explore their world from an early age. They do not compartmentalise their explorations as mathematical or otherwise. However, they will encounter mathematical ideas such as number, quantity and shape. Mathematics is an essential area of understanding and knowledge in our everyday lives as adults and this is also true for children. The National Curriculum (DfEE, 1999a: 60) states 'Mathematics equips pupils with a uniquely powerful set of tools to understand and change the world. These tools include logical reasoning, problem solving skills and the ability to think in abstract ways'. Lee (2006) states that mathematics empowers and enables us to take control of various aspects of our lives. It is also a creative discipline, capable of being used flexibly to communicate precisely. Mathematics can also be seen as a web of ideas that are continually refined and developed. According to ACME (2008: 4) the 'big ideas' of mathematics for young children include 'place value and the number system, conservation of number and measures, equivalence relations and dimensionality' (see chapters in Part 2).

Parents and carers will often intuitively draw young children's attention to mathematical ideas by pointing out and talking about numbers, quantities, shapes and sizes as part of everyday life. This will be continued when they sing and recite rhymes to, and with, their children and as they play with their children using a variety of toys and objects (for example, wooden bricks and other construction toys, soft toys, small-world toys and toy versions of real objects like tea sets). Mathematics features in the routines of everyday life, such as getting dressed and putting on two socks or laying the table and getting three plates out. Children begin to use vocabulary that reflects understanding of mathematics such as when they ask for more chocolate, sweets or chips. From these early mathematical experiences and ideas, children will gradually extend their understanding to more formal mathematics.

How do young children learn mathematics?

A number of theorists have proposed ideas about how children learn generally, and these ideas can be related to the learning of mathematics. Piaget (in Donaldson, 1978) believed that children construct their own knowledge and understanding through their interactions with their environment. This is called a constructivist theory.

Vygotsky (in Atherton, 2011) is often referred to as a social constructivist. He emphasised the need for a child to have guidance from a 'more knowledgeable other' and to have opportunities to interact socially with peers as a means of learning. He also proposed the idea of the 'Zone of Proximal Development', which is that a child can work with someone else to achieve something that they could not achieve on their own, thereby learning through this process so that eventually they are able to perform the task by themselves. This is sometimes called scaffolding (Bruner, 1966; Wood, 1998). Similarly, Gifford (2008) refers to cumulative learning, meaning that learning needs to build on previously learnt ideas and that presenting children with something too advanced will not be effective.

Mathematical learning is associated with the development of mathematical understanding. Barmby et al. (2009) see this as a continuum where children add to and refine previous understandings. This builds on the work of Bruner (1966) who identified the idea of the spiral curriculum, where children meet an idea at one level and then later meet the idea again but are able to study it at a deeper level and achieve a better understanding of it. His influence can be seen in many mathematics curricula documents and in the practice of teaching mathematics. Bruner also suggested that children go through three phases when learning. The enactive phase is when children engage with something concrete in order to explore and manipulate ideas; this could be related to kinaesthetic learning. The second phase, iconic, is when children begin representing the ideas in a more abstract way. This can be supported in mathematics by using models and images so that eventually children can visualise some of them internally to assist their thinking. Finally, children come to the symbolic phase where they can use abstract ideas and ways of representing the mathematics.

Liebeck's (1984) ELPS approach is related to Bruner's enactive, iconic, symbolic phases in some ways. The E stands for Experience – children need practical experience of the ideas to start with. L is for language, and this is where Liebeck's approach differs from Bruner's; Liebeck emphasises the need for children to learn the language of mathematics, highlighting the need for adults and children to talk about the ideas. She then recommends that children go on to represent mathematical ideas through pictures (P) or diagrams before moving on to formal recording of mathematics through the use of symbols (S). Similarly, Gifford (2008) emphasises the importance of multisensory experiences for learning. Froebel (in Beckley, 2011) also emphasised the importance of practical activity for children's learning, including gardening and use of building blocks. This influence can be clearly seen currently in many nursery settings in the UK.

Skemp (1971) described two ways of understanding mathematical ideas that he called 'instrumental' and 'relational understanding'. Instrumental understanding is a shallower form of understanding. For example, we might develop an instrumental understanding of how to add, subtract, multiply and divide using a set procedure or algorithm by memorising the steps required. However, we might not understand how the procedure worked or why the various steps in the procedure are needed. One of the difficulties with this level of understanding is that if our memory of the procedure failed, we would be unable to continue. In contrast, a relational understanding of these procedures would mean that we understand how and why the procedures work.

The importance of practical activities

The work of Piaget, Bruner and Liebeck all emphasises practical activity as a starting point for learning with young children and Gifford (2008) reports neuroscientific support for this approach, too. Children are naturally curious and explore the world around them. They love to play. Adults working with young children can build on this in order to support mathematical development. One way to do this is to ensure that appropriate toys and other resources are available for children to play with and for the adults to recognise the mathematical potential of these toys and resources. Adults can then observe children interacting with the resources and provide additional resources or play alongside children using appropriate vocabulary and asking appropriate questions to maximise this potential.

- What sort of toys and resources will be helpful in supporting children's mathematical development?
- Do they have to be especially produced for mathematics?
- Which everyday toys that young children play with might also help to develop mathematical ideas?

CASE STUDY

Farm set

Oliver, aged 5, and Daniel, aged 3, both had identical new farm sets. They played together creating fields of different sizes and shapes with the eight fence sections. They created various shapes and sizes and arranged animals in the fields talking about how many animals would fit and whether they wanted big or small animals in the various fields. In each set there was a tree and the boys sometimes included the trees as field boundaries to increase the different shapes they could produce. At one point they used a section of fence to create a common boundary between two fields, leaving two fence sections out. Oliver announced that they had a 'square field and a triangle field'. He went on to talk about the triangle field being smaller than the square field. Then he said that 'triangles are always smaller than squares'. I asked him if this was always true and said I thought I could draw a really big triangle. He rushed off to find pen and paper and drew the largest triangle he could on a sheet of A4 paper, then he cut this out. He then gradually cut into the triangle creating smaller and smaller triangles. He also drew three rectangles, which he called squares on another piece of paper and wrote 'small to [middle] size to big' and told me that he could draw squares in lots of sizes. Taking another piece of paper, he drew a series of five triangles, each one slightly larger than the one before, a similar set of six circles and finally four squares (see Figure 1.1). This demonstrates that he has a good understanding of ordering sizes and that a shape can come in any size, contradicting his previous statement that 'triangles are always smaller than squares'. Daniel, at 3 years old, did not choose to draw anything but was content to talk about the sizes of the animals describing them as big and little and counting a set of four big horses accurately. I attempted to develop his vocabulary by talking to him about 'middle-sized' animals; he appeared to listen but did not use this vocabulary himself.

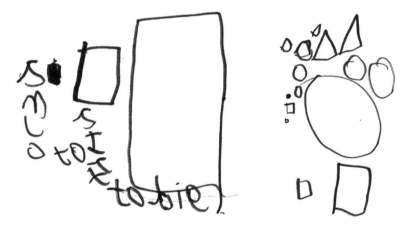

Figure 1.1 *Oliver's drawings of shapes of different sizes*

Resources, models and images

The case study is an example of the use of toys that are not made specifically for mathematics. However, various resources have been designed specifically for this purpose. Many of these are designed as models which, together with mathematical

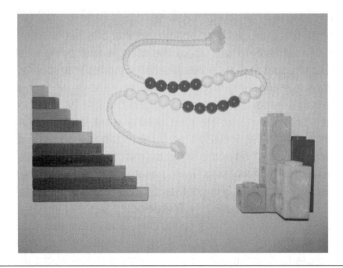

Figure 1.2   *Bead string, Cuisenaire rods and interlocking cubes*

talk, can support children in building up mental images of mathematical ideas. This type of resource includes objects such as interlocking cubes, Cuisenaire rods and bead strings (see Figure 1.2). Some paper-based resources are also published to support children in building up their own images and mathematical understanding. These include number lines and hundred squares. Delaney (2010) recommends that resources should be used in two different ways. One of these is by a teacher or adult for demonstration of an idea along with explanation. He also recommends that children should engage with resources, directly playing with them, handling them and talking about them so that they can build up their own conceptions of the mathematical ideas.

Higgins (2008) recommends that ICT can be helpful for children in learning about mathematical ideas, if it is carefully selected and accompanied by appropriate talk. Some computer programs can help children in counting and developing early calculation and ideas about shape. Calculators can also be judiciously used to support the development of mathematics, as can interactive whiteboards.

CASE STUDY

Hundred square

Children in a Reception Class aged 4 and 5, had been introduced to the hundred square (see Figure 1.3) by their teacher. Later in the week during a child-initiated session, a group of children chose to draw and make marks on mini whiteboards.

1	2	3	4	5	6	7	8	9	10
11	12	13	14	15	16	17	18	19	20
21	22	23	24	25	26	27	28	29	30
31	32	33	34	35	36	37	38	39	40
41	42	43	44	45	46	47	48	49	50
51	52	53	54	55	56	57	58	59	60
61	62	63	64	65	66	67	68	69	70
71	72	73	74	75	76	77	78	79	80
81	82	83	84	85	86	87	88	89	90
91	92	93	94	95	96	97	98	99	100

Figure 1.3 *Hundred square*

Harry (aged just 5) had chosen a whiteboard with a 10 x 10 grid marked on it. He fetched a copy of the hundred square that the children had been using previously. He started to write numbers on the whiteboard grid, trying to copy from the hundred square. He wrote 1 and 2 successfully then wrote 3 the wrong way round. He missed out some numbers and wrote some of the teens numbers in the top row. In the square under the number 1, he wrote 100, although he found it difficult to fit the three digits into the small square. I asked him to explain what he was doing. He did not appear to realise that he had missed writing some numbers but he appeared to have a good understanding of how the hundred square worked and how the numbers are traditionally arranged in it. Josh, aged 4 years and 11 months, came over to join in the conversation. He pointed out that the 100 should be in the bottom right-hand square and added 'because that is the end number'. He went on to say, however, that when we're counting 'We can go past one hundred [and] we can go on counting forever because it never stops'. Harry rubbed 100 out from the second row and wrote it in the bottom right-hand square. This demonstrated both children had been supported in their mathematical understanding through the use of the hundred square and that both had a good understanding for their age of the number system and how it works.

Starting with children's interests

It is important that children develop positive attitudes to mathematics in the early years; therefore they need to be interested and to enjoy mathematical activities and experiences.

Much of the documentation produced by the National Numeracy Strategy (DfEE, 1999b) and the Primary National Strategy (DfES, 2006) in England has recommended that children should be given opportunities to solve 'real-life' problems in mathematics. However, it could be questioned whether a problem within a classroom or early years setting is in fact 'real-life'. It may be preferable to use the term 'meaningful contexts' for problem solving as this can also include fantasy or imaginary contexts, such as stories that are meaningful for children but fictional. In the case study described earlier in this chapter, Oliver and Daniel were engaged in mathematics in a context that was meaningful for them on that particular day as they had just received new farm sets as presents. You will be able to identify other play situations and toys where there is potential for mathematics arising from the children's play. Play and mathematics is the subject of Chapter 3.

Giving children a degree of choice can help them to build up their independence; this in turn will help them to develop persistence and resilience, which are necessary in the learning of mathematics and in problem solving within mathematics, the wider curriculum and beyond. Children need a self-image as a successful learner (Gifford, 2008) and the affective aspect of learning mathematics is extremely important. Adults need to build children's confidence in mathematics as well as their competence.

Schemas arising from children's interests

Carruthers and Worthington (2006) built on Athey's (1990) work on schemas. These are repeated behaviours during play that demonstrate children's exploration of particular ideas and concepts. Schemas include enclosing things, connecting and transporting. Their research involved asking parents to keep diaries of children's schemas. Adults working with children in various early years settings also took note of children's schemas. Carruthers and Worthington recommend that adults working with young children should work with and extend children's schemas. They give an example of where a child was in a spiral schema, extending this by encouraging her to examine snail shells carefully and to stir fruit into plain yoghurt. They also identified that children may represent ideas associated with their present schema, leading to further exploration of the idea and therefore to deeper learning. They contrast children exploring shapes through their play when they are interested, with a teacher holding up a shape and telling the children that it is a triangle.

- Think of a child in the age range of 0–8 years that you know well. What are their current interests?
- What would be a meaningful context for them?

Routines of the day can also provide meaningful contexts for mathematical development. These could include:

- getting dressed
- laying the table
- tidying up
- preparing a snack.

Often, just by listening and talking to children at these times, mathematical language and vocabulary can be developed. For example, we might talk with children about the sizes of different objects. Sometimes, the situations could be developed into problems for children to solve. Examples of questions we might ask children when laying a table are:

- 'How many plates do we have?'
- 'How many plates do we need?'
- 'How many more plates do we need?'

The first of these is a simple counting question. The second could be more challenging if the people needing the plates are not all present and the child has to count from their imagination. The third question could combine the first two and involve some addition or 'counting on'. Adults can assist children to answer these questions through modelling by thinking aloud.

Stories, songs, poetry and rhymes can also provide meaningful starting points for mathematics. Beyond counting books, some stories have been written especially for the purpose of developing children's mathematical understanding. However, mathematics can also ensue from reading a story that is not directly written with mathematics in mind. An example is *Mr Magnolia* (Blake, 2010). Although it is not obviously a counting book, it works in that way. Mr Magnolia starts the story with one boot, he has two sisters, three creatures in his pond, and so on. There is also scope for discussion of sizes when looking at the pictures. The opportunity to discuss items that come in pairs could also lead to work on odd and even numbers or counting in twos. Giant stories can also lead to discussions of size (see Chapter 13) and perhaps to children solving problems by working out how tall the giant is from a foot or hand print.

Many children will enjoy joining in with songs and rhymes and these can provide a meaningful context from which to explore some mathematical ideas. 'When Goldilocks went to the house of the bears' supports counting to three and talking about different sizes. Very early adding and subtracting can be supported by singing 'Two

Little Dickie Birds'. You can find books (sometimes with a CD) of songs especially written for supporting mathematical development in young children.

Out of doors and further afield

Young children learn all the time and in different environments. They will be used to this before they join a more formal learning setting such as a nursery, pre-school or school situation. Many children love to play outdoors and much mathematical learning can take place outside, taking advantage of the spaces in the natural and built environment. This could be in an outdoor area adjoining the setting or further away, necessitating a journey. Locations for outdoor learning can be familiar or unfamiliar. Similarly, there are interesting opportunities for learning in different indoor locations. Different locations will appeal to children's interests and can be useful in motivating children to think in different mathematical ways. More consideration will be given to these ideas in Chapter 5.

Linking mathematical and other learning

Linking mathematical activities within a setting with home and other experiences a child has outside of the setting encourages meaningful learning. This involves getting to know the children well as individuals including their current preferences and interests. Therefore, it is also useful to build productive relationships with the children's parents or carers. Good communication is then far more likely and parents and practitioners working within settings can help children to continue their interests and can talk to the children about them and therefore make learning deeper and more effective (see Chapter 8). Communication between adults within a setting is also very important, especially if a child will come into contact with a number of different adults within a week. Feedback from all adults is also vital if one adult has the key responsibility for the planning of mathematical learning, resources and experiences.

Links between mathematical ideas

Research into effective teachers of numeracy (Askew et al.,1997) has shown that the most effective teachers of primary mathematics are those who believe that it is important to help children to see the links and connections between different mathematical ideas, different representations of mathematics and children's existing methods and understandings. Teaching is based on dialogue between the teacher and the child and between children to ensure that these connections are highlighted.

Barmby et al. (2009) believe that children develop mathematical understanding through adding mental connections between ideas by representing the mathematics and reasoning. Adults working with young children will often intuitively assist them in making connections, such as helping children to add numbers together by counting. However, if adults are aware of the importance of this, they can capitalise on the opportunities to assist mathematical development. Chapter 10 highlights links between the four operations and it is essential for children to become aware of these.

Links between setting-based and outside experiences can also involve topical themes to be explored in a mathematical context. Young children will not see learning as separated into subject categories and one activity may help their development in several different areas. We have mentioned the development of children's mathematical vocabulary and language several times, because it is bound up with thinking and therefore learning, but this also means that through assisting a child with developing this vocabulary they will be developing their language more generally. Gifford (2008) also highlights this aspect and the way that adults can model mathematical thinking and talk through thinking aloud and helping children to articulate in 'sustained shared thinking' (Siraj-Blatchford et al., 2002).

Figure 1.4 lists some topical themes and related mathematical activities together with the mathematical vocabulary that could be highlighted.

Theme	Possible mathematics activity	Possible mathematical vocabulary
Autumn	Collecting, sorting and grouping leaves	Sort, group, the same as, different
Christmas	Exploring and creating symmetry in decorating Christmas trees	Symmetrical, match, shape
The Olympic Games	Comparing numbers of medals for different countries	More, fewer, the same as, lots, none
Holidays	Exploring and counting sand castles	Big, small, size
India or Hinduism	Exploring and creating Rangoli type patterns	Pattern, shape, curve, straight
National Book Day	Using a story as a starting point for mathematical ideas	Page numbers, order, ordinal numbers, e.g. first, second
Bonfire Night	Making and describing a firework picture, counting and describing position and direction	Over, high, up, down, close, far

Figure 1.4   *Themes and mathematical activities*

C A S E   S T U D Y

Rock pool activity

One summer term I was teaching a class of 4–5 year olds and had chosen the theme of summer holidays to base activities around. I wanted to give the children opportunities to develop positional vocabulary, so I decided to set up the sand or water tray to resemble a rock pool. Stones, pebbles and shells were collected from a beach and washed thoroughly. A large shallow dish of water was placed at one end of the sand tray; this was surrounded by the rocks and pebbles. Sand was then distributed to make a more natural appearance. Children had a collection of sea shells and plastic sea creatures, including crabs and other shellfish, a seahorse and starfish. Groups of children then arranged the sea creatures and shells as they wished in the tray. As they did this an adult talked to the children and discussed where they were placing them. Clipboards and paper were also provided and many of the children drew representations of the rock pool and the creatures, again practising the positional language as they drew and described their pictures. They used phrases such as:

'The crab's under water'

'The starfish is coming out from under the rock'

'I've put the shell on the top of the sandcastle'

I encouraged children to use the phrase 'in between' by modelling sentences for the children, 'The seahorse is in between two rocks'. Some of the children were also later heard using this phrase.

Children solving problems

Problem solving is important in all areas of learning, but perhaps particularly in mathematics where it provides opportunities for children to develop mathematical thinking skills and to apply their understanding in a meaningful way. It encourages children to draw upon their previous experiences when considering possible ways of solving a particular problem and deciding a course of action. Problem solving features in many of the other chapters in this book, with a particular focus on problem solving within children's play in Chapter 3.

- What constitutes problem solving in mathematics for very young children?

For children to appreciate mathematics as meaningful and relevant to them and their everyday lives and not just a preparation for the future, they will need to be involved in using and applying mathematics to solve problems. Problem solving for very young children should consist mainly of practical problems. It is sometimes easy to think of problem solving in school mathematics being word problems. These would only be relevant for some of the older children within the age group considered by this book, and even then practical problems should be the focus. Problem solving is a key feature of the curriculum guidance from each of the countries of the UK. Children have often been asked to solve some problems by using and applying their recent learning in mathematics lessons. However, young children will often come across problems to solve in their play and daily activities. Sometimes these can lead to the children learning mathematics. Starting with a problem can also be a very effective approach for older children and is regularly used in the Netherlands in 'Realistic Mathematics Education' (van den Heuvel-Panhuizen, 2001).

Children will need to learn problem-solving skills such as:

- identifying the mathematics required
- simplifying
- decision making
- representing
- organising and checking
- recognising patterns
- communicating in different modes
- predicting
- justifying
- explaining
- conjecturing or hypothesising
- generalising.

Some of these will need to be modelled by adults. For example, we might demonstrate to children how to draw a table to organise their results. However, at times children will also need freedom to approach a problem in their own way with opportunities to discuss methods and approaches with others.

Children solve problems of a mathematical nature through their lives and play as and when they occur. Adults may also set up problems for children to solve. Children will sometimes take these ideas forward into their play later on. Figure 1.5 suggests some problem-solving opportunities and gives some examples of problems children may engage with.

(Continued)

(Continued)

Problem-solving opportunity	Examples
Building with construction toys	Children will often look for a brick or a piece of a certain size to fit a gap.
Tidying up	An adult may ask 'Have we got all the scissors?' This might result in a child making sure that each place in the scissor rack has a pair of scissors in it or saying that one pair is missing.
Adult suggested problem after a story	After listening to the story of The Three Bears, children might be challenged to use junk modelling materials such as recycled cardboard packaging boxes and pieces of fabric to make beds for teddy bears. This could be supported by talking with the children about whether the various teddies will fit the beds.

Figure 1.5 *Problem-solving opportunities*

Progression in children's mathematical ideas 0–8

As described in Chapter 9, babies have a sense of quantity and as they get older children will gradually build up more experiences and develop their mathematical ideas. Some of this will happen almost naturally and despite what adults do. However, ultimately it is important that children's mathematical progress is maximised. Progress could be seen as cumulative learning (Gifford, 2008). Talk and developing mathematical vocabulary is essential for this maximising of progress (see Chapter 2). Many parents intuitively talk to their children about mathematical ideas and will help their children to progress, for example they will count for and with the child and encourage the child to count further than they have previously. They will use words to describe sizes and praise the child when he or she talks about a big dog.

Once a child joins a more formal setting such as a nursery, pre-school or school, it will be more important for the adults to identify and enable progression; this is more complicated when working with larger numbers of children. Children need new opportunities that build on their previous knowledge and understanding supported by development of their mathematical vocabulary. It is therefore essential that adults understand what children already know, understand and can do in order to provide appropriate challenges, resources and other support for children in their play and in the activities that adults encourage the children to take part in. This understanding is gained through assessment of children's learning (see Chapter 7). However, it is not just adults understanding where children are in their mathematical development that is important. This must feed through to planning the next stages for children's learning. This may be short-term planning in deciding what question to ask the child or what challenge to set immediately, or it may be longer term, in deciding what mathematical opportunities should be presented to the child the next day, next week or next term.

By the time children are 8 years old, they will need to be able to count accurately in steps of different sizes, forwards and backwards. They will have met and begun to understand the four operations of addition, subtraction, multiplication and division. They should have some knowledge and understanding of shape, space and measures. They should also be able to use and apply their mathematical knowledge and understanding in a variety of contexts to solve problems. It is also helpful if children of this age can remember and recall some mathematical facts rapidly, such as number bonds and multiplication tables (see Chapter 10), so they can use them in later mathematics and problem solving.

Remembering and mathematical learning

Alloway (2006) conducted a literature review into the effects of children's memories on their mathematics. She found that children with poorer working memories struggled with mathematics learning. This would suggest that adults should assist children in this area by giving very limited numbers of instructions at any one time, breaking tasks down into bite-sized pieces and providing memory aids. Children will also need to learn strategies for supporting themselves independently when their memory fails them.

It is vital that young children develop positive attitudes to mathematics in order to prepare them for success in future mathematical development. In order to promote these attitudes children need to be motivated, stimulated, engaged and interested so that they enjoy their mathematical learning.

Learning through mistakes and misconceptions

Using children's misconceptions

Bell's (1993) research, albeit with older pupils, showed that addressing misconceptions through discussion during teaching improves achievement in the short and longer term. Letting pupils initially demonstrate misconceptions was also shown to be more effective than trying to get children to avoid them.

Ryan and Williams (2007), Cockburn and Littler (2008) and Swan (2001) advocate that children can learn effectively through their own and others' mistakes and misconceptions if they are exposed and handled sensitively. Adults can assist this learning by being aware of typical errors that children make in various areas of mathematics, not planning to avoid these but rather to highlight them and use them positively in the learning setting. Building up a positive and supportive ethos and culture (Drews, 2011) is important in the learning setting so that children do not feel humiliated if they make an error but gradually begin to appreciate the value of persistence, resilience and the efforts of other children. Spooner (2002) advocates placing children in situations where they feel in control of identifying errors and misconceptions. Ryan and Williams (2010: 147) recommend that adults working with children take 'a positive view of errors and misconceptions as productive starting points for learning'.

According to Koshy et al. (2000), children make different types of mistakes when they are engaged in mathematical activities. It is possible for them to make an error where they have a good understanding of an idea but they are perhaps distracted and something goes wrong. However, a mistake might instead be the result of a misconception. These can be described as partial conceptions based on incomplete or immature reasoning (Ryan and Williams, 2010; Swan, 2003; Thompson, 2008a) and ideas about mathematics resulting from incorrect assumptions or over-generalisations. Swan clarified that few misconceptions are completely wrong and they often apply in more limited circumstances. An example of this is the view that multiplication always makes a number larger. This works for numbers greater than 1, but not for numbers less than or equal to 1, for example $8 \times 1/2 = 4$. Ryan and Williams (2007) describe misconceptions as 'the result of intelligent engagement'. Barmby et al. (2009: 4–5) regard misconceptions as 'evolving understandings' and as important to children's progression in learning mathematics; 'working through misconceptions is an important part of the process of developing understanding'. With children in the 0–8 age phase, Thompson (2008a: 207) suggests that misconceptions can be thought of as 'limited conceptions'. Challenging misconceptions is necessary so that children can progress with their mathematics and later ideas are built on firm foundations.

Drews (2011) highlighted that it is essential to devote time to confronting misconceptions because deep-rooted ideas will be hard to shift and require a change of mind-set. She recommends that children should be rewarded for having the courage to test out mathematical ideas and this is more important than getting correct answers or presenting work neatly. If misconceptions are not tackled, it could be counter-productive to future learning and progress.

Littler and Jirotkova (2008) warn that adults involved in teaching mathematical ideas should not be tempted to teach short cuts that can later lead to problems for children, as un-learning ideas is very difficult. An example of this is that it can be tempting to teach children that to multiply by 10 they can 'add a zero', however this will not work once a child is multiplying numbers with decimals. The assessment of children's misconceptions is explored in Chapter 7. Specific misconceptions and errors are discussed in the chapters of Part 2 of this book.

Summary

This chapter has explored why it is important that children learn mathematics and described principles, based on theories, of how children learn mathematics. The role of adults in supporting learning and maximising opportunities within children's everyday lives, touching on their play and the routines they participate in, has been discussed. The importance of building on children's interests in order for mathematical learning to be relevant, interesting and engaging and of enabling positive attitudes was emphasised. Progression in learning mathematics is essential as children get older and move through into later primary and secondary education and then for their lives as adults. Children learn through mistakes and misconceptions and adults can use these in positive ways to maximise effective learning.

Further reading

Thompson, I. (2008) *Teaching and Learning Early Number*, 2nd edn. Maidenhead: Open University Press.

Sections 1, 2 and 7 are relevant to the ideas discussed in this chapter. It is a readable and accessible book and will give you more detail in many areas.

Carruthers, E. and Worthington, M. (2006) *Children's Mathematics: Making Marks, Making Meaning*, 2nd edn. London: Sage.

Mathematical schemas are explored in Chapter 3 of this book. It will help you to put the idea of building on children's interests into action. Other chapters in the book will also be of interest such as bridging the gap between home and school mathematics.

MacGregor, H. (1998) *Tom Thumb's Musical Maths*. London: A and C Black.

In this book new words have been written to familiar tunes to aid mathematical learning.

Moseley, C. (2010) 'Stories for primary mathematics', *Mathematics Teaching*, 219: 16–17.

Moseley suggests some stories to use as starting points and what mathematics may be accessed through them.

2

Children Talking about Mathematics

Jill Matthews

 Chapter Overview

In this chapter you can read about:

- The nature of effective communication and its importance in developing young children's understanding of mathematics
- The interplay between talking about, and doing, mathematics
- Ways in which adults can support young children's ability to talk about their mathematical thinking.

Learning to communicate mathematically

Communication is a social and purposeful interaction between the child and another. Such interactions are situated within a particular context and develop an apparently shared understanding of that context at that time. However, understanding of the language used in a particular way within a certain context on a specific day does not guarantee that the child will understand the same vocabulary the next day, in a different situation or, indeed, be able to use the words or signs themselves to express their own understanding. It is only through multiple interactions in a variety of contexts that children are able to develop richer conceptual understanding and knowledge of associated language.

Bruner (1983) suggested that the underlying motivation for communication by babies is a biological predisposition to ensure survival and that adults are attuned to respond by structuring and modelling language in such a way that it becomes meaningful to children and enables them to communicate in a purposeful and increasingly sophisticated way. Communication depends on a complex combination of sounds (or signing), tone, gesture and facial expression (or body language) which have a shared meaning within the cultural norms of the family. Adults respond to these behaviours, and the reciprocity enables the infant to adapt and refine the behaviours (Schaffer, 1996, 1997). Adults adapt their responses to the child's particular behaviours, and these are modified further as the child matures. It is this reciprocity and mutual sensitivity which provides the key to a child's social development and the foundations of their ability to communicate with others.

The fact that all children seem to be able to gradually develop a communication repertoire, which becomes increasingly complex, appears to support the idea that this is innate. Key factors underpinning such development include not only being receptive to communication through words and gestures but also being supported by adults in interpreting communications within the context in which they occur. Early communication is largely gestural, accompanied by some vocalisation; naming things and pointing. It is clear that children need to develop their ability to take part in dialogic interaction with a significant adult right from birth. Context and familiarity, rhythm and routines are important. The significant factors are the initiating signals and the response; the active and reciprocal sensitive participation by both the child and the adult. In situations where little or no response is given to a child's signals, it has been found (Beckett et al., 2006) that the child ceases to make the signals and eventually does not look for opportunities to communicate with others. Institutional deprivation of stimuli and language has significant effects on children's cognitive development and, in circumstances where positive intervention is attempted past a certain age, only a limited remediation has proved possible. At 14 months, words and gestures are both used but as adults encourage vocalisation, this becomes more dominant.

CASE STUDY

Stacking toy

Jenny's son (aged 9 months) had just started sitting reliably. He was starting to reach for things purposefully. He knew when something was too far away and left

(Continued)

(Continued)

it or rolled himself closer. When he picked something up, he would change it into his other hand and put it in his mouth. Jenny was showing him a new stacking toy. He had played with the rings for about 10 minutes and had taken all the rings off the post, examined them and mouthed them. Jenny started to show him how to put the rings over the peg.

Jenny: Look at this ring. It's the blue one. Can you put the blue ring here over the post? Like this ... Now you do it ...

[Jack looks at the ring and puts it to his mouth.]

Jenny: Yes, it's the blue ring. The biggest one. Can you put it over the post like I did? ... Shall I help you? There ... good boy! Well done. Aren't you clever? Shall we try with another one? ... Which colour shall we choose ... ? The green one?

[She points to the green ring and then looks back at the baby. Jack is looking away at the other rings which are spread on the floor.]

Jenny: No, which one?

[Jack points.]

Jenny: The red one? OK.

[She gives the red ring to Jack. He puts it to his mouth and then to the other hand and looks at it. He gives it back to her.]

Jenny: Shall I put the red ring on the post for you?

[Jack takes the ring back.]

Jenny: Shall we put it on top of the blue one ... ? Look, it's smaller than the blue ring ... The red ring's smaller ...

[She continues to engage with Jack whilst he is still interested. After about 10 minutes, Jack's attention wanders and Jenny puts him in the push chair and they go for a walk to the shops.]

Jenny plays with him with the stacking toy for a few minutes daily until he loses interest. She maintains a similar dialogic patter to that transcribed above allowing significant pauses which give Jack time to make some kind of response. Jenny waits for his reaction before she commences her next utterance.

Three months later Jack has mastered stacking the rings on the post and can do this independently and without prompting. He can pick up a ring specified by colour (blue, green, yellow, orange and red) showing that he has understood these words.

He has been introduced to key words and phrases: 'bigger than', 'smaller than', 'the biggest' and 'the smallest' within the context of the rings and, with prompting, he is beginning to stack them in graduated order according to size. However, there is no evidence to suggest he understands the meaning of these terms beyond his mother's patter/commentary within the context of the toy.

- How does Jenny's rich interaction with her baby extend both his physical and mathematical development?
- Identify the key features which made the interaction purposeful.

By the end of the second year, most children are beginning to use phrases and to mimic their adult carers. They are rapidly extending their active and comprehending vocabulary, particularly of labels for objects, including categories of objects, for example tins, boxes, animals, dogs. Hearing new words depends on the child's ability to distinguish individual sound segments within a string of words. Adults play their part by adjusting their speech and simplifying the grammatical structures of their utterances so they can be heard and understood by the child.

The comprehension of new words depends on the context in which they are heard. Children's comprehension is in advance of their speech (Wood, 1998). Wells (2009) suggests that by modifying their speech, adults increase the chances of their children understanding what they say and provide good models for the children's own language construction. Adults also need to use contextual clues to make a good guess at what the child is trying to say, to check with the child that the meaning is what he intended and then to make an appropriate response. There may be a mismatch between the meaning intended by an adult and the meaning received by the child. Donaldson's (1978) work showed how children could misunderstand what was being asked of them because they did not understand the language within the context of the situation.

Adults should introduce the specific language of mathematics to young children in meaningful, realistic contexts as part of their everyday experiences. They need to ensure that the child is able to construct meaning within the given context and then build on that situated learning by applying the vocabulary to different situations and within their own play. This means that adults need to verbalise what is happening, what they are doing and why, to widen the child's exposure to an extended contextual vocabulary.

In the following case study examples:

- Consider how well the adults use opportunities to develop the boys' mathematical language.
- How are mathematical ideas explored?
- How might this prepare children for future mathematical experiences?

CASE STUDY

The supermarket

Example 1

Dom and Jo (with 3-year-old Max in the child's trolley seat) walk up and down the aisles of the supermarket purposefully. They have a list and go round in a particular order. While Dom pushes the trolley, Jo finds the things she needs for the week, snacks for lunches and their evening meal for that night. Max starts to grumble and reaches out for things at the end of the aisles. He attracts Dom's attention.

Dom: Are you alright, mate? Are you hungry?

Max: Crisps ....

Dom: You want some crisps, mate? Jo, I'm giving him some crisps.

[He opens a multipack and gives one to Max.]

Dom: You going to give me some then, Max? ... Ta ... Good boy.

[Max enjoys the crisps. They keep him quiet until the checkout, when he starts to grumble again. Dom takes him out to the car. Jo bags up the shopping, pays and then pushes the trolley to the car. Dom helps her load the shopping into the boot and then they go home. While they unpack the shopping, Max is put in front of the television.]

Example 2

Jason and Jane (with 3-year-old Carl in the trolley). They have a list and move up and down the aisles purposefully. The contents of their trolley are similar to that of Dom and Jo.

Jane: Right, we're in the fruit aisle. What shall we get? Carl, what do you like? ...

Carl: Bananas?

Jane: What do you think, Jason? OK? Bananas? How much are they? Look, they're 68p loose. Shall we have these yellow ones or the greener ones? Carl, what do you think?

Carl: Yellow

Jane: Yes, I think so too. The yellow ones ... Which bunch shall we have? This bunch has 1, 2, 3, 4, 5 bananas. This one is smaller it has 1, 2, 3, 4. Let's weigh them. Look at the dial. Which bunch is heavier? This bunch weighs more. Shall we take the bunch with five bananas ... ? Yes I think so too.

[And so it goes on, round the aisles until they reach the checkout.]

Jane: OK, we've got to unpack now. Carl, can you make sure I get everything out of the trolley, please? And Daddy can put the stuff in the bag. He'll sort the stuff so we know where they go when we get home. Now we've got to pay ... Oh dear, £127.00! That's a lot, isn't it? It's more than last week.

[When they get home, they unpack together and Carl is allowed to put the biscuits and cereals in the bottom of the cupboard. They sit down together with a drink and watch something on the television together before Jane starts to get the tea.]

Effective communication and the development of mathematical language can be encouraged through social interaction within the context of the child's immediate environment and experiences. Parents and carers play a crucial role in supporting children's language development and understanding of their surroundings and environment (see Chapter 8). The interactions do not need to be long or extended but they do need to incorporate appropriate turn-taking and to be focused on something that has attracted the child's attention or that the child and adult are doing together. Such interactions provide a framework for the child's interpretation of their environment and a means of constructing verbalised thought (Wells, 2009). The shopping case study above illustrates how mathematical ideas can be explored within an everyday, realistic context.

As the child starts to use language productively to communicate their own thoughts and meanings, they can then use their active language and experiences by re-enacting them in their independent play. Hughes (2012) identifies the criteria of what constitutes play and emphasises that the nature of play is not solely what the child does but is more to do with why and how the child becomes engrossed in a particular 'play' activity. He suggests that play is an 'irresistible urge' which helps children to master their environment and that play activity stimulates neural growth, thus improving the capacity and organisation of the brain. Young children can often be observed talking aloud to themselves as they play. Hence, it is important to provide opportunities for play within nursery and early years' settings which mirror the real-life experiences which most children will have encountered. Playing with peers enables children to rehearse their own experiences but also to come into contact with alternative and slightly different conceptions which may provoke a cognitive conflict and stimulate further internal thought and understanding (see Chapter 3).

Promoting mathematical understanding through talk

Many mathematical concepts can be experienced and understood without verbalisation (Wood, 1998: 226). Shapes can be recognised and matched just by looking. Young children can recognise simple bead patterns, for example, and continue them correctly without explanation. Objects can be sorted according to the child's own ideas (for example, colour, hard or soft, shapes). Quantities that are 'more' or 'less' can be gauged by eye. However, the foundations for working together and talking about their learning are laid when children are very young. Nutbrown (2011) suggests that children form schema through social interaction and that the quality of the response given by adults facilitates cognitive development. The role of the adult is to extend children's experience and vocabulary, thus enabling them to participate as fully as possible in learning. Helping a child to verbalise what they are doing and to establish this as a routine habit can reap benefits when they subsequently engage in more abstract learning of mathematics in school.

As they move from their familiar home environment to that of a nursery or preschool setting, children have to adapt to new surroundings, new carers and a new social setting with possibly different boundaries for behaviour and communication. Where verbal interactions between parent and child are usually on a comfortable footing, with participants sharing equal status within the dialogue, the interaction is now with a responsible adult in charge. The interaction becomes more hierarchical and develops a sense of control or instruction. Where once the language used may have been exploratory and informal, based on the context, setting and previous knowledge, the language used in the new environment may be more formal, use words in a specific way (for example, mathematical vocabulary), and the grammar and syntax may be different. The child needs to acquire the ability to communicate effectively within this new environment, vertically with the adult in charge and horizontally with peers on an equal footing.

The impact of language and communication difficulties

Wood (1998) found that the overall achievement in mathematics of deaf children lagged behind that of children without a hearing impairment, although they were able to perform well on tests of mathematical ability if the test was not couched in complex written language. Wood (1998: 227) suggested that they found learning more difficult because 'the process of *communication* with their teachers is difficult' and 'their acquisition of *knowledge* was consequently impeded'.

Currently, some 7% of children start school with a language delay (Roulston et al., 2010) and are unable to construct proper sentences in their spoken language. The proportion is significantly higher in areas of social and economic deprivation. This statistic obviously has significant implications for the learning potential of these children and adjustments to teaching provision have to be made. Within educational settings, adults need to support the development and precision in the use of mathematical language, as well as the development of mathematical conceptual understanding.

The Cockcroft Report (DES, 1982) stressed the importance of mental mathematics and recommended that young children should not be allowed to move too quickly to written work in mathematics (paragraph 316). The Report highlighted the significance of giving children time to rehearse their thinking using their previous knowledge, allowing children to use informal methods in mental calculation and opportunities to discuss their thinking and processes.

Alexander (2004) describes how structured dialogue, where a teacher facilitates the pupil's exploration of their thinking through open questioning, not only enables the pupil to confirm and articulate understanding but also enables other pupils to engage with the discussion because the language is accessible to them. Ryan and Williams (2007) extend this further by promoting the use of dialogue to challenge mathematical understanding and to resolve misconceptions (see Chapter 7). 'Concept cartoons' (Dabell, 2008) provide a possible context for such dialogic learning. These 'cognitive drawings' or 'visual disagreements' use a cartoon-style design to present mathematical conversations inside speech bubbles' (p.34). The children can talk about which person in the cartoon they agree with and explain why. The discussion can be used to challenge thinking and explore misconceptions.

CASE STUDY

Water play

Four children (aged 4–5 years) are playing around the water tray outside the class-room. There are various plastic beakers, bottles, jugs, funnels, cartons, etc. Some of the plastic containers with screw lids contain water. There are numerous empty washing-up bowls. Anna, an adult, is observing them. Two boys are playing inde-pendently but both are filling different containers with liquid and are fascinated by how the water flows, by the light refracting and how they could regulate the pressure inside the bottles to create a vacuum and suck liquid back into the bottles. Two of the girls are playing together. They seem to be re-enacting a birthday party and are pouring liquid from an old 2-litre lemonade bottle into five of the beakers.

Jess: Have we got enough drink?

Amita: I fink so? We need these cups ... 1, 2, you and me ... and Harry and Max ... and Anna. Anna, are you coming to our party? D'you wanna drink? It's Coke, OK?

Jess: How many?

Amita: 1, 2, ... Harry and Max... that's 1, 2, 3, 4, ... and Anna, one more?

Jess: 5... Have we got enough drink?

Amita: Pour it out and see. That's a big bottle of Coke you got there ... Careful ... Don't spill any.

Jess: It's hard, it's too heavy ... I'll try this one [selects a 500ml bottle] ...... that's better.

Amita: Got enough?

Jess: I think so ... Oops, I put too much in that one ... What do you think? Is that too full?

Amita: Na. Jus' right. Anna, come and have a drink at our party. Harry, Max, come on. Sit down and we'll pass round the drinks.

[After the drinks and the washing up, Anna asked the children why they put down the 2l bottle.]

Jess: It was too big and heavy.

Anna: Why do you think it was heavier than the one you used?

Jess: It had too much drink in it. I couldn't pour it.

Anna: I wonder how much more drink it has than the bottle you chose in the end?

Amita: It was a lot more. We couldn't hardly pick it up ... Phew!

Jess: My mum always buys the big bottles and I can't pour my drink at home. She says I'm going to make a mess.

Anna: Do you think we could find out how much more drink the big bottle contained? I could help if you like.

Amita: You can lift the big bottle and we could pour it into lots of beakers.

Jess: Yeh, but I like pouring. You could pour into this (carton) and we could pour it into beakers by ourselves.

Amita: But it would be better if we had it in the small bottles ... and then we could pour into cups and then we would know how much bigger it was.

If you were Anna, consider:

- How you could build on the learning opportunity presented here
- What mathematical vocabulary you could introduce
- How this could be developed as a theme
- How might this prepare children for future mathematical experiences.

As children enter more formal school settings the teacher's freedom to teach in an opportunistic way may be reduced and often a more closely prescribed curriculum agenda prevails. Subject teaching can further remove mathematics from real-life contexts and render it more abstract to pupils. Regrettably, opportunities for dialogic learning can become less frequent as children are expected to conform to codes of behaviour conducive to whole-class teaching. However, it is vital that teachers establish a positive ethos for learning within their classes that encourages and facilitates shared learning experiences and constructive and focused inter-pupil communication as well as teacher–pupil or perhaps preferably pupil–teacher talk.

Children coming from a range of differing home environments need to learn together new parameters of engagement. The teacher then needs to focus on individual learning needs and to create inclusive activities to foster and extend mathematical understanding. Previous learning and real-life contexts should provide the learning hooks as starting points to cue pupils into new concepts. New vocabulary needs to be introduced orally and explored, tried and tested in various ways by pupils until they are comfortable with it. Establishing a shared understanding of the specific vocabulary is essential to support and develop new learning. The aim is to enable children to use mathematical terms to express their thinking and understanding with clarity.

Some helpful approaches for developing children's mathematical vocabulary include:

- Encouraging children to invent their own games or vary existing games, thereby using vocabulary to negotiate rules and strategies (e.g. playing dominoes which show one more than the previous number rather than matching the numbers)
- Visualisation activities in which children have to describe arrangements, patterns or relationships for another child to visualise (see examples in Figure 14.2 in Chapter 14)
- Encouraging discussion during practical activities (for example, using construction kits or floor robots) in pairs or small groups
- Engaging children in mathematical talk about stories or displays (see Chapter 6)
- Collaborative problem-solving activities (for example, the river-crossing problem in Figure 3.4 in Chapter 3)
- Providing role-play areas (for example, a garden centre, vet's surgery) rich in mathematical opportunities
- Engaging in discussion with children as a 'play-partner' during child-initiated play.

Puzzles with a definite answer are a good way of getting children to use and apply their shared knowledge to reach a solution. Children also like to use and apply the number facts (for example, number bonds and multiplication tables) they have learned within different situations. Working together, they can explore ideas and share thinking without the pressure of working independently. The tension associated with producing a correct answer is reduced because of the collaboration. Crucial to the learning experience, though, is the opportunity to share the solution and the reasoning which underpinned the solution with others. Adults need to avoid lapsing into a curtailed adult-led initiation–response–feedback interaction (Sinclair and Coulthard, 1975) that would restrict extended explanations. Alexander (2004) suggests that supporting children to articulate their thinking through extended explanations is the key to securing understanding. Children need to feel confident within the classroom environment to be able to express their thinking without worrying about the accuracy of their answers. Pratt (2006: 6) argues that children need the freedom to 'make sense of their mathematics together through discussion and reflection'.

Summary

Mathematics should be learned and taught within the context of meaningful experiences. Practical activities and experiences should precede mathematical tasks which are more abstract. Activities should involve mathematical talk between learners and between learners and adults. The foundations for mathematics are laid in the opportunities young children are given to explore their understanding of concepts using mathematical vocabulary. Adults have a crucial role in preparing and resourcing suitable opportunities for children to develop and refine their mathematical thinking through discussion.

Further reading

Ryan, J. and Williams, J. (2007) *Children's Mathematics 4–15*. Maidenhead: Open University Press.
In Chapter 3 the authors outline an approach to developing and refining mathematical understanding through discussion.

Dabell, J. (2008) 'Using concept cartoons', *Mathematics Teaching*, 209: 34–6.
In this article Dabell explores how he has used concept cartoons in his teaching to encourage children to talk and explore their understanding.

Wheeldon, I. (2006) 'Peer talk', *Mathematics Teaching*, 199: 39–41.
Wheeldon discusses improving the quality of mathematical talk within small groups.

3

Play and Mathematics

Clare Wiseman and Karen Vincent

 Chapter Overview

In this chapter you can read about:

- Why play is important
- How play supports early mathematical understanding
- How adults can support children's mathematical development through play.

The importance of play

Everyone, with few exceptions, engages in play. Play and playful language are a natural part of our lives. Play is an elastic concept that allows us to experiment and hypothesise; when we cook, we may play with the approximate quantities of ingredients in familiar recipes. The nature of play changes as we develop from infancy, through childhood, adolescence and into adulthood, but the power that play has to engage, motivate, inspire and challenge is continuous. For any child, play is important for holistic development – good quality play supports positive learning outcomes, not only in the cognitive domain, but also in the emotional, social and psychomotor domains (Anning et al., 2004). Play helps us to achieve a sense of well-being and happiness. It enables us to be inspired and motivated, and is therefore ultimately empowering.

The power of play in enabling children to learn has been examined and debated by many educationalists, academics and practitioners and continues to be embedded within current national curricula documents for young children. This chapter explores the importance of play for cognition and learning and how early mathematical understanding can be enhanced through play.

Play and learning

Play can allow young children freedom, flexibility and motivation to discover the world around them. For example, children's playgrounds can provide spontaneous opportunities for an early understanding of concepts such as height, speed, direction, shape, space and comparison.

However, it cannot simply be assumed that when a child is playing they are automatically learning (Wood and Attfield, 1996). Therefore, if we accept that play is important because it contributes to the child's development, the theories which attempt to explain the contribution that play makes to a child's learning are significant (Bruce, 2001; Moyles, 2010).

Much early childhood practice has been informed by constructivist or social constructivist views of learning and play that stem largely from the work of theorists such as Piaget (1962), Vygotsky (1978) and Bruner (1990) (see Chapter 1) who supported the principle of the child as an active learner. Current practice recognises that all aspects of the child's learning and development – the cognitive, emotional, social and psychomotor domains – are important, simultaneous and complementary. For example, water and sand play offer children a safe environment in which to experiment with ideas of volume, capacity and mass in a way that is meaningful and thereby children begin to construct and adapt their own ideas about such concepts. Bruner (1986, in Smidt, 2011) suggested that play was important for children as it allowed them to learn from first-hand or real-life experiences – crucial during the early stages of development when the infant is constantly trying to explore the world with the senses. These experiences form a bank of ideas and memories from which to make comparisons with new experiences and adjust existing understanding to form new learning.

The following case study exemplifies children engaging in free-flow play. It illustrates several of Bruce's (1991, 2004) 12 features of such play (for example, trying out most recent learning, pretending, making up rules, making props, playing together, and carrying out a personal play agenda).

CASE STUDY

The long jump

After watching athletics on the television, Chris (5) and his sister Lucy (3) are playing outside. Chattering and laughing, they re-create the long jump event. They remove the cushion from the sun-bed and lay it on the grass, making a 'pit' for the long jump. They then run up, take off and see how far they can jump along the 'pit'. The children are completely absorbed in their game and demonstrate self-confidence and imagination by pursuing their activity through negotiation with each other and without adult input. They soon realise that they need to find a way to mark their landing positions in order to compare the lengths of the jumps. Chris and Lucy use sticks to do this and re-enact the raking of the sand with a toy garden fork. Chris begins to recognise that the longer and faster he runs up, the more successful his jumps are. He encourages Lucy to do the same, telling her, 'The faster you run, the more far you will go'. Lucy copies Chris, although she cannot match the length of his jumps.

This play episode allows Chris and Lucy to control their learning, expand existing schemas and discover new understanding in a way which is pertinent to their immediate interest (see Chapter 1). The role-play element is intrinsically motivating and mathematically rich and also promotes exploration of mathematical vocabulary. Their learning through this self-directed play is a socially-centred activity, where joint involvement facilitates the construction of new knowledge and builds on existing understanding (Anning et al., 2004).

> • Consider other playful activities that you have observed which may support mathematical learning. Which features of Bruce's (2004) free-flow play were evident?

Characteristics of early mathematical play

The Piagetian orthodoxy that young children have very limited understanding of the nature of mathematics has been challenged in recent decades and research has demonstrated that human beings are born with a range of mathematical competences (Pound and Lee, 2011). Therefore, mathematical learning can, and should, begin from the very earliest stages of development. Chapter 8 outlines how parents intuitively and informally introduce the child to mathematical concepts through everyday routines and play at home. Playful activities and situations can provide an appropriate context in which children can spontaneously explore complex mathematical ideas. Whilst acknowledging that individual children can, and should, initiate and control their own play, the role of dialogue and interaction with others is important if they are to learn from their experiences (Gifford, 2005).

Figure 3.1 illustrates how early mathematics may be embedded and recognised in different types of play activities.

Play Activity	Possible Mathematics Learning
Small world play – the toy train set and track; cars and car park; toy town	Comparison of distance; parallel, curved and straight lines; angle; position; direction; movement; building in three dimensions; problem solving
Outdoor play – the playground, park, garden	Counting actions, rather than objects – hops, jumps, skips (see Chapter 9); speed; distance; direction; orientation; position; movement
Pretend play – playing 'shops'	Sorting; categorising; counting; simple calculating; handling money
Making 'props' for play – mobile phones/TV remote controls/ calculators from 'junk' Making 'covers' and 'blankets' for teddies, dolls and other toys	Number and symbol recognition; matching; ordering number; pattern; 'stable order' principle (see Chapter 9) Shape; size; surface area; pattern; fractions; measurement; estimation; problem solving
Structured play – board games and outdoor games such as hop scotch	Pattern; sequence; counting; position; simple calculation; problem solving; movement; direction; estimation
Sand and water play	Volume; capacity; conservation of amount; comparison between quantities; estimation; fractions

Figure 3.1   *Mathematical learning in different play activities*

- How might adults support children's mathematical learning in the different types of play activity in Figure 3.1?

The following case studies (along with the previous case study – 'The long jump') illustrate how mathematical learning can be stimulated and developed through play activities, particularly in the early years.

CASE STUDY

Wooden building blocks

Fifteen-month-old Amy sits on the floor surrounded by a pile of coloured, wooden cuboids of varying sizes. She randomly sweeps her hand through the blocks, picking some up and feeling their texture and weight. Amy explores what happens when she stacks bricks on top of each other until the pile crashes to the floor, and repeats this over and over with varying degrees of success. Amy tires of her play; the adult passes her the bucket for the bricks and offers to help Amy tidy them away. Amy drops bricks into the bucket one by one; taking turns with the adult who counts each brick placed in the bucket. Amy claps her hands when the last brick is in the bucket. The adult praises her and encourages her to place the lid, in the correct orientation, on top of the bucket.

Figure 3.2 *Amy plays with the bricks*

This episode demonstrates how early ideas around counting, shape and measurement can be explored by very young children using simple toys. Whilst it is not possible to know exactly what a child is thinking, particularly when lacking the language to articulate this, we can gain insights about their thinking through observing their actions.

Early ideas about counting

The development of number understanding in very young children is not a singular process, but rather several overlapping processes involving the development of verbal, motor and cognitive activities (Munn, 2008). Munn suggests that children's beliefs about counting and its purpose should be identified when assessing their learning. Through her play, Amy is exposed to several important ideas associated with counting, even though she does not have the language skills to verbalise her thinking. These might include:

- Objects can be counted.
- Counting activities have a beginning and an ending and may be purposeful.
- A new word is spoken for each object dropped into the container.

Such early counting experiences, especially involving play and interaction, lay the foundations for understanding counting (see Chapter 9). Vygotsky's (1978) model of learning, where the child acts as the 'apprentice' spontaneously learning from the 'expert' (see Chapter 1), can be seen here.

Early ideas about shape and space

When Amy handles the cuboids she is learning at the Sensory-motor Stage (Piaget, 1962). At this stage of cognitive development, Piaget argued that the child's learning is developed through interactive schemas which are gradually refined, as the child assimilates and accommodates information about objects, people, environment, time and space. In this play episode, Amy develops the understanding that her environment consists of three-dimensional objects. The blocks have vertices, straight edges and faces, which appear as different two-dimensional shapes, depending on their orientation. She is also assimilating the idea that shapes exist in different sizes and that grasping the larger ones requires both hands, whilst smaller blocks can be manipulated with one hand. Early ideas about comparison of objects by mass and size are explored and may underpin later mathematical understanding.

Amy also begins to discover that the blocks sometimes fit together to form new shapes and structures. When she tries to balance them, she quickly deduces that she must place flat surfaces together, or the tower of bricks will collapse. She may also learn through experience, trial and error, and adult support that the bucket lid needs to be oriented precisely.

Early ideas about measurement

Nutbrown's (2011) research suggests very young children begin to learn about concepts through the pursuit of particular patterns of behaviour and interest with mathematical roots. Amy is investigating a vertical schema (see Chapter 1) concerned with increasing the height of the tower she makes with the building blocks. Repeatedly she uses motor skills to add further blocks until they will no longer balance and they topple to the floor. Amy is beginning to make connections between the addition of blocks and the growth of the tower. She may also be assimilating ideas about balance and stability. These early explorations of the concept of height through experience and the linking of action and thought may support later understanding of measurement and comparison.

The 'long jump' and mathematical learning

This play episode, stimulated by a televised athletics event, provides a variety of early mathematics learning opportunities. Importantly, the children may begin to see that mathematics is integral to our culture, activities and pastimes. As Tucker (2008: 36) suggests: 'Play has several important functions in mathematical development as it promotes an understanding of the cultural role of mathematics along with the varied activities in which it has a significant part'.

This experience affords Chris and Lucy with opportunities to expand their thinking and understanding about measurement. Chris already has well-developed schema for length and knows some associated vocabulary. He unconsciously acts as what Vygotsky (1978) would call 'the more knowledgeable other' (see Chapter 1) by scaffolding Lucy's understanding and experience of relevant vocabulary (for example, 'longer', 'far', 'shorter', 'more', 'less', 'faster') within an informal, meaningful and motivating context.

The children also make connections between speed and distance, using their physical play to compare the lengths of their jumps and striving to make longer jumps each time. Haylock (2010: 283) argues that 'The foundation of all aspects of measurement is direct comparison, putting two ... objects (or events) in order according to the attribute in question'. Later, when Chris and Lucy learn about measurement more formally, their previous play experiences may enable them to make connections and assimilate new ideas.

Early ideas about problem solving

In Chapter 1, we noted that problem solving for very young children must be meaningful; play provides a natural and accessible context for this. In the earlier case study, Chris and Lucy spontaneously participate in solving problems within their play.

McGrath (2010: 196) asks 'when is a problem not a problem? Whether it is a problem or not is determined by the child's experience'. Young children are capable of sophisticated, creative thinking and they encounter many challenges in their everyday lives, which they strive to overcome. McGrath, (2010: 204) cites Montague-Smith (1997) as suggesting that 'everyday tasks are problems for young children as they are still making early connections'. When solving problems, young children are also developing learning dispositions. The ability to concentrate, focus and strive for a goal is an important element of learning and is illustrated in the next case study.

CASE STUDY

The dishwasher

Amy, now 20 months old, enjoys standing on her chair at the sink to 'wash up'. She washes her dish and cup several times until it is time for dinner. When her mother returns the chair to the table, she climbs onto it independently in order to eat. After dinner, she watches her father open the dishwasher to stack the dirty dishes. He discusses what he is doing with Amy, thereby increasing her understanding and linking the actions to her developing vocabulary. Later, Amy decides that she would like to continue to wash up. Instead of moving her chair in order to reach the sink, she decides that a far better solution (see Figure 3.3) is to open the dishwasher and stand on the door!

Figure 3.3 *Amy's solution*

This is an ingenious solution to a real-life problem experienced by a young child. Amy applies a sense of logic to the situation in order to overcome the challenges. She is fascinated with getting up high and exploring 'being up there', which Athey (1990) described as dynamic vertical schematic behaviour. Amy enjoyed climbing and had the intrinsic motivation to apply her skills to this new situation. She experienced a sense of agency which empowered her to achieve her goal. By applying her reasoning she discovered a new way of reaching the sink and thus learned more about her world. What is so interesting is the link that she has made between her previous strategy of standing on the chair to that of standing on the dishwasher door. The idea is ultimately creative in linking the two objects in terms of their ability to raise her up higher.

Polya (2004: 5-6) proposed a four-stage sequence for solving problems:

1. Understanding the problem
2. Devising a plan
3. Carrying out the plan
4. Looking back.

If we apply Polya's work, we can see that Amy understood the problem (reaching the sink in order to wash up). She devised a plan (open and use the dishwasher door as a substitute for the chair). She carried out the plan (stand on the dishwasher door) in order to reach the sink. While we are not able to see explicitly whether she looked back over her plan, as the dishwasher door was not high enough to enable her to reach the water in the sink, we can suppose that she learnt that this only partially solved the problem. Because her skills of estimation were not sufficiently developed, the plan was not as successful as she hoped and subsequently the chair was the favoured option.

Older children learning mathematics through play

Young children's play is often spontaneous, self-directed and embedded in the child's own interests and immediate environment. While older children may have less opportunity for spontaneous activity, play-based learning is still important. Children's motivation and enthusiasm for play remains powerful throughout the primary phase of schooling.

Play activities, planned or serendipitous, are crucial in ensuring that older children are able to continue to explore, experiment with, discover, understand and consolidate mathematical ideas and concepts. However, tensions may exist between play-based approaches to learning mathematics and a plethora of learning objectives to be covered.

Briggs and Hansen (2012) provide a comprehensive list of types of play to enhance learning in the primary school phase. Figure 3.4 explains some of these categories of play and offers examples of how these forms of play may encourage the development of mathematical ideas.

Type of Play	Example of Mathematical Development
Exploratory play The child explores a specific context or resource.	**Playing with calculators** Children can play with calculators to stimulate discussion about numbers. Such exploration may arouse children's interest in large numbers, negative numbers and fractional numbers. It may help children to recognise number patterns, develop their understanding of place value or stimulate mental calculation. (Williams and Thompson, 2003)
Games play These include physical games, card and board games, computer games.	**Using a target game to reinforce number operations** Children can use magnetic 'darts' or bean bags to play a game similar to traditional darts. Scores can be subtracted from a given number to reach zero or, to practise addition skills, a target score must be reached. The dartboard can be adapted to use numbers up to 12 and more than one 'dart' can be thrown at once and the two scores multiplied if children are to practise times tables. (Briggs and Davis, 2008)
Play in different environments Children experience different environments including indoor and outdoor spaces, their local environment and virtual environments.	**Beachcombing** Children may be invited to collect objects of interest found on the beach. They can sort and categorise the objects that they find (shells, seaweed, driftwood, cuttlefish, etc.). Later, they could construct a three-dimensional chart representing the categories of objects collected, interpret this and share their results.
Role play For older children this may be more aligned with drama activities, where the stimulus is created by adults and the children have an opportunity to practice and develop a 'role'.	**The river-crossing problem** Children are asked to solve the following logic problem: 'An Inuit, an arctic hare, an arctic fox and a clump of tundra grass have to cross a gap in the ice in a kayak without any of them being eaten by the others. Only two of them will fit in the kayak. How can they cross safely?' 'One approach was to get groups to act out the problem with one member of the group directing the others acting the parts. Everyone has an opportunity to contribute to the discussion.' (Briggs and Davis, 2008: 103)

Figure 3.4 *Play activities for older children and mathematical links*

- What additional structured mathematical equipment could you allow children to explore in a playful way and what would the mathematical learning be?
- How might other traditional indoor or outdoor games be used to create opportunities for mathematics learning or the consolidation of mathematical skills?
- Which parts of the environment could you safely use to encourage children to play and develop mathematical ideas?
- What other opportunities may exist for mathematical problem solving through drama and role-play activities?

The role of the adult in supporting children's mathematical development

Adults need to provide an environment, dialogue, resources and ethos that support mathematical learning. They should encourage and value all forms of play as meaningful learning experiences for children.

Sustained shared thinking

The Researching Effective Pedagogy in the Early Years project (Siraj-Blatchford et al., 2002) found that good outcomes for children are linked to adult–child inter-actions that involve 'sustained shared thinking' and open-ended questioning, which extend children's thinking. Siraj-Blatchford et al. (2002: 8) have defined sustained shared thinking as 'an episode in which two or more individuals work together in an intellectual way to solve a problem, clarify a concept, evaluate activities, extend a narrative etc. Both parties must contribute to the thinking and it must develop and extend'.

'Sustained shared thinking' is explicitly referred to in England's Early Years Foundation Stage (DfES, 2007b: DfE, 2012a), particularly with regard to developing children's creativity and critical thinking.

Adults' interactions with children need to be sensitive and encouraging during play. Adults should observe children carefully and listen to them in order to nurture their thinking. Using appropriate open-ended questions such as 'why do you think …?' and 'what might happen if …?', will enable children to further develop their ideas. Observing babies and young children at play can provide adults with sometimes surprising, but valuable, information about children's ideas, experiences and developing mathematical understanding (see Chapter 7).

However, adults working with older children and aiming to encourage a play-based approach to learning mathematics, may have to consider who will have 'control' over the learning. The play may be planned, structured and guided by the adult, or the children could be the decision-makers, promoting self-directed and child-led learning.

Adults involved in planning for, or structuring, play activities need to be clear about what particular mathematical learning the play could provide and ensure there is clarity of purpose. Additionally, a decision may also be required about whether there is to be an 'end-product' or whether the process and involvement in the play is sufficient for learning to occur and for the adult to assess this. Planning how and when mathematical learning is to be assessed during play activities and how this will be recorded is important.

Interventions by adults during play will alter the outcomes of the learning for the children involved. Adults will therefore need to make decisions about when interventions are desirable. They should also consider the nature and purpose of any interventions. An adult may take the role of a questioner, challenger, model, demonstrator or co-learner, or the adult may play alongside the children. Briggs and Hansen (2012: 65), summarising Dockett and Fleer (1999), suggest that there are

> three roles of adults in play-based learning environments. As a *manager*, the adult manages the resources, time and space. This would also include being aware of risks such as checking equipment and internet safety. As a *facilitator*, the adult mediates, promotes equality and interprets children's play. As a *player*, the adult engages with the children in parallel play, co-playing and play tutoring.

In different types of play, the role undertaken by the adult will need to be flexible and reflective if learning through play is to be optimal.

Summary

In this chapter we have explored the value of play in different aspects of children's mathematical learning and development and illustrated this through a discussion of case studies. Alongside a discussion of each child's mathematical learning, we have highlighted the importance of the adult's role in scaffolding and supporting children's thinking through sensitive, personalised interactions. We noted the importance of engaging in 'sustained shared thinking' (Siraj-Blatchford et al., 2002)

(Continued)

(Continued)

with children and provided opportunities to consider how aspects of your own practice can be developed to enhance children's learning. We have also considered how older children can be encouraged to learn mathematics through play and how the role of the adult is key in ensuring that all children from birth to 8 years are offered an environment that nurtures and values play as a means of learning. As they develop and learn in different contexts, these early experiences enable children to make connections, apply their understanding, and form firm mathematical foundations for later mathematical learning.

Further reading

Bruce, T. (2005) *Early Childhood Education*, 3rd edn. London: Hodder and Stoughton.
Chapter 5 explains more about schemas and their relationship with Piagetian theory.
Montague-Smith, A. and Price, A. (2012) *Mathematics in Early Years Education*, 2nd edn. London: Routledge.
This book explores early mathematical concepts in relation to theory and practice along with a wealth of activities that will enhance your planning and assessment.
Briggs, M. and Hansen, A. (2012) *Play-based Learning in the Primary School.* London: Sage.
This book explains the value of play as an effective medium for teaching and learning across the curriculum. It offers suggestions about how to plan and facilitate play-based learning to increase motivation and engagement and includes case studies of how mathematics can be learned through play.

4

Children Representing their Mathematics

Clare Wiseman

Chapter Overview

In this chapter you can read about:

- How children begin to understand that mathematical thinking can be represented
- Progression in children's representation of mathematical thinking
- How children can be encouraged to represent and record their mathematical thinking
- How adults can interpret young children's mathematical representations.

Mathematical communication

The work of socio-constructivists Vygotsky (1986) and Bruner (1990) has shown that an important part of learning is interaction between the learner and others. Such interaction requires communication and negotiation; this may take the form of actions, spoken language or written language which provides symbols for understanding ideas and concepts. This chapter is concerned with how the written language of mathematics can be nurtured and developed in young children.

Like any other language, mathematics is communicated using symbols, which have to be decoded and interpreted by the reader in order for meaning making to happen. The symbols used in mathematics are to some extent arbitrary and often have an alternative meaning in another context and for the young child. For example, the symbol '+' can trigger associations with particular religions, first aid, the location of 'treasure' on a map, a meeting point for two roads, a 'kiss' or simply two lines in space. For the young child there is no logical reason why this sign should also have a particular mathematical application; this needs to be explored and understood.

There has been some concern that children are too hastily introduced to formal methods of recording their mathematical thinking in advance of true understanding of the abstract ideas that this complicated code represents and this may be detrimental to their later mathematical understanding (Pound, 2006). However, children meet many aspects of mathematics in their everyday lives and through their play (see Chapters 1 and 3) and sometimes look for a way of recording, representing and giving permanence to their thinking. This chapter presents an outline of how young children may begin to do this.

Enactive representations

Initially, children represent thoughts and ideas using their senses, actions and movements, involving concrete or real objects. For example, the child lining up a row of teddies or toys is using actions and objects to represent thoughts around sorting, classifying, quantity and pattern; the child sorting shapes into a sorter is using senses and objects to explore and represent thoughts about how three-dimensional objects look, feel and work in space. Nutbrown (2011) further explores this idea of movement and actions as a mode of learning for children. She describes how young children develop schema (early patterns of behaviour) to discover, experiment with and investigate the world around them and begin to develop understanding and knowledge in areas of literacy, mathematics, science and the arts. Children involved in basic activities and actions such as stirring, spinning, turning taps or simply watching the clothes in a washing machine go around are developing an early understanding of shape, space and rotation. Similarly, children who explore the outside environment and engage in climbing up and down, crawling, turning, running or going backwards and forwards are increasing their awareness and early understanding of concepts such as height and length. It is unlikely that at this stage children will be able to verbalise, explain or represent their thinking in terms of conventional signs and symbols. However, attending to the way that children move around, organise toys and objects and explore their environment may reveal something about their emerging mathematical understanding.

> - When observing children playing, consider how their actions and behaviours might reveal their emerging understanding of mathematical concepts.
> - Which mathematical ideas have you seen evidence of?

Engaging with written mathematics

Hughes (1986) argued that young children have considerable mathematical understanding and language before they begin formal schooling and that this understanding is communicated through everyday, informal language and in response to the child's familiar world. Like Hughes (1986), Carruthers and Worthington (2006) suggest that, in a similar way to that in which children first learn about literacy in the home and have access to literacy practices through written language (packaging, newspapers, signs, advertisements, leaflets, letters, texting, email), so too will children begin their learning about mathematics in the home. They highlight the work of Tizard and Hughes (1984) to illustrate how language use at home helps children to change experience into understanding. Practices in the home and early years settings can provide opportunities for young children to begin to explore forms of written symbolic language, demonstrating what is significant to them and revealing their thinking in a visual form.

Carruthers and Worthington's (2006) research suggests that children need to become 'bi-numerate' (2006: 2), translating between their informal 'home mathematics' and symbolic 'school mathematics', in order to communicate their personal understanding of mathematics in a written form. However, Hughes (1986) indicates that there is a large gap between these forms of mathematics which children find difficult to bridge. Hughes (1986) cites the work of Bruner and Kenney (1974) to reinforce his recommendation that some of these barriers to mathematics learning for children could be removed if they were encouraged to use their own methods of representing their mathematical thinking, often referred to as mathematical mark-making.

Mathematical mark-making

The progression into mark-making is an important stage in development. It demonstrates that the child's thinking has evolved to the stage where they understand that they can make marks to represent something else and as a tool to make their thinking visible. It also allows them to use expression and emotion, which has a central role to play in cognitive development (Matthews, 2003).

In the same way in which children need to explore and experiment with mark-making as a developmental stage in the process of becoming literate (where children move through informal representations of their ideas through 'scribble', painting, drawing and emergent or developmental writing before they are able to understand and employ the accepted rules and conventions of writing), children also need to make marks to represent their mathematical ideas as part of the process of becoming numerate. Children are 'meaning makers' (Wells, 2009) and have a desire to communicate and represent their developing understanding. The opportunity for children to make their own meaning out of interactions and experiences and experiment with idiosyncratic representations is important in mathematical development too. The development of personal strategies for use in problem solving and calculation is essential before children are introduced to abstract, symbolic and formal written mathematics (Carruthers and Worthington, 2008).

Representing and recording mathematics

'Recording' and 'representing' mathematics are different. Carruthers and Worthington (2006) suggest that children *recording* the outcome of a practical activity or recording something that has been mentally calculated is of limited value and is more concerned with the *product* of the mathematical thinking. In contrast, they suggest that a child's own representations support deep understanding by providing visual feedback, thus supporting their mathematical thinking, meanings and understanding about all aspects of written mathematics and symbols. Children's *representation* of mathematics allows for the *process* of the thinking to be revealed, rather than the *product* of the thinking (see Figure 4.2) where the process (a count-all strategy) by which the child has reached a total amount is evident. In a sense, children's mathematical graphics are their thinking process on paper. While the exactness of the mathematics is important when children are *recording* mathematics, it is the quality of the mathematical thinking and understanding that is important when children are *representing* mathematics.

Children's invented representations

The tins game

Hughes' (1986) research showed that young children (including those children who are already familiar with conventional symbols to represent number) employ their own invented, meaningful symbols to represent their ideas about concepts of counting and quantity. The 'tins game' required children to label four tins, each of which had either zero, one, two or three bricks inside. Hughes analysed and categorised the marks that the children made to represent these quantities as follows:

1. **Idiosyncratic responses:** Children understood that marks convey meanings which are personal. These marks may be described as 'scribble', but are nonetheless an important stage in early mark-making.
2. **Pictographic responses:** Children produced marks that resembled a picture of what they could visualise inside the tins.
3. **Iconic responses:** Children produced marks (for example, tally marks, circles) that showed one-to-one correspondence (see Chapter 9) with the amount of bricks in each of the tins.
4. **Symbolic responses:** Children (mostly 7 years or older) produced some form of conventional mathematical symbol to represent the number of bricks in each tin.

Hughes (1986) noted that where children had used personal, invented symbols to record the contents of each tin, they were able to still interpret the marks successfully up to one week later. This suggests that if children use their own marks for representing mathematical thinking, their understanding and learning is more meaningful and permanent.

The Williams Review focused attention on the need for adults to 'support children in making mathematical marks as part of developing their abilities to extend and organise their mathematical thinking' (DCSF, 2008: 2). This key recommendation from the Report draws extensively on the work of Carruthers and Worthington (2006). Carruthers explains that: 'We have observed that children make mathematical marks as well as marks for writing ... we believe this is the very beginning of the process of children understanding the abstract symbolism of mathematics' (DCSF, 2008: 35). Therefore, for those working with young children, an understanding of how to encourage, respond to and develop children's mathematical mark-making is essential.

Taxonomy of children's mathematical graphics, 0–8 years

Carruthers and Worthington (2006) charted the development of children's mathematical graphics. Their taxonomy (available at http://www.childrens-mathematics. net/taxonomy.pdf) demonstrates how children may progress from early exploration

(Continued)

(Continued)

of representations through play (enactive or multi-modal representation – representing thinking through actions, senses, movement and speech) to their own invented mark-making (may be described as 'scribbles'), and subsequently towards more conventional marks such as drawings, letters, numerals and symbols.

Interpreting children's mathematical marks

Figure 4.1 shows how Bobby (age 5) is experimenting with and combining numbers, symbols, letters and drawings to represent his thoughts and ideas around people and objects that are meaningful and important to him in his environment.

Figure 4.1 *Bobby's tractor*

Children begin to represent their mathematical ideas about numbers and symbols, using numbers as labels, to represent counted (see Figure 4.2) and uncounted quantities. The taxonomy proposes that representations of counting precede representations of mental calculations. Carruthers and Worthington argue that 'children all need to be

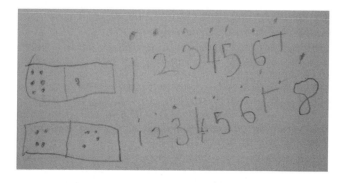

Figure 4.2 *Bobby's dominoes*

freely representing quantities that are counted before moving on to early operations in which they count continuously' (2006: 130). At this stage, children may not yet understand and represent the separation and combining of sets (see Chapter 10) and thus show ideas around calculation as counting continuously. Thompson (2008b: 98) refers to this strategy as 'counting-all'. When trying to find the total number of items in two groups children may recognise that each group can be counted separately, but will begin at one and count all the items continuously to find the total. In Figure 4.2 Bobby is adding together the two sides of the dominoes and is developing a sense of addition by combining the two sets, but, at this stage, is reliant on a count-all strategy (see Chapter 10) to find and represent the total.

After this stage, when children will move on to develop more efficient strategies for addition and subtraction (such as counting-on, or counting back) they will still need opportunities to explore symbols in their own ways before they are introduced to the standard symbolic representation of addition and subtraction (numerals and the +, – and = signs). Children's exploratory symbols may be 'implicit', where addition or subtraction is implied rather than written; children may use their own personal symbols to represent a calculation (for example, a line, a star, a box), or they may represent the calculation using 'narrative action' pictorially to show the idea of change (for example, a drawing of a hand adding or removing some items, or an arrow pointing to some numerals). Carruthers and Worthington (2006) suggest that when children use 'narrative action' (p. 112) it allows them to reflect on the operation and its function, thus indicating that they are making connections between concrete objects, drawings, signs and the idea of transformation or change. Children representing their mathematical thinking at this stage may also be 'code switching' – moving between informal, non-standard representations that include pictures and personal marks from the language that is already understood and including some standard symbols from a 'second language' of abstract mathematical codes in which they are not yet fluent (Carruthers and Worthington, 2006: 121).

From this stage, the taxonomy demonstrates that children may begin to progress to representing their mathematical thinking using standard symbols for operations with small numbers, usually supported by jottings and often returning to earlier forms, usually iconic representations, for 'security and fitness for purpose in a particular context' (Carruthers and Worthington, 2006: 130). In Figure 4.3 Isobel (age 6) employs both a standard symbolic representation of addition, alongside the security of iconic representation. From here, children are eventually able to move into representing their mathematics in mostly standard and formal ways, and should be able to make choices and decisions about how best to record and demonstrate their mathematical thinking. However, as Thompson (2008c: 158) argues, even at this stage, children 'should be working in an environment that attaches value to idiosyncratic written methods and should be praised for inventing their own notations and jottings'.

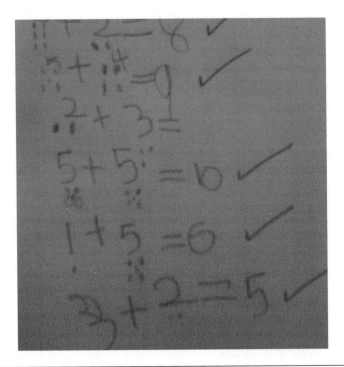

Figure 4.3 *Isobel's calculations*

- How could you encourage young children to represent their mathematics in ways which are meaningful and purposeful to them?

The following case studies illustrate Carruthers and Worthington's (2011) taxonomy and will help you to consider how young children demonstrate and represent their mathematical understanding in ways which are meaningful, purposeful and provide a foundation for later progress towards more conventional mathematical representations.

CASE STUDY

Jose's numbers

Jose was sitting with two friends, talking about birthdays and their ages. Jose had just had his fifth birthday and had received several cards featuring the number five. His birthday was acknowledged both in the classroom and during the whole school assembly, thus connecting home and school learning. Later, he drew a picture (Figure 4.4) to represent what he had been doing earlier in the day. A conversation with him revealed that the graphics represent Jose and his two friends (one of whom is 'still four and a half'), his past and current ages and one hundred because 'that's an important number'.

Jose's graphics reveal much about his understanding of number. Applying Carruthers and Worthington's (2011) taxonomy we can see that Jose is in the early stages of

Figure 4.4 *Jose's numbers*

exploring mark-making and attaching mathematical meanings to his graphics. He is 'exploring with symbols' to represent number and writing numbers for his own purpose. He understands that 'numerals can be used as labels' and to 'represent quantities counted'. For example, Jose recognises that 'five' is a label to show his age and also to represent the number of birthdays he has had.

The drawing may also indicate Jose's emerging understanding of fractions. He has used his own invented symbol to explore and represent how 4½ can be written. This marks an important milestone in his mathematical understanding. During early stages of children's mathematical development, formal teaching about fractions would be inappropriate. However, children will meet the language of fractions in social contexts, especially in sharing activities with objects, food or toys (see Chapter 11). More particularly, in our society where birthdays are anticipated and celebrated, children soon begin to understand and attach meaning to the idea that their age is an important factor in decisions that are made for them and about them. For example, children are often told 'when you are five you will be able to … '. Furthermore, because it is important to most children and it is a term that is commonly used, they naturally begin to understand that being 4½, for example, is somewhere between two important birthdays which are represented by numbers. The recognition that values between whole numbers exist and can be represented is the very beginning of understanding fractions and decimals.

The learning environment plays an important role in supporting Jose in the development of his motivation and ability to represent and communicate his thinking to others through written symbols. Not only is he afforded the time, space, materials and opportunity to engage in this activity, but his mark-making is valued and nurtured by the class teacher who discusses his picture with him and praises him for his efforts. He is also immersed in surroundings which provide him with multi-sensory experiences of mathematics. There are both concrete and abstract materials for him to explore; the semi-abstract number track mounted on the classroom wall provides examples of mathematical representations which Jose can use, discuss and incorporate into his own personal representations of number.

CASE STUDY

Sam's data handling

Within a topic about 'Harvest', Sam's class had been considering 'fruit'. The class teacher had encouraged the children to discuss their favourite fruit. She also introduced them to bar charts as a way of recording preferences and a class bar chart for 'Favourite Fruit' was compiled, showing individual preferences for different fruits.

Several days later, during child-initiated time, Sam decided that he wanted to make his own bar chart. Paper, pens, clipboards and other writing materials were readily available in the classroom and Sam independently collected the 'tools' that he felt would enable him to record his findings. Sam then, idiosyncratically, gathered data from other children and recorded his findings, as shown in Figure 4.5.

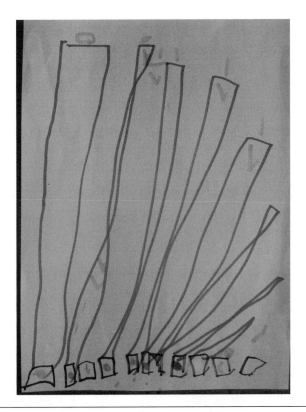

Figure 4.5 *Sam's graph*

Sam's representation of his findings in his form of a bar chart demonstrates that he understands that:

- data can be collected
- he needs a way of keeping track of responses to his question 'What is your favourite fruit out of … ?', and he uses ticks, dots and tally marks to achieve this

- mathematical data can be represented graphically
- bar charts use columns
- bar charts can be used to communicate mathematical data.

In this self-initiated activity Sam has experienced the first three of the four stages of the data-handling process: collecting, organising, representing and interpreting data (Haylock, 2010) (see Chapter 15). An adult could support Sam further in his learning by discussing with him what his bar chart shows about the original question he had posed. The important role of dialogue as part of developing mathematical understanding is highlighted in Chapter 2. Care needs to be taken about attributing mathematical understanding when examining children's representations in isolation. It is crucial that a sensitive observation and dialogue between the adult and the child supports the understanding of what is represented; the mathematical interpretation of the mark-making needs to be that of the child, not the adult (see 'In Practice' below).

This case study also underlines the importance of providing an enabling environment for children which will allow them to experiment with mathematical graphics. Carruthers and Worthington (2006) propose that in order to foster children's attempts to communicate their thinking through marks on paper the learning environment needs to be both physically and psychologically open to children's initiatives. Access to a range of physical resources for representing, coupled with an ethos of encouragement and empowerment for children, as demonstrated in Sam's classroom, will enable children to create mathematical meaning through play and exploration.

Figure 4.6 provides suggestions about how adults can provide learning environments which support rich representations of mathematics.

The Role of the Adult	In Practice Examples
To provide a model for recording and representing mathematics. To notice an appropriate point in the children's development where a specific aspect of mathematical representation may be meaningfully modelled.	• The adult 'playing' alongside children with the small world toys may model how to sort, match, order and group the toys into chosen categories. • An adult 'playing' alongside children in the outside area may model to children how to use tallies to keep a record of laps completed, points scored, or items collected. • The children in the flower shop role-play area want to know how to make labels to represent prices for their goods. This may lead to the adult specifically supporting the children by modelling how a price label could be written using standard numerals and notation. Similarly, the adult may see this as an opportunity to plan an activity which would encourage the children to experience examples of price labels in the environment and use these as models for their own representations.

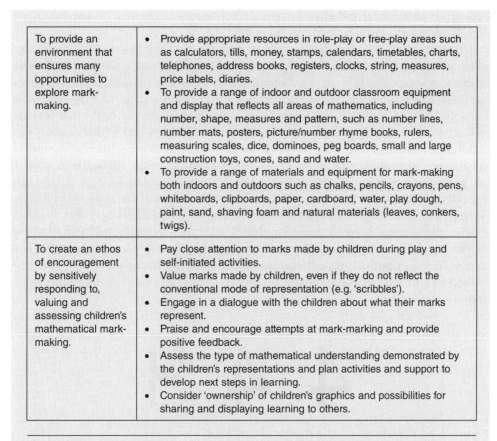

To provide an environment that ensures many opportunities to explore mark-making.	• Provide appropriate resources in role-play or free-play areas such as calculators, tills, money, stamps, calendars, timetables, charts, telephones, address books, registers, clocks, string, measures, price labels, diaries. • To provide a range of indoor and outdoor classroom equipment and display that reflects all areas of mathematics, including number, shape, measures and pattern, such as number lines, number mats, posters, picture/number rhyme books, rulers, measuring scales, dice, dominoes, peg boards, small and large construction toys, cones, sand and water. • To provide a range of materials and equipment for mark-making both indoors and outdoors such as chalks, pencils, crayons, pens, whiteboards, clipboards, paper, cardboard, water, play dough, paint, sand, shaving foam and natural materials (leaves, conkers, twigs).
To create an ethos of encouragement by sensitively responding to, valuing and assessing children's mathematical mark-making.	• Pay close attention to marks made by children during play and self-initiated activities. • Value marks made by children, even if they do not reflect the conventional mode of representation (e.g. 'scribbles'). • Engage in a dialogue with the children about what their marks represent. • Praise and encourage attempts at mark-marking and provide positive feedback. • Assess the type of mathematical understanding demonstrated by the children's representations and plan activities and support to develop next steps in learning. • Consider 'ownership' of children's graphics and possibilities for sharing and displaying learning to others.

Figure 4.6 *Role of adults in supporting mathematical mark-making*

Conventional representations of mathematics

Although giving children the opportunity and encouragement to represent and record their mathematics in an open and personal way is important, most children will be aware of environmental print around them which includes the standard numerals and mathematical symbols that are conventionally used in our society. Children will reach a stage of development when they will want to be able to begin to use conventional representations to communicate their ideas. In the same way in which it is crucial for children to understand and use the alphabet and punctuation accurately to communicate, it is also essential that children understand that standard mathematical symbols can be used with precision for the same purpose. However, an important transitional stage is to permit children to operate with a degree of fluidity, allowing them to move between both informal and formal mathematical representations, or, to use Carruthers and Worthington's term, to 'code switch' (2006: 119).

Before children can be introduced to writing the 10 numerals (0–9) that are used in our number system, their fine motor skills and handwriting abilities must be sufficiently developed. Children need many opportunities to practise and refine such handwriting skills within diverse activities such as making patterns in the air, writing with chunky chalks on the playground, tracing and copying, and using a range of resources such as flour and water mix, paint, large pens and whiteboards. Once children have mastered some of the skills needed for writing, children should be encouraged to practise writing numerals regularly. Some of the numerals (0, 1, 4, 7) are generally easier for children to reproduce; other numerals (2, 3, 5, 8, 9) cause considerable difficulty for some children and it is common for some numerals to be reversed until children reach about 7 years old (Carruthers and Worthington, 2006). Adults also need to draw children's attention to the visual variations in the way in which numerals are presented in everyday life (see Figure 4.7). It is therefore important to support children by identifying such features of numerals in evidence in the environment and providing models of numerals through display and resources.

Figure 4.7 *Variations of the numeral for 'four'*

Children will also need to acquire an understanding of how mathematical operations are recorded in a standard way. As discussed at the beginning of the chapter, many of the signs and symbols that are used in mathematics are, to a large extent, arbitrary, and this can cause difficulties for young children. Children will be gradually introduced to the standard signs that are used to indicate addition (+), subtraction (−) and equivalence (=). However, as Carruthers and Worthington (2006) caution, it is unhelpful to introduce such symbols to young children before they have developed an understanding of the concept being represented and have had purposeful opportunities to develop their own method of representing it. Adults', or peers', representations may act as models, demonstrating to children how their repertoire of marks for showing simple calculations can be extended to include conventional abstract symbols. The regular implementation of this, in situations that are authentic for the children and are accompanied by a dialogue between those involved (see 'In Practice' featured earlier in this chapter) will provide support for transition between children's own methods for representing calculations through to the use of standard forms.

Mathematical symbols can be particularly problematic for young children, due in part to the variety of associated vocabulary that may be used for any one symbol, but also because the same symbol can represent a variety of meanings depending on the context in which it is used. For example, the = sign has a range of associated vocabulary ('makes', 'equals', 'is', 'leaves', 'totals') and can represent a complex network of ideas and experiences (Haylock and Cockburn, 2013). Adults need to support children to make connections between practical mathematical situations, the images or diagrams used to represent them, the conventional mathematical symbols used and the associated vocabulary. Encouraging young children to write and re-tell 'maths stories' (with pictures), alongside practical mathematical activities, will help them to make associations between the mathematical situation or operation and the conventional symbols and language used to express this.

- When and how should children be introduced to conventional forms of mathematical recording?

Summary

This chapter has explained why it is important that children are given opportunities and encouragement to represent their mathematical thinking, and has particularly highlighted the need for adults to be aware of children's own personal and idiosyncratic methods for representing mathematics. It has also shown the need for young children to be given time and space to develop their own methods of mathematical representation, before being required to adopt the very formal, abstract and complicated code of conventional mathematical symbols. The work of Carruthers and Worthington (2006, 2011) has been explored in some detail to help to illustrate how even very young children can begin to represent their mathematical thinking and understanding and to help provide a framework which can be used by those working with young children to analyse the mathematical marks that children make.

Further reading

Carruthers, E. and Worthington, M. (2011) *Children's Mathematics Network*. Available at: http://www.childrens-mathematics.net/ (accessed 16 January 2013).

Visit the website to find out more about the work of Carruthers and Worthington and for many more examples of children's mathematical graphics and detailed information about their taxonomy.

Tucker, K. (2010) *Mathematics through Play in the Early Years*, 2nd edn. London: Sage.

Chapter 3 of this very accessible book will give you further support in interpreting the meaning behind children's mathematical graphics, and ideas about how to stimulate and support mathematical graphics through play.

5

Mathematical Learning Outside the Classroom

Helen Taylor

 Chapter Overview

In this chapter you can read about:

- The value of taking young children outside to develop mathematical understanding
- Different outdoor environments for learning
- Aspects of mathematics that might be enhanced through learning outside
- Managing children's learning and mathematical development outdoors.

Why outdoors?

Many children enjoy opportunities to be and to play outside, opportunities that some may rarely experience. They may feel less constrained than within the classroom. Running and making a noise is allowed and there are opportunities to do things on a larger scale than is often possible inside, enabling children to develop their gross motor skills, a prerequisite to developing the fine motor skills needed for writing numerals. Education outside has been recommended by many over the years including Pestalozzi (1746–1827), Froebel (1782–1852) and McMillan (1860–1931). These pioneers of outdoor education recognised its benefits for children's health and well-being as well as their learning. Laevers (1994) also highlighted the positive effects on children's well-being. Boys, particularly, seem to value and benefit from outdoor activity and learning (ESTYN, 2011; Ouvry, 2003).

Connecting school or setting mathematics with everyday life is essential if children are to learn mathematics effectively and be able to use their learning in other contexts. Adults need to help children to make these connections. Taking children outdoors is a good way of doing this and can help children to see the purpose of mathematics and to learn actively. For example, children may have been learning names of simple geometrical shapes in the classroom from brightly coloured plastic shapes which may seem disconnected from the real world. However, while outside, they might begin to recognise these shapes in the natural or built environment. Children may have the additional opportunity to move materials and resources around more freely outdoors and this may lead them to making connections and being creative.

Loose parts

Nicholson (1972: 6) identified the importance of variables or 'loose parts' in creating an environment where children can become engaged and involved:

> In any environment, both the degree of inventiveness and creativity, and the possibility of discovery, are directly proportional to the number and kind of variables in it.

This has come to be known as the theory of 'loose parts'.

Outdoor learning also lends itself to learning across curriculum areas as children use 'loose parts' imaginatively to build with or to represent other items. Young children do not compartmentalise learning into subject-based boxes so these opportunities may seem more natural to them. Adults planning and recognising learning, can easily make links between mathematics and science, design and technology, geography, physical education and other curriculum areas. Figure 5.1 shows children who have constructed a tunnel in the woods, using the 'loose parts' of branches and sticks, in the process talking about aspects of shape and size.

Outdoor experiences enable children to practise and develop mathematical language. Often, this will relate to shape, space or measures. Children are often eager to point out something they have noticed and attempt to describe where it is in the environment using words such as near, far, by, next to, in front and behind. They may talk about the size of objects, for example describing an ancient tree as 'really big' or

Figure 5.1 *'Can I squeeze through?'*

a log they have picked up as 'heavy'. Adults may be able to extend children's language in these situations by challenging children to find something heavier or lighter. Outdoor observations present opportunities for awe and wonder in the changing environment and awareness of 'the nature of pattern and time' (Pound and Lee, 2011: 103).

Playing outdoors often leads children to be curious and thus into solving problems (Boaler, 2009), such as finding objects that will fit in terms of size, the number of objects or children that can fit into a space, or working out how they can balance or fix something.

CASE STUDY

The see-saw

Figure 5.2 shows Carrie and Susie (both 4 years old) playing in the woodland within the school grounds. They had inserted a fallen branch unevenly into a fork in a tree and one child climbed on each end. The children said they were on a

(Continued)

(Continued)

see-saw. However, because of the way they had inserted the branch one end of the see-saw was higher than the other. Jake came along and climbed on to the higher end with Carrie. The children insisted that Susie was heavier than Carrie and Jake together. Their teacher reminded them of using balances inside the classroom and asked them to think about other reasons for one end being higher than the other.

Figure 5.2   *'Who is heavier?'*

Advantages of outdoor play include children having opportunities to work with others, to co-operate and to talk to each other. Outdoor play, although not necessarily directly and solely mathematical, gives opportunities for developing mathematical language amongst more general language development. Children are able to extend mathematical ideas and to share them through playing with and alongside other children. Collaboration and oral communication skills are essential. Connections can also be made between outdoor play that will support children's mathematical learning and stories. The traditional tale of *The Enormous Turnip* and the modern story of *Grandpa's*

Garden (Fry, 2012) will support mathematical talk and link to outdoor mathematical contexts. Imaginative contexts combined with the outdoor environment can boost children's concentration (ESTYN, 2009).

Digital cameras are ideal for recording outdoor mathematical learning and can be used by adults or children to collect images to discuss indoors later. Digital counters might be used for surveys, digital stopwatches for timing events, mobile phone applications for identifying compass directions and digital microphones for recording sound patterns.

Different outdoor environments and mathematical opportunities

Views from windows may provide mathematical opportunities. Some classes and groups have a bird-feeding station near to a window and this can provide opportunities for children to count birds of different species and to talk about the capacities of different feeders as they fill and refill them. The view from a window might give rise to discussion about the relative heights of tower blocks or trees. Shapes may be identified and discussed in the natural or built environment. Passing vehicles may be counted.

> - Look out of the window of your setting. What can you see that might generate mathematical opportunities or discussion?

In the last 10 years, many early years settings have developed their outside area, usually an area immediately outside the classroom or setting door where provision is continuous and accessible all year round. Children can be involved in planning the development of such areas (Pound and Lee, 2011); this can create valuable mathematical opportunities to discuss space, shape, numbers and money. Sometimes there is a covered area where children can shelter from rain or sun. Frequently these areas are set up as an extension of the classroom, where children can come and go as they choose, with resources that children can use during child-initiated time and during adult-directed activities. Resources should be changed, just as they are inside, to encourage children to interact with them in different ways and to encourage learning. For example, many outside areas have a water tray which might be set up with different objects so that children can investigate whether they float or sink – a scientific activity. However, subsequently it might be set up with containers of different shapes and sizes so that children can tip water from one container to another to experience ideas of capacity.

Figure 5.3 suggests some resources that could be provided and the mathematical ideas and vocabulary (Ouvry, 2003) playing with them might encourage. Alongside these resources, children can have access to paper on clipboards, pencils, pens, crayons and other stationery items to record their mathematical ideas. It is also important to ensure, however, that outdoor provision complements and extends opportunities offered indoors rather than mirroring it (Ouvry, 2003; Stevens and Scott, 2002).

Resource	Activity	Areas of Mathematical Learning and Vocabulary
Water tray with containers of different shapes and sizes	Pouring	Capacity
Sand tray • with containers • with other toys, e.g. plastic dinosaurs, spades or toy vehicles	Pouring Building Creating	Capacity Position, direction and movement Shapes
Bikes, trikes, scooters, cars, etc.	Riding round obstacles or a course Children can be encouraged to 'park' vehicles in numbered bays	Position, direction and movement Recognising numerals
Climbing frames	Climbing up, over and through	Position, direction and movement Shape
Large construction sets	Building Creating	Position, direction and movement Shape Measures
Bean bags, buckets, hoops, balls, skittles, etc.	Throwing, bowling, scoring, inventing and playing games	Position, direction and movement Shape Measures Counting, addition
Washing lines	Children can be encouraged to hang numbered objects on the washing line in the correct order	Position, direction and movement Shape Measures Recognising numerals
Painted designs on the play surface, for example numbered snakes, hop-scotch, number lines	Running, jumping, hopping, skipping, throwing, bowling	Position, direction and movement Shape Measures Recognising numerals Counting, addition

Figure 5.3 *Developing mathematical learning using resources for outside areas*

The wider grounds of a setting can be used to help children to develop mathematical ideas.

- Take a walk (or an imaginary walk) around the grounds of a setting that you know well. What mathematical opportunities can you identify?

Figure 5.4 suggests mathematical development which could take place in or be inspired by different areas in the grounds.

Area	Mathematical Opportunity
Car park	Counting Recognising shapes Recognising numerals Looking for patterns, e.g. on car wheels
Pond area	Pond dipping, sorting and counting small creatures and plants
Garden	Counting Looking for patterns in flowers and other plants, creatures and seasons Talking about relative sizes and positions Talking about capacity when filling containers and watering
Playground markings	Talking about position, direction and movement when following lines Counting and scoring with addition when playing games
Climbing frames	Recognising shapes, talking about positions and sizes
Field	Counting daisies Talking about measures including length and speed
Entrance to building	Recognising numerals and shapes
Trees	Talking about measures, shapes and counting Sorting leaves and seeds like conkers and acorns Den building leading to problem-solving discussion related to shape, size and numbers
Mathematics trails round the grounds	Different types of trail can be devised to encourage children to notice and work out different things, including shape, counting and calculating
Maze	Pound and Lee (2011) suggest that mazes and labyrinths encourage adults to model and children to use positional language and that children can be involved in constructing their own mazes

Figure 5.4 *Developing mathematical learning within the school grounds*

Some settings have a wooded area within the grounds; others may be able to arrange for children to make regular visits to woods or Forest Schools. The idea of Forest Schools, where nature and the outdoor environment are used to give children freedom and space to play and discover natural phenomena (Williams-Siegfredsen, 2007), originated in Scandinavia but has become increasingly popular in the UK in recent years. Forest Schools provide children with opportunities for physical, personal, social and intellectual development (Joyce, 2012; Knight, 2009; Maynard, 2007; Tovey, 2007).

Forest Schools

Murray and O'Brien (in Knight, 2009) have researched extensively about the benefits for young children of being involved in Forest Schools, at first in Wales (2004) and then applying the techniques in England (2005). Knight then undertook a project focusing on the same outcomes in order to facilitate comparison of the outcomes. Although their studies did not highlight any particular mathematical learning or development, they did highlight some general benefits which would be applicable to children learning mathematics as well as other subject areas. These benefits included confidence, social skills, language and communication, motivation and concentration, physical skills and knowledge and understanding.

This chapter concentrates on the mathematical development that might be encouraged and developed by activities in woodland. Little research focuses solely or mostly on this area, but White (2008), Ouvry (2003) and Warden (2005 and 2007) recommend that using natural materials will encourage children to develop intellectual skills and support mathematical thinking and development of schemas (see Chapter 1).

Outdoor activities and mathematical learning

Rachel Taylor (2011), a Reception class teacher at a small primary school, tried to find out whether the children in her class would learn outdoors and to measure their progress towards achieving the Early Learning Goals (DfES, 2007b). She noticed children's achievements in applying mathematical vocabulary introduced within the classroom and in problem solving. Whilst collecting wood for their camp Jonathan said, 'This stick is nearly as tall as you, Miss Taylor. Could you help me carry this, please, because it is too heavy?' Adam then commented on Jonathan's piece of wood saying, 'That stick is too big; we need small, bendy ones to fill the gaps'. The children were often observed counting and calculating, as for safety reasons only a small number of children were allowed in certain trees at a time. They often worked out that they needed two children to come down then it would be their turn. On one occasion, the children became fascinated by the size of some of the trees and decided to measure them (see Figure 5.5); string was provided to extend the activity.

Figure 5.5 *Measuring trees*

CASE STUDY

Using the woods in the school grounds

Another primary school has a wooded area within the school grounds. The Reception class, their teacher and two teaching assistants spent every Thursday morning in the woods. The teacher saw the woods as an extension of the class-room and she believed that during each morning the children should spend some of the time undertaking an adult-directed activity and the rest of the time on child-initiated activities. One week, the adult-directed activities related to, and developed, some of the ideas about mass children had been working on in the classroom. They had compared objects inside, talking about whether they were heavier or lighter. The children had also made bags out of paper, which they attached to canes with one bag at each end. They had compared the mass of two objects by placing them in the bags and deciding which end of the cane was going down for the heavier object. They took these bags on canes outside with them and extended the work in the woodland area (Figure 5.6). One child was surprised to pick up a large log which was quite light, prompting talk about whether large objects are always heavy and smaller things lighter. The children used language such as 'This one's really

(Continued)

(Continued)

heavy! I can't even lift it', 'This feather is tiny'. Clipboards with paper and pencils had been taken into the woods and some children chose to record their findings in their own way (see Figure 5.7).

Figure 5.6   *'The big stick is heavy'*

Gradually children became involved in self-initiated activities, many of which were problem-solving activities about measures. Children were observed making various structures, including a tunnel. 'Will this fit?' was often heard, followed by, 'I need a really big one'. They were persistent and followed through ideas; they helped each other and explained to others what they were trying to do or to look for, so practising mathematical vocabulary and displaying the problem-solving attitudes and behaviours that will be required in later mathematics.

They had previously enjoyed making maps in the forest. Initiated by children making their own maps using paper attached to clipboards, this had developed into a large class map of the woodland area on a large piece of card. Grid lines had been drawn on it and squares were labelled A–E along the bottom and 1–4

Figure 5.7 *'Three heavy and five light things'*

up the side. Significant features of the area were marked on the map and some of the children were able to identify that the seating area was in D4 and the fire pit was in C2.

Walks from the setting may provide opportunities for mathematical learning.

- Undertaking traffic surveys including counting and data handling.
- Looking at street furniture such as post boxes provides numerals and times to discuss.
- Signs and notices support numeral recognition.
- A park may provide similar opportunities for activities to those suggested earlier.

(Continued)

(Continued)

- Indoor destinations for walks, such as a post office, shop or garden centre, also offer mathematical learning opportunities.
- The built environment provides many talking and starting points for mathematics. Opportunities include counting and calculation, identifying and talking about shapes, symmetry and measures, and data handling. Some buildings are rich in containing a variety of shapes; a cathedral or church may have tall pillars and arch-shaped windows, with different shapes inside them and the floors may be made up of interestingly-shaped, tessellating flagstones.

Occasionally, it may be possible to take children further afield. Beaches are a favourite destination that can provide rich mathematical opportunities. The NCETM website (https://www.ncetm.org.uk/resources/9268) refers to mathematical opportunities at the beach and a range of other outdoor experiences:

- Capacity can be explored through using buckets and other containers of sand and water.
- Competitions can be held to see who can build the tallest sandcastle.
- Shells and pebbles can be collected, counted and sorted in different ways.
- Seaweed can be compared for longer and shorter pieces.
- Marks made in the sand can be used for games and lead to talking about shapes, position, direction and movement.

Children's farms are popular destinations with opportunities for mathematical activity, for example:

- Counting animals
- Comparing sizes of different animals and their babies, alongside the relevant language development
- Talking about shapes in the natural and built environments
- Talking about position, direction and movement as they describe animals to each other (see Chapter 15).

When planning a visit further afield, it is sometimes easy to forget about mathematics and to focus on other areas of the curriculum. However, children can help in preparations for visits and these can provide additional mathematical activities, such as working out how many coaches are required or how much something will cost.

Managing children's mathematical learning outdoors

Recognising and providing opportunities for outdoor learning of mathematics is sometimes challenging. The additional organisation that is required to take children outside can daunt adults who are trying to promote progress in mathematics. Health and safety is a primary concern when taking children outside for learning (Ouvry, 2003; Warden, 2005, 2007). Using areas of the grounds that are not usually dedicated to learning, such as the car park, should necessitate additional considerations, and this also applies to areas that are not used every day or that present additional potential hazards such as pond areas. Taking children off-site will require further consideration, including higher adult to child ratios. Adults taking children outside and off-site should refer to the setting's policy and make sure all procedures are followed. Dressing appropriately for the weather conditions is essential. Some settings keep a stock of all-in-one cold or wet weather suits for children to wear outside, they encourage the children to bring a pair of suitable boots to wear outside and have a few spare pairs for those children who do not have them. Knight (2009: 4) quotes Farstad in saying that 'there is no bad weather, only bad clothing'. Parents may worry about their children being out-of-doors, because of the weather, ill-health or perceived time-wasting. Carruthers (2007) recommends outdoor learning for children with Special Educational Needs and disabilities as it can provide opportunities for risk-taking that they might not otherwise have. Staff therefore, need to allay parents' fears and communicate effectively with them so they understand what their children are doing and how they are learning and developing, as well as how they are being cared for in the out-of-doors (see Chapter 8).

Outdoor contexts provide opportunities for free play and adult-directed activities (as illustrated in the case studies), just as the classroom does. Adults can plan appropriately for progression for individuals, small groups and the whole class. They can also observe children and intervene occasionally and sensitively in their play to enable them to progress while following their own current interests (see Chapter 1). Bilton (2002) advised that outdoor space needs to be managed in a similar way to indoor space in order for children to gain maximum benefit from it, including by providing appropriate resources for children to extend their play and experiences.

Assessment and recording based on the observations by adults is possible outdoors just as it is inside (see Chapter 7). Pocket-sized notebooks are useful here and writing in pencil is recommended to avoid smudging in the rain. Cameras are also useful, along with a note or digital microphone recording of what a child has said when a particular achievement is noted for the child. Children may also choose to represent their mathematics if stationery is available for them (see Chapter 4).

Summary

The value of children learning mathematics outdoors was explored. Links were made to children's lives, to providing meaningful and enjoyable opportunities for mathematical learning and to enabling them to learn mathematics in a way that also promotes their physical development and general well-being. Different outdoor locations were considered for their mathematical learning potential, starting in and very close to the setting, moving into the grounds and then further afield. Outdoor contexts provide good opportunities for children to practise mathematical vocabulary. Children become very involved in their activities, frequently displaying high levels of persistence in solving their own practical problems, often in the areas of shape, space and measurement. The extra effort in organising children's learning of mathematics outdoors was recognised, however the benefits for children's learning make this worthwhile.

Further reading

Pound, L. and Lee, T. (2011) *Teaching Mathematics Creatively.* Abingdon: Routledge.
Chapter 9 clearly justifies using the outdoor environment for the learning and teaching of mathematics. The scope of this book covers the whole primary age range, so some of the practical suggestions and examples are for older children, but many of them are directly applicable and others could be adapted.
The National Centre for Excellence in Teaching Mathematics website, available at https://www.ncetm.org.uk/resources/9268 (accessed 15 February 2013) recommends a wider range of different types of outdoor learning experiences.
The Learning Outside the Classroom website, available at http://www.lotc.org.uk/why/early-years/ (accessed 15 February 2013) provides an additional rationale for using the outdoor environment for learning and how this can provide motivation and challenge, particularly with problem solving.
Warden, C. (2005) *The Potential of a Puddle*. Auchterarder: Mindstretchers.
Warden, C. (2007) *Nurture through Nature*. Auchterarder: Mindstretchers.
Warden's books focus particularly on the potential for under threes learning in the outdoor environment and include some beautiful photographs.

6

Mathematics and Display

Bridie Price

 Chapter Overview

In this chapter you can read about:

- The purposes of display in the teaching and learning of mathematics
- Types of display and their impact on the teaching and learning of mathematics.

Children's experiences of displays

Children experience displays in a number of different ways in a variety of settings. They may be used to seeing their achievements and efforts displayed at home, possibly a picture held in place with magnetic letters and numbers on the refrigerator or they may have entered an art or writing competition at the local library and then seen their work displayed for others to see. Children observe adults checking information displayed by a shop, for example opening and closing times or the price of goods. They see how adults appear interested in photographs of distant places displayed in a travel agents' window or how they enjoy looking at art work exhibited at a local library, and so on. These displays are designed to capture people's attention and may contain text, symbols, photographs or other images. In some instances displays contain audio or video.

Displays can also be used to stimulate learning and some provide interactive opportunities. For example, a football team poster may encourage a child to record 'home and away' scores and calculate the team's position in a particular league to determine whether it will move into another league at the end of the season. In some settings displays are used to present a welcoming environment and may encourage a child to feel secure, creating a sense of belonging. Some children will therefore have a variety of experiences with displays for a number of different reasons which may have included some mathematical ideas.

- Consider some of the ways children may encounter different types of display.
- Consider how the displays you have seen support and/or develop mathematics.

Using displays to support mathematical learning

To support and develop children's understanding and enjoyment of mathematics they require a mathematically rich learning environment (see Chapter 1), which could include the use of displays. The mathematical learning environment can impact on the quality of a young child's informal knowledge of mathematics (Osana and Rayner, 2010) so it is important to consider how this environment is used effectively to engage and motivate children. Displaying children's mark-making at home or looking at a calendar together and talking about what will happen on certain days helps to engage children in mathematics and demonstrates its relevance and value. Provision of appropriate mathematical resources which are readily available and accessible enable children to choose and use equipment as and when required. If we want children to engage with a display we need to consider their access to it. For instance, if we want to support young children's counting skills the height and type of display will need careful consideration as children may need to touch, point or move the items to be counted (see Chapter 9). The vocabulary used in displays will need to be appropriate for the children concerned or they may require an adult to demonstrate how to engage with these displays. Observing an environment from a child's perspective and adapting it where appropriate would enable adults to consider children's access and potential engagement with displays. When resources and displays that offer the potential for engaging in mathematics are provided within learning environments children will often respond. Carruthers and Worthington (2006) identified that when they included resources which encouraged writing, mark-making and talk that were related to mathematics then children incorporated these within their play, whereas this was not evident previously. Mathematical displays which encourage children to interact with them provide such opportunities for encouraging children's responses.

Role-play areas can provide numerous opportunities for displaying and developing mathematics (see Chapter 3). These areas could be set up for a number of reasons depending on age groups and interests but will include opportunities to engage in and discuss mathematics:

- Café – children observe and create menus with price lists
- Cinema – observe and/or create displays for opening and closing times, ticket prices, screen numbers
- Beach shop – children make up prices for spades, buckets, etc. to display in the shop
- Post office – printing own stamps for sale and displaying these together with prices.

- Consider how you would incorporate displays in a role-play area on a chosen theme to develop mathematical learning for children of different ages.

Types of mathematical displays

Displays for celebration

Celebrating a child's achievements or effort through display demonstrates that their contribution is valued, and this could lead to an increase in a child's self-esteem and motivation (Kershner and Pointon, 2000; Muijs and Reynolds, 2005). At home their pictures and other recorded achievements might be displayed on the refrigerator held in place by magnets or displayed on their bedroom walls. For some children, similar displays used in other settings such as a playgroup, nursery or school could create links between the setting and home. When we consider displays which celebrate children's mathematics efforts or achievements these could encourage a more positive attitude to mathematics and help develop children's perceptions of themselves as mathematicians. Conversely, if their contribution is not displayed this might lead to a child developing a negative attitude towards mathematics. A child may be used to displaying their own achievements in some settings aware that it will be valued but if they are unable to do this in other settings this could have a negative effect on children, too.

Displays can include completed and on-going work. The latter offers the opportunity for further discussion and reflection and gives adults opportunities to assess children's current understanding and to identify any issues that require further attention. Involving children in presenting and celebrating alternative methods and solutions to problem solving can support the development of adaptive expertise within the setting. Children's ability to solve mathematical tasks will become more flexible and creative through using meaningfully acquired strategies (Rittle-Johnson and Star, 2007). Torbeyns et al. (2005) demonstrated that when children were offered two different strategies to solve single-digit addition problems children effectively adapted their mathematical knowledge to fit the problem. By celebrating children's different approaches and methods through display adults are clearly indicating that they value these strategies. Askew et al. (1997) found that one of the attributes of effective teaching of mathematics was an attention to making connections with children's methods, then valuing and sharing these. This type of display presents an opportunity to discuss these methods with children, enabling them to develop their mathematical understanding by adding to, refining or creating new connections with things they already know (Barmby et al., 2009). In this way the use of the display can be planned into future activities. This allows time for adults and children to engage with the display and demonstrates its role in the teaching and learning of mathematics.

- Think about some of the displays you have seen which celebrate children's achievements and efforts in mathematics. Consider what each display is celebrating.
- Do they demonstrate how the children arrived at a solution to a problem?

Stimulus display

Displays can be used to engender curiosity and stimulate further enquiry. Curiosity is important in learning as it leads to wanting to find out more about something, to investigate, enquire and seek information. It can lead to a more active engagement with learning rather than a passive acceptance. Polya (2004) argued that children's curiosity should be challenged by 'setting them problems proportionate to their knowledge' (p. v). To develop independent thinking, support and guidance through the use of stimulating questions could be offered to help children solve their problems. To develop mathematical thinking displays could be used to present a mathematical problem or puzzle for children to solve or offer prompts for them to respond to, for example 'Is it always, sometimes, never … ', or 'Find as many possibilities … ', or 'Is this true or false? Why?' (see Figures 6.1 and 6.2) or the display could encourage children to notice the prevalence of certain numbers in society. In using display in this way children are encouraged to develop a sense of enquiry and it demonstrates that mathematics is more than finding the right answers. The emphasis in this type of display moves away from an adult as a 'sole giver of knowledge' (Carruthers and Worthington, 2006: 143) to include the child in exploration within mathematics.

Figure 6.1 *Factor bugs – 'Larger numbers always have more factors: true or false?'*

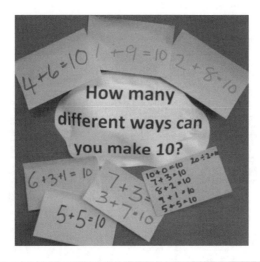

Figure 6.2 *Different ways to make 10*

The following are some examples of themes for displays to encourage children's curiosity or stimulate further enquiry:

- Numbers are Everywhere! How many numbers can you find in your home? On the street? In shops?
- Shape Detectives! What shapes can you find at home? Outside?
- Maths is All Around Us! What maths can you see? (see Figure 6.3)

(Continued)

(Continued)

- What Can You Do in a Minute? How many times can you write your name? How many star jumps can you do?
- Which One is the Odd One Out? Why? (show a series of numbers, for example 5, 9, 10, or shapes)
- Stories and Rhymes – How many stories/rhymes can you remember which include numbers? Do some numbers occur more often?
- What is the Biggest Number You Know? Briggs and Davis (2008) suggest that this type of question will encourage children to talk to each other about the largest number they can count to, write or read.
- 'What's the Same? What's Different?' – a collection of objects could be displayed on a table for children to explore.

Figure 6.3   *'Maths is all around us! What maths can you see?'*

Displays can be used to stimulate children's curiosity or encourage them in developing their mathematical thinking. At home children might pin posters of their favourite sportsperson to their bedroom walls which not only provide them with information about this person but also present questions which encourage children to complete research. These questions could involve aspects of mathematics such as 'When was the person born?', 'How many years ago was that?'. Other questions, depending on the particular sport involved, could involve fastest times, distance travelled, highest jumps, or most goals scored. In educational settings displays might offer a selection of answers to a given problem and invite children to find a solution from these and justify their reasons for their choice. For instance, children could collect three-dimensional shapes (for example, food packaging) and create a selection of different nets for a display, thereby making some connections between mathematical ideas and objects/materials they see in the world around them (Cunningham, 2007). The inclusion of questions such as 'Which nets will make up these shapes?' or 'Can you find any other nets that could make up these shapes?' will provide a mathematical challenge. Making appropriate resources available would also support children in finding solutions. The use of the resources will enable children to explore and manipulate ideas physically or to represent their ideas through pictures and diagrams. In other cases displays might be used to encourage children to think of possible questions. For example, a number or shape might be placed on display and children are invited to consider what the possible questions could be.

Using a display in educational settings to present a mathematical topic at the start of a unit of work may encourage children to explore the topic for themselves. For a 'Shapes in the environment' topic, children could look for shapes in their locality and take photographs, draw pictures or cut out pictures from newspapers or magazines, write about what they already know about shapes or they may be encouraged to ask questions about what they want to find out and contribute these to the displays. The display could then be developed, possibly including relevant vocabulary for the shapes they have included in the display, responding to the questions asked by other children or identifying the pictures of shapes found by others. The display acts as a stimulus to learning and a form of assessment. It also provides a record of what the children discovered in the environment related to an aspect of mathematics and to the mathematics explored in the educational setting, therefore enabling children to make connections (Donaldson, 2007). Displays such as this focus on making connections and uses mathematics as a means of making sense of the world (Pepperell et al., 2009). However, adults need to draw children's attention to displays and the mathematics within them, encourage their participation in using displays and demonstrate that they value children's engagement with them. In educational settings consideration would therefore need to be given to the allocation of time for children to engage with these displays and how and when their responses would be shared.

- Think about a display which has stimulated mathematical thinking. How was this achieved? In what ways did children engage with the display? How can you identify such interactions?
- How would you cater for children's responses and include these into the display?

Informative displays

Support for children's mathematical learning can be provided through the use of informative displays. Some children will be familiar with this use of display. As mentioned earlier, they may have experience of looking at opening and closing times of shops, or they might be familiar with reading information about books or films on poster displays or they could have number friezes or times tables charts pinned on their bedroom walls. Such displays offer prompts for children's learning. For instance, a display featuring the names of the days of the week acts as a reminder to younger children or displays of mathematical vocabulary provide opportunities for children to become more familiar with the correct terminology (see Figure 6.4).

Figure 6.4 *Information display*

Vocabulary displays could be used to discuss any differences in understanding that the children might have (Mooney et al., 2012b). Children could also be encouraged to use them when articulating their thinking and so move them towards using more abstract language (Pepperell et al., 2009). Some displays offer modelled examples of mathematical procedures (for example, how to complete a division calculation through 'chunking'), with the intention of supporting children's mathematical learning. Other types of information displays used in educational settings may feature children's explanations of how a resource or method was used and provide examples which can be used for assessment purposes (see Figure 6.5). Placing these explanations alongside the resource discussed enables children to make meaningful connections which may later support their mathematical learning.

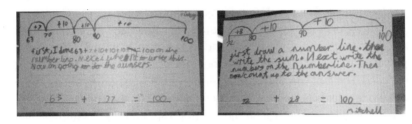

Figure 6.5   *Children's writing to show how they used the Empty Number Line*

Displays which provide information could be considered as 'scaffolds' within what Vygotsky (in Atherton, 2011) called the Zone of Proximal Development (see Chapter 1). The display is used as the 'more knowledgeable other' to bring the child's knowledge to a higher level. When the child is more confident in this aspect of learning the scaffold will no longer be required. Again, children need to be made aware of these displays and how they can support their mathematics. Some information displays may, however, encourage children to follow procedures and thereby create an instrumental understanding of mathematics rather than developing a relational understanding (Skemp, 1971) (see Chapter 1). Adults will also need to consider whether some children might become too reliant on such displays and how they might address this so that mathematical understanding is developed. In other instances children could create their own information displays. Preparation of displays will involve children in considering and checking the information they have and want to display and so deepen their understanding. Involvement in planning and creating displays offers children greater ownership and promotes increased engagement with them.

CASE STUDY

Two-dimensional shape display

The teacher wanted to provide opportunities for the children (aged 6–7 years) to build on their learning of two-dimensional shapes. They were mainly identifying two-dimensional shapes from their appearance (van Hiele's (1986) level 1 'Visualisation', see Chapter 14) and she wanted them to progress towards considering the properties of shapes and for some to consider the link between the number of sides and the number of corners a shape has. Children worked in pairs to construct a two-dimensional shape using Geostrips. They were encouraged to count each side of the newly-constructed shape and stick a numbered label on each side as it was counted. Then, using numbered labels in a second colour, they similarly counted the corners. The questioning which followed enabled the children to consider what they had discovered. The children's constructions were placed on a wall display to remind them of the lesson and to use as a prompt for future learning. The questions asked during the session together with the names of the shapes were also included. Some of the shapes were displayed in tilted orientations and not all shapes were regular (see Figure 6.6). Having planned for the children's involvement in creating the display, the teacher hoped that this would engage the children in using the display to support their learning. It also provided information to support later learning as the teacher regularly referred to such displays.

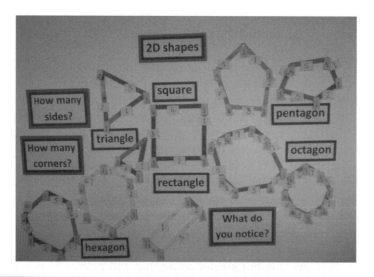

Figure 6.6 *Properties of two-dimensional shapes*

The case study above demonstrates how the teacher clearly identified a need to display children's mathematical learning but also wanted the display to serve as a reminder of the mathematics addressed during this particular activity. Some children, particularly visual and kinaesthetic thinkers, are more likely to benefit from such effective use of models and images where key mathematical concepts are clearly illustrated (Clausen-May, 2005). The importance of presenting children with a variety of examples including non-prototypical images (see Chapter 14) was acknowledged by expecting children to explore shapes in different rotations so as to minimise later misconceptions. Hansen (2011) suggests children may experience difficulties in identifying shapes in different orientations if they have not had such exploration experiences. OfSTED (2008: 9) indicated that 'Effective teachers anticipate pupils' likely misconceptions and are skilled in choosing resources and particular examples to expose misconceptions and check that their understanding is secure'. Adults can draw on their understanding of difficulties which children experience to create displays which may help to address these, though not necessarily to avoid them (see Chapter 1).

Sharing information

A Home–School Knowledge Exchange project set up in Bristol and Cardiff explored what mathematics took place at home and school and considered ways to develop the sharing of knowledge between these (see Chapter 8 for further details). It was recognised that learning took place in both but could be enriched by better connections (Winter, 2010).

Nurseries and schools can use displays as one way of informing parents about mathematics taking place in their setting, not just through displaying children's achievements but by providing information about the use of particular resources, different mathematical procedures or mathematical events (see Figure 6.7). The displays could also be used to show what mathematics takes place at home. In this way, displays can used to share mathematics from both contexts so that children's learning can be better supported (see Chapter 8).

Interactive displays

Many of the displays mentioned previously provide opportunities for children to interact with them in a variety of ways. Children may offer written or other visual contributions, or participate through explorations or investigations of resources/games provided with the display. Children may talk about displays with others or refer to them as a

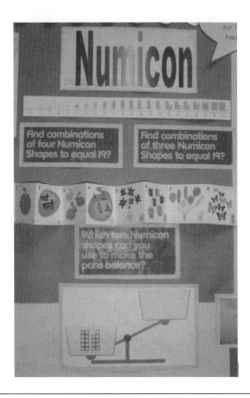

Figure 6.7 *'We have been exploring all the ways that Numicon can support our learning and had some fun too!'*

prompt during mathematical activities. At home, children might draw a number of pictures or make marks to represent numbers on a number frieze or to attach to the fridge door using a corresponding magnetic number. Children in nurseries may respond to a display featuring a photograph of a stack of five chairs together with the number five by stacking five chairs. Displays can be used as teaching aids to engage children in the mathematics present in the display. For instance, when identifying or recognising numbers, young children could be encouraged to illustrate aspects of a story or rhyme they have been sharing together and to use this to support their counting skills. Other interactive displays may include the use of advent calendars enabling children to identify and order numbers. Some might feature 'washing lines' for children to place numbers in the correct order (see Chapter 9) which could be adapted for different age ranges. Children may be involved in counting the total amount of money displayed on a purse and then checking the answer displayed underneath a corresponding flap. Such displays could be used as teaching aids and, if displayed at an appropriate height, by children to explore independently.

CASE STUDY

Adding two groups of objects

Figure 6.8 *Interactive spring display*

The display (see Figure 6.8) was linked to a current topic on 'Spring and life cycles' and the children (aged 5 years) were invited to draw and decorate sheep, flowers and trees which were then placed on the display (celebrating children's work). The display was then used to support children in identifying how many items were in each set by counting. A number symbol was identified by the children to represent this amount and placed next to the set formed. This step was repeated for another set. Addition and equals symbols were introduced to form a number sentence. Children were asked to find the total number of animals in both sets by counting on from the number in the first set (see Chapter 10). A number line was included below the display and used to aid this calculation. Other groups were formed for the children to add together. The children were informed that throughout the next few days the display would be adapted and different sets would be made for the children to add together if they wished.

At this point a game was introduced. Some frogs were to be placed on a game board depicting lily pads in a pond. The children used a spinner to find how many frogs to place on a lily pad and how many to put in the pond. Their task would be to count the number of frogs on the lily pad, the number of frogs in the pond and then find the total number of frogs. The game was introduced to offer a hands-on experience of the calculating skills used when engaged with the display. A whiteboard and pens were provided and children encouraged to make marks to represent their thinking.

The teacher in the case study above created a 'stimulating environment for pupils' which demonstrated 'a clear understanding of appropriate teaching strategies' when teaching early mathematics (DfE, 2012b). Links to their learning about spring and life cycles ensures that connections are made and a meaningful context created. Involving the children in the development of the display may have motivated some children to engage more fully as they were working with items that they had made, thus creating a relevant, interesting context and offering some form of ownership (Hegarty, 1996). By moving and counting the pictures and then writing the numeral beside the set created, the teacher was linking pictures and symbols. Using number lines or number tracks within displays supports children in exploring aspects of counting (see Chapter 9) or when calculating (see Chapter 10). Children chose to play with the frog game and look at the display during child-initiated time. This reinforced the mathematical learning which took place earlier while providing a motivating experience for children which encouraged engagement with mathematics (Drews and Hansen, 2007).

In many classrooms display boards can be placed too high for children to have direct interaction with the display. However, in this instance the teacher recognised this limitation and used the display as a teaching and learning resource when directly teaching the class. She also ensured that the children could have a hands-on experience of the same calculating skills by offering the frog game.

CASE STUDY

Three-dimensional shapes

The use of display was planned as part of a lesson to encourage some 6–7 year old children to become involved in the construction of three-dimensional shapes. A town-planning scenario was used to enable children to use nets of cuboids to make the buildings for the town. The children were then asked to consider rooftops for their buildings. Again, some nets, together with three-dimensional shapes and real-life examples of three-dimensional shapes, were made available. In her role as 'Town Planner', the teacher asked the children to consider making a number of other buildings (for example, lighthouse, school). At this point children had to create their own nets. Children's investigations about the nets required to create the buildings involved the use of both prior knowledge from previous sessions and the use of a trial-and-improvement strategy. The use of appropriate questioning by the adult encouraged both mathematical dialogue and the use of relevant vocabulary among the children.

The display (see Figure 6.9) was constructed by the children on the floor so they could also use it within their play activities. They took ownership of it and it was

Figure 6.9 *Town planning*

not uncommon for children to bring their parents into the classroom to observe their efforts.

By considering display at the planning stage the adult was able to maximise the children's involvement throughout the series of sessions and identify how this would develop and support children's mathematical understanding. The children had a purpose in planning and creating the display, engaging in both the construction of appropriate structures together and thoughtful consideration of the properties of the shapes.

As we can see, displays serve a variety of purposes and can be used in many different ways. Sometimes one display may serve a variety of purposes; for example, it may celebrate children's work but also provide a stimulus to children's learning. When discussing the use of resources Delaney (2010) makes a distinction between teachers using resources as a teaching tool and children using them to support their learning. Displays are used in similar ways so adults and children should be clear about their intended purposes. Kershner and Pointon's (2000) research demonstrated that the intention of some displays was not explained to children and so they were unclear about their purpose. Many of the displays mentioned earlier combine both purposes indicated by Delaney (2010), thus optimising their use in developing mathematical learning.

Summary

This chapter has identified a number of different types of mathematical displays and has considered the impact of such displays on supporting and developing children's mathematical understanding. The importance of organising displays so that children have access to them and are encouraged to engage with them has been considered. The case studies illustrate how displays have been planned to support and develop the teaching and learning of mathematics. The final section of the chapter considered how displays may be used as a teaching and/or learning tool and the importance of ensuring that children are clear about the intention.

Further reading

Stone, P., Fisher, L. and Marshall, E. (2012) 'The benefits of engaging in researched informed practice', *Mathematics Teaching*, 227: 31–33.

One of the research studies in this article considers how mathematical dialogue can be promoted through the use of a suitably designed role-play area.

Tarr, P. (2004) 'Consider the walls', *Young Children*, 59(3): 88–92. Available at: http://journal. naeyc.org/btj/200405/ConsidertheWalls.pdf (accessed 10 February 2013).

This article critically examines the quality and quantity of commercial materials used in displays generally and invites teachers to determine whether they contribute to children's learning.

Assessing Children's Mathematics

Helen Taylor and Karen Vincent

 Chapter Overview

In this chapter you can read about:

- Purposes and audiences for assessment
- Different types and methods of assessment
- Recording assessment
- Collaborative approaches to assessment
- Involving children in their own assessment.

What is assessment?

Assessment is a mental process whereby a situation is observed and interpreted in order to ascertain its quality. Headington (2011: 73) says, 'Assessment is about measuring or judging, what someone knows, understands and can do'. An adult might observe a child to determine how far they were able to count. They might decide to help the child to count further by modelling the next few number names and encouraging the child to repeat them or to join in, either immediately or later. This is an example of assessment *for* learning, or formative assessment, as the adult was using the information gained from observing the child at the time of teaching, to promote learning and progress (Black and Wiliam, 1998). It involves thinking about what a child needs to do to learn more (Hodgen and Askew, 2010). Lee (2006) observes that the better the quality of evidence about a child's understanding, the more effectively adults can plan for progress. However, if the adult had observed the child counting, recorded the extent to which the child could recite the number names accurately, but not used the opportunity help the child to progress, this would be an example of assessment *of* learning, or summative assessment. Summative assessment, a summary of what a child knows, understands and is able to do (Hodgen and Askew, 2010), is often used at the end of a particular stage in a child's learning; this might be when they leave a particular setting to move on to another one. A grade or level may be assigned. Summative records can be used by staff in the subsequent setting as they plan the next learning steps for the child. Headington (2011) asserts that the challenge for teachers is to use assessment evidence effectively and to demonstrate appropriate accountability. So in terms of improving learning, assessment evidence should be used to inform planning, thus assessment and planning become a cyclical process (Bottle et al., 2005).

Monitoring is associated with assessment. Monitoring children's learning is an ongoing process where adults get a general feel for how groups of children are learning at any one time; this might be followed with detailed, precise assessment for individuals within the group. For example, a teacher of 6 year olds asked her class to place number cards 1–30 in order on a prepared 5 x 6 grid. Children decided whether to work their way across rows or up and down columns. When they started the activity, the teacher walked around the classroom to monitor how they were doing and noticed two children who seemed to be struggling. She asked these two children to work with her to assess their learning; she discovered that the children were confusing the numbers 12 and 21. She was then able to assist them in making progress. In this way, the teacher monitored the learning of the whole class but assessed the learning of the two children, thus demonstrating that assessment is more detailed and precise than monitoring.

Why do we assess? Purposes and audiences

In 1988 a Department for Education and Science task group identified four purposes for assessment: diagnostic, formative, summative and evaluative. Each of these plays a part in accountability. In finding out what a child knows, understands or can do an adult can:

- Plan effective next steps in children's learning
- Set appropriate targets for and with children
- Address difficulties or misconceptions that children experience
- Report to others about the child's learning and progress.

The first three on the list mainly use formative or diagnostic assessment and the fourth one is mainly about summative and evaluative assessment.

- Before reading on, list the people who may be interested in the outcomes of mathematical assessment.

Depending on the particular setting, you may have listed some of the following:

- Feedback to children can help them to recognise their progress, encourage them and help them to think about their own learning. This will also assist them in developing independence through becoming able to identify their strengths and areas for development.
- Reporting to parents orally and in writing, formally and informally will be appropriate at different times.
- Members of staff within the setting need to share knowledge about the children in order to facilitate progress. At times practitioners will report to a senior member of staff such as the nursery manager or head teacher enabling monitoring of children's progress across the setting.
- Staff in other settings will need information, especially at the point of transfer, such as when a child leaves a pre-school setting to start school or moves up a class.
- Outside agencies need information about the learning of an individual, for example if an expert comes to assess and provide advice to support a child with special educational needs or a disability. They sometimes need information on a cohort of children, such as for inspection or compiling national statistical data.

Methods of assessment

Questioning

Asking a child questions can enable an adult to interpret children's mathematical thinking and learning. The questioning may take place alongside another assessment method such as observation. Different types of questions can elicit assessment data which varies in quality and quantity. Open questions generate more information than closed. For example, we might ask a child what 2 plus 3 equals, the child might reply with '5', we would then know that on this occasion the child guessed correctly, knew, or was able to work out the correct answer to this calculation. If the child replied with the incorrect answer or said, 'I don't know', we would then know that the child did not know the answer, could not quickly work it out, or did not understand the question.

Alternatively, asking 'Can you think of some pairs of numbers that total 5?' allows greater scope for answers, including:

1. 0 and 5, 1 and 4, 2 and 3
2. 1 and 4, 2 and 3
3. 2 and 3, 1 and 4, 4 and 1, 3 and 2.

Answer 1 shows a systematic approach to the question and knowledge and understanding of 0 which is missing from the others. It may also reflect the child's implicit understanding of commutativity (see Chapter 10), which may also apply to answer 2 but appears to be missing in answer 3. Answers 2 and 3 do not reflect understanding of 0.

A closed question can be followed with others to gain additional assessment information. 'What does 2 plus 3 equal?' may be followed with 'How did you work it out?' This will give an insight into the mental methods the child is using. Answers may include:

1. I got out 2 counters, then I got out 3 counters, then I put them together and I counted them all, 1, 2, 3, 4, 5.
2. I put 2 in my head, then I put up 3 fingers, I remembered 2 and counted 3, 4, 5.
3. I thought it would be easier to start with 3 so I put it in my head and put up 2 fingers and counted 4, 5.
4. I just know it.

These answers demonstrate children's thinking and help adults to plan next steps. Answer 1 shows a child at the early stages of addition, counting all (see Chapter 10). Once confident in this, the child will need to move on to the more efficient strategy of counting on as demonstrated in answer 2. Answer 3 also demonstrates counting on and implicit knowledge of the commutative property of addition. Answer 4 could be interpreted in different ways; it may indicate that the child has memorised the fact or it could mean that the child is unable to articulate their method. A teacher of 5 year olds, might ask a group of children how they worked something out and see puzzled faces. To enable children to describe their methods, she could describe one method and ask other adults to articulate different methods, thus modelling the process; later the children may begin to articulate their thinking, helping the teacher to plan for future progress.

Questions can be classified in a number of ways and it is helpful to ask a variety of them in order to engage and assess children in a range of mathematical thinking. Bloom's taxonomy (1956, updated Krathwohl, 2002) emphasises the importance of asking children questions and setting them tasks for remembering, understanding, applying, analysing, evaluating and creating. Gifford (2005) suggests that indirect questioning, such as wondering aloud (for example, 'I wonder if I can find all of the triangles') and making provocative statements (such as 'I bet you can't count all of these'), can be helpful in eliciting explanations and assessment information.

Observing children

As responsible and respectful educators we should assess young children in play-based, practical and problem-solving activities as far as possible. Non-stressful situations are more likely to allow children to demonstrate what they know, can do and understand. Observation helps us get to know each child; therefore, time should be invested in order to build up a picture of their skills, abilities and interests. Papatheodorou et al. (2012) consider that observation offers us an opportunity to examine and re-examine previous knowledge, assumptions and understandings to reach new meanings. Children need to be included in this activity where appropriate and, through conversations regarding their views and abilities before, during or after the activities, new and deeper understandings can inform future planning and work. Reflecting upon these observations and conversations will enable highly effective provision for young children.

There is a world of difference between an adult-led assessment that tests a child to see if they can count the blocks and observing a child playing, pretending the blocks are 'food' for the teddies and noticing that they are counting the blocks to see if they have enough. The latter example has real meaning for the child, stemming from an intrinsic desire and understanding of the need to be able to count to solve a problem. Further observations may indicate that the child is able to tell the difference between the number of teddies and the number of blocks and the need to acquire some more.

Observations should contribute towards a holistic picture for each child and so adults usually aim to collect observations of children within and across areas of learning. Over time, a picture of a child's strengths can be built up, using observations from a range of adults including parents, as well as asking children what they think. Many settings use these to compile a 'learning journey' portfolio for each child, demonstrating what children can do, both in the setting and at home. Parents and children are encouraged to contribute to these regularly through sharing photographs and anecdotes (see Chapter 8).

There are many different forms of observation but they can be categorised into planned and unplanned observations. Parker-Rees et al. (2010) describe these as hunting and gathering. The hunter type is when adults know what they want and seek it and the gatherer type is where adults immerse themselves in a situation and pick up information incidentally. For planned observations, adults decide beforehand the purpose and approximate duration of the observation.

Palaiologou (2008) highlights the difficulty of distancing oneself from the action and not making assumptions about observed behaviours. For example, it is inappropriate to note that a child who can recite number names to 100 can count to 100. The adult does not know that they are able to count 100 items accurately. Recording of observations may be through notes, photographs or film or a combination of these and other recording methods. Analysis and reflection should follow, when considering the next steps for the child.

- Plan to undertake an observation of a child playing where some mathematics is involved. Knowing why you are observing a child is important. Think about your reasons for doing the observation.
- Consider whether and how you will explain the purpose to the child. They may behave differently when being watched.
- Consider whether you will interact with the child and make notes later or observe 'from a distance'.
- Consider the best way to capture an accurate representation of what happened. Would a camera help?
- What will happen if other children require your attention whilst you are doing an observation?
- Decide how you will share your observation. Will it be with other adults or the children?
- Consider the implications and next steps.

Different types of observations

Narrative observation

A narrative observation is usually a short, planned, intensive observation of a child or group of children resulting in a written description. Another adult being available to attend to children's needs is helpful to avoid distraction. Recording should be detailed, accurate and factual and include spoken expression as well as interactions with resources and other children (see for example, Palaiologou, 2008; Papatheodorou et al., 2012).

CASE STUDY

Planned, narrative observations

Both Terry, the teacher, and Chris, a teaching assistant, complete two planned, 10-minute narrative observations each day. They use a form for recording which enables links between the observed behaviours and the curriculum to be recorded (see Figure 7.1). Sometimes, photographs are taken to illustrate the observed activity, providing additional evidence for the child's learning journey.

Reason for observation	Observation of choice and independence during child-initiated play	Curriculum Links
Child/date/context	Notes	
Rory 21 June 2012 11am Outside bikes and trikes	Rory is riding around the playground on his bike. He calls to his friend Peter 'The yellow one's free. Come on!' (Peter joins him riding around the perimeter of the playground). Rory leads, pedalling quickly for about a minute or two. He laughs and smiles as he calls out to his friend, 'We're going fast!' He stops at the side of the playground next to a pile of plastic cones and begins arranging them on the playground. 'I'm making a race course', he calls to his friend. Peter joins him. Both boys begin placing cones randomly on the playground and then jump back on their bikes to ride in-between the cones for another minute or two. Suddenly Rory stops, gets off his bike and goes over to the writing area under the canopy. He collects some blank pieces of paper, a felt pen and some sticky-tape from the drawer and takes them back over to Peter who has remained with the bikes. Rory begins to write the number one on a piece of paper and goes over to a cone to stick it on with the sticky-tape. Peter says the number aloud. 'Now I need to do number two', states Rory. He looks for reassurance to help him to write the number two in the form of a number line painted along the fence. He studies the number two carefully before attempting it on his piece of paper. Rory continues to write each number sequentially up to ten, pausing only at number five and again, checking the number line for reassurance. Peter assists by sticking each number card onto a cone at random, naming each number as he does so. As Peter sticks the last numeral card onto the last cone, Rory shouts, 'You've got to ride from one to ten', excitedly to Peter. Both boys jump back on their bikes and continue to ride, travelling from cone number one to cone number ten in the conventional order and back down through the sequence again.	Communication Physical skill Collaboration Independence Writing numerals Recognising numerals Ordering Counting backwards and ordering

Figure 7.1 *An example of a completed narrative observation form*

(Continued)

(Continued)

Terry and Chris observe child-initiated activity to assess a child rehearsing their skills and abilities independently of adult support. Self-guided activity illustrates the child's level of intrinsic motivation and perseverance, which are key indicators of being able to learn successfully.

In this example, it is possible to identify Rory's learning and development in several curriculum areas. Specifically within mathematics, Rory communicated effectively, showing an awareness of Peter's need to understand the game; 'You've got to ride from one to ten'. We can begin to see that Rory may be exploring the concepts of encircling, around and in-between as he rides around and between the cones demonstrating spatial awareness. He is able to count from 1 to 10, recognise the numerals and order them forwards and backwards. He is intrinsically motivated in developing the task and has a real purpose for writing numerals. He is able to form most numerals correctly seeking assistance when required. He is able to collaborate with Peter, working together with a shared sense of purpose and is able to seek out materials. From this it is possible to plan relevant learning opportunities for Rory, including consolidating and improving his numeral formation, particularly for 2 and 5. This could be done in a variety of ways, perhaps capturing his interest in the bikes and trikes. Water could be poured onto a tarpaulin, enabling Rory to ride over the water and use the tyre marks to make the numeral 2 or 5 on the playground. Alternatively, large paintbrushes or brooms could be used. Extending Rory's understanding of number might involve removing the odd or even numbered cones to encourage counting in twos or starting at the number 2 and extending to the number 12.

Incidental observation

During planned narrative observations, children may not engage in any mathematical play or interaction. Incidental, unplanned or anecdotal observations are helpful when children demonstrate particular skills or competencies. As events occur, adults may realise that a specific incident represents an important development for that child and choose to record it. Papatheodorou et al. (2012: 161) discuss how 'it is important for those who work in early years settings to become empathetic and observant practitioners who are tuned into children'. Some adults use sticky labels for short written descriptions to aid the process of collecting this information. For an example see Figure 7.2 which is related to the following case study.

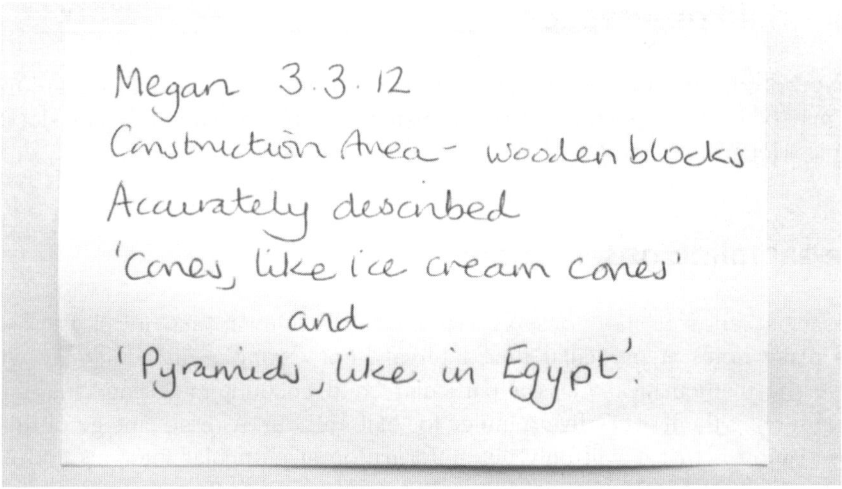

Figure 7.2 *Example of a sticky note record*

CASE STUDY

Incidental observation

Jamila, a teacher, noticed Megan (aged 5) playing in the construction area of the classroom. Megan demonstrated that she was able to name several three-dimensional shapes whilst building. She made a castle using cuboids, cones, cylinders and pyramids. 'I know what these are', she stated, 'These are cones, like the ice cream cones my Mum buys and they are pyramids. They have these in Egypt, don't they? I went there on holiday last year.'

From this, Jamila was able to deduce that Megan was able to connect the three-dimensional pyramid shape with the pyramid she saw on holiday. She had explored the characteristics of shapes and was able to use some mathematical vocabulary to describe them. Jamila provided 'junk' materials in the creative area to enable Megan to extend her understanding of joining three-dimensional shapes and ensured that each shape was named by an adult as she used it to extend her understanding to include cylinders and cuboids. She also planned teacher-directed activities using play dough and shape construction kits to emphasise the names of the three-dimensional shapes.

Target child observation

This type of observation focuses on an individual, working as part of a group. The focus may be on social interaction or competency with the mathematical task (see for example, Hobart and Frankel, 2009).

Time-sampling observations

These are a series of short observations usually relating to activity choices, where adults make notes at particular time intervals. For example, an adult may wish to observe the mathematical ideas a particular child encounters during child-initiated time, observing them every five minutes for half an hour. A disadvantage of this type of observation is that it will only give information at particular intervals and not on what happens in between. Recording these observations onto a meaningful grid may help interpretation later (see for example, Hobart and Frankel, 2009; Palaiologou 2008; Papatheodorou et al., 2012).

Event-sampling observation

This is similar to the technique described above but adults note down every time there was an interaction, for example, every time the child changed activity or spoke to someone else (see for example, Hobart and Frankel, 2009; Palaiologou 2008; Papatheodorou et al., 2012).

Rich tasks

Providing, and observing children engaged in, 'rich tasks' enables adults to find out how to help children learn (Hodgen and Askew, 2010). 'Rich tasks' include problems where the answer is not obvious, and children need to discuss and articulate different ideas. One example is asking children, 'Which is the odd one out?' They could be presented with a series of numbers such as 2, 7, 8 and 14. Several answers could be correct. Another idea is to present questions in an unusual way (Lee, 2006), for example a missing number question such as:

- $? + 5 = 8$, or
- $4 + ? = 6$.

All these involve exposure and discussion of possible mistakes, thus promoting understanding.

Assessment through children's representations of mathematical ideas

Carruthers and Worthington (2006) state that young children represent maths in multi-modal forms (see Chapter 4). Listening and talking with children about the marks that they make enables adults to assess a child's thinking. 'It is easy to disregard scribbles and what appears to be idiosyncratic responses' (Carruthers and Worthington, 2006: 90). Talking with children about their representations enables adults to begin to make sense of observations and to set them within context, leading to provision of resources and activities to extend children's thinking.

Recording the outcomes of assessment

Outcomes of assessment are not always recorded, for example, when informal unplanned assessment takes place and the adult immediately intervenes and helps a child. However, often it is necessary to record because retaining all assessment information mentally is difficult. Assessment outcomes may be reported in recorded formats such as the annual report to parents or for passing on to another setting or member of staff. Reports are compiled by looking back at records of learning over a period and summarising the progress children have made. It can be rewarding to read records detailing children's earlier learning, thus recognising their progress. Therefore a manageable system for record-keeping is vital. Montague-Smith and Price (2012: 211) suggest that it is useful to record 'significant achievement', including when a child does something for the first time, when they are especially interested in something and when there is evidence of understanding of a mathematical idea. Records should be dated and include notes of observations of the child engaged in mathematical activities and comments against assessment criteria showing a child's understanding and skill development. Assessment criteria include specific mathematical milestones that children are expected to reach or specific aspects of mathematics that may be listed in a curriculum, for example, the child can recite number names in order from 1 to 6 or the child can double the numbers 1 to 10.

What to assess

Purposes and audiences will dictate what is assessed. Many assessments will be unplanned, as adults notice a child engaged in an activity and observe and talk to the child to gain a better understanding of what that child knows, understands and is able to do, in order to plan the next steps. At other times, an adult might plan to assess a child involved in a particular mathematics-centred activity to find out something specific, for a particular audience or as part of formal compulsory assessment. Examples of this include the Early Years Foundation Stage profile in England and end of year or key stage assessments in schools. Montague-Smith and Price (2012) emphasise that children's problem solving should be assessed as the processes of mathematics are as important as knowledge of the subject.

It is helpful to assess children's learning when they make errors, although Lee (2006) reminds us of the necessity of doing this sensitively and building a supportive ethos in the setting. Through noticing and analysing errors adults can gain a better understanding of the child's learning and thus help the child progress (see Chapter 1).

Learning from children's misconceptions and errors

Ryan and Williams (2007: 16–27) undertook a large-scale research study into children's mathematical misconceptions and errors, using test results from 15,000 children and smaller-scale work observing teachers developing children's discussion about errors. They were able to categorise errors and misconceptions in four ways. 'Modelling' errors may occur when children do not understand or represent the context of the mathematics appropriately. To exemplify this, Ryan and Williams refer to Hughes' (1986) work where young children are unable to answer 'bald' mathematical questions like 1 add 2, but, once they are presented in a meaningful context such as 'I've got one brick and I get two more', even if the bricks are not visible, children are more likely to be able to answer the question. For the second category, 'prototyping', they give an example of young children only recognising equilateral triangles orientated with one side parallel to the bottom of a page or the floor as triangles. 'Intelligent over-generalisation' results in some common misconceptions such as taking the smaller digit away from the larger digit in two-digit subtraction e.g. $22 - 19 = 17$. Ryan and Williams labelled their final category 'process, object and structural conceptions', for example, difficulties with recognising that the answer to 'how many?' is not an instruction to go through the counting process, but rather to give the cardinal value of the set.

Ryan and Williams recommend that teachers use children's misconceptions and errors positively in the classroom by giving children opportunities not just to correct errors but to refine understanding through discussion of mathematical ideas. Adults should listen carefully to children's responses in order to build on their current ideas and understandings. Questions and tasks can be used wisely to promote this discussion, starting with what they call a 'problematic' where children may hold different points of view. Ryan and Williams refer to this as diagnostic teaching because errors are probed and analysed using the four categories above to reveal the underlying causes and teaching is planned to address these rather than just treating the symptom or error at a shallow level.

- Note down some difficulties, errors or misconceptions that you have seen children experiencing recently.
- Try to establish why the error or difficulty has occurred. Using appropriate chapters from Part 2 of the book may help here.
- Do you think the errors result from misconceptions? Can you categorise them using Ryan and Williams' four categories?
- What steps would you plan to enable the children's progress?

Collaborative approaches to assessment

It is helpful for all adults working in a setting to be involved in the assessment of children's mathematics. Hence, good oral or written communication is essential.

Figure 7.3 provides an example of a sheet that could be used to record information for passing to the supervisor or class teacher for use in future planning.

Date....................................

Learning intention.......................................

Activity details

....

....

....

....

....

Assessment record

Child's name	Did the child achieve the learning intention?	Notes and comments as appropriate

Thank you for your help with this. It will be used in planning next steps in learning for the children.

Figure 7.3 *Exemplar recording sheet for group activity*

Involving children in their own assessment

If our aims for children include that they should become increasingly independent learners, we need to teach the appropriate skills. This will include involving children in their own assessment so that they become aware of their own strengths and areas for development in mathematics (Glazzard et al., 2010; Headington, 2011). Sensitive, timely feedback helps children to reflect on activities and learning. This should include encouragement and praise for what the child has done well and a challenge to enable progress.

Black and Wiliam (1998) identified that involving children in self- and peer-assessment, after sharing clear learning objectives and success criteria and allowing time for consolidation and reflection, could be very beneficial for children's learning. Lee (2006) explains that children, who understand what they are learning and the steps they need to take to learn it, can also begin to assess their learning and that of others. Articulation of this leads to deeper understanding.

If adults are familiar with common errors and misconceptions, they can decide whether to try to avoid or minimise them for children or can plan to teach children appropriately once an error has been made. Enabling children to discuss errors and misconceptions is a helpful way forward. With young children this needs to be handled sensitively and one way of doing this is to anonymise the mistakes. Use of a puppet (Gifford, 2005) or a 'naughty teddy' (Thompson, 2008a: 210) can be beneficial.

CASE STUDY

Maths Monkey

Anne was working with her class on counting. Most of the children, aged 4–5, were good at reciting the number names in order but sometimes made errors in counting quantities of objects. Anne placed a number of pebbles on a table in a random arrangement. With the children watching, she brought out Maths Monkey, a hand puppet. Maths Monkey whispered in Anne's ear and Anne relayed what he said to the class. He wanted to practise his counting but he was shy and unsure so he needed the children's help. They agreed. Maths Monkey then had several attempts at counting the pebbles, making a different mistake each time. The children were asked to explain the error to a talk partner and then to share with Maths Monkey.

The children in the case study shared and articulated their understandings of counting in a safe environment which they thoroughly enjoyed. Working with a partner enabled them all to participate and talk. Lee (2006) recommends using exemplar pieces of work for children to assess and this is a practical example suitable for young children.

Asking children to assess their confidence levels after a mathematical activity can also be helpful (Lee, 2006). Children might indicate by thumbs up, down or horizontal how confident they feel with an idea. If they have recorded on paper, they might use a traffic light system at the end to indicate very confident (green), fairly confident (orange) or lacking in confidence (red). This will not be completely accurate in all cases. When adults know the children well, they will be able to ascertain whether children's confidence is misplaced.

Summary

'Good quality assessment takes time to work out and quality assessment of children's learning goes beyond the superficial: it probes further' (Carruthers and Worthington, 2006: 198). Effective assessment is an essential element of effective learning and teaching. It allows the adults working with children to plan for progression and appropriate learning for all individuals in their care. In this chapter we have considered what assessment is, why we assess and the purposes and audiences for the assessment. Methods of assessment that are part of normal setting activities were discussed with an emphasis on observation as a key assessment data collection approach with young children. It is important to assess children's errors and misconceptions accurately in order to provide suitable learning opportunities to overcome difficulties, thus enabling children to progress at later points. Involving children in their learning through assessment was highlighted as an effective strategy for enabling progression.

Further reading

Ryan, J. and Williams, J. (2007) *Children's Mathematics 4–15: Learning from Errors and Misconceptions*. Maidenhead: Open University Press.
This book reports on a large-scale research project involving errors and misconceptions from 15,000 pupils and smaller-scale projects observing teachers extending children's mathematical ideas through discussion. Although this book focuses on older learners, it has some very interesting and practical ideas that can be applied for younger children.
Montague-Smith, A. and Price, A.J. (2012) *Mathematics in Early Years Education*, 3rd edn. London: Routledge.
Chapter 8 of this book is about planning and assessment of young children's mathematics. It includes some useful charts of concepts alongside suggested assessment checkpoints and key questions that adults could ask children to elicit assessment information.

Thompson, I. (2008) *Teaching and Learning Early Number*, 2nd edn. Maidenhead: Open University Press.

In Chapter 15 Thompson applies much of the research in this area to working with pre-school and school-aged children up to the age of about 7. There are some useful examples of misconceptions, typical of many children's mathematical ideas.

Clark, A. and Moss, P. (2011) *Listening to Young Children: The Mosaic Approach*, 2nd edn. London: National Children's Bureau and Joseph Rowntree Foundation.

This book views children as 'experts in their own lives' (p. 6) and is a helpful source of information for the many different ways of listening to young children and using their views in your work.

Working with Parents

Helen Taylor and Jill Matthews

 Chapter Overview

In this chapter you can read about:

- The key role of parents in early mathematical experiences and learning
- How mathematical understanding is situated in everyday interaction between parents and children
- Practical ways to encourage parents to become involved with their children's informal mathematical learning
- Ways in which practitioners can support parents' understanding of how their children develop mathematical understanding.

The key role of parents in early mathematical experiences

From birth, parental engagement with their children relies (often unconsciously) on mathematics in its widest sense. The rhythmic patterns of innate sucking responses and reciprocal eye contact between mother and infant suggest that even babies a few days old have a predisposition to turn-taking. Communication between parent and child develops at a phenomenal rate as the child's ability to anticipate and respond to stimuli increases. At these early stages, it is important to encourage multi-sensory experiences so that the development of the number of synapses (the wiring of nerve connections) is maximised. The most important phase of developing brain connections through experience is believed to be from birth to 3 years of age (Riley, 2007). Once these synaptic connections are established, they contribute to the child's ability to engage with its environment through sensory and social activity. Traditional nursery rhymes which involve use of the hands and fingers provide one such activity.

CASE STUDY

One, two, three, four, five

Jenny was playing with her 9-month-old son while changing his nappy (see Figure 8.1). She was singing the traditional rhyme '1, 2, 3, 4, 5, once I caught a fish alive ...'. She touched the baby's toes on each foot as he counted, '1, 2, 3, 4, 5' and '6, 7, 8, 9, 10'. The baby's gaze tracked the counting and the toes touched. The baby watched intently as the rhyme built up to the climax. 'Which finger did it bite? ... This little finger on the right!' Squeals of delight and squirming showed that the baby was anticipating the foot about to be touched.

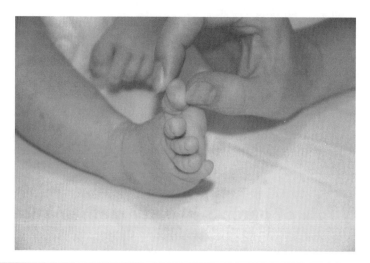

Figure 8.1 *One, two, three, four, five*

- How significant is the multi-sensory approach to developing the child's familiarity with the sequence of the number words?
- How could this develop a child's ability to count in a meaningful way?

Parents and everyday mathematics learning in the home

Just as parents play a key role in developing their children's ability to comprehend and use language, they also have opportunities to engage them with informal mathematics in daily life. These opportunities include normal family activities ranging from noticing patterns in their surroundings and changes that occur, telling the time, using computers, recording television programmes, setting a table, shopping, cooking, using measuring instruments and telephones. However, Bottle (1999) believed that while parents involved children in mathematical activity at home, it was not a high priority for parents.

Social interaction between parent and child during normal activities provides the child with a context in which to situate learning and thus build understanding of mathematics in a meaningful way (Askew, 2012). Cognitive pathways are constructed which link together the developing conceptual understanding, activity, context and the associated language.

CASE STUDY

Baking

Claire baked buns with 3-year-old Misha. They weighed ingredients using pan balance scales. Three eggs were used as the mass against which butter, castor sugar and flour were measured. Claire modelled the weighing of the butter, first putting too much in so the pan went down, then taking out too much so that the eggs went down. She talked through what she was doing all the time as if she was talking to herself ... thinking aloud. Misha watched and then joined in with the talk ... 'too heavy', 'too much'.

Misha spooned flour in and out of the pan. She told her mother that it was 'too heavy, take some out' ... and knew when the balance was 'jus' right'.

- What does Misha understand about weighing and differences in mass?
- Do you think she would understand the vocabulary in a different context?
- How did Misha's mother support her learning?

Working with parents

Parents are a child's first educator and they know their children best. Therefore, it is vitally important that others involved in children's education build on parents' knowledge and understanding of their child. Some children spend considerable time with other adults who are carers or members of the extended family, so although we are using the term 'parents' in this chapter for ease, the points also apply to others in a caring role.

Many settings aim towards creating a partnership between parents and practitioners for the benefit of the child, necessitating two-way communication. Whereas practitioners have traditionally seen a certain level of communication with parents as part of their role, this may have been limited to occasional formal opportunities. Parents may be unsure of their role in supporting their children's mathematical development and may lack confidence in talking to staff. Practitioners may also recognise the practical difficulties of gaining information about large numbers of individual children and using this effectively in supporting mathematical development. However, responsibility resides with practitioners to create opportunities and the open ethos to encourage parents to feel at ease and recognise that they have a valuable role in mathematics education for their child. So working effectively with parents involves the establishment and maintenance of a partnership between practitioners and parents in supporting children's mathematical learning (Pound, 2006).

Carraher et al.'s (1985) study showed 'disconnection' where children can fail to make mental links between mathematics that they do in school and informal mathematics met at home and elsewhere. Such disconnection may mean that children find it difficult to apply their learning from one situation to another. Working with parents to assist children in making these connections will deepen children's mathematical learning and understanding.

Culturally, in England it is acceptable for adults to say they are 'no good' at mathematics, and common for parents to tell a teacher that they struggled with mathematics at school and therefore they are not surprised that their child is struggling (Atkinson, 1992). Expectations of their child's mathematical learning and achievement are, therefore, low among some parents. Clemson and Clemson (1994) suggest that children easily adopt their parents' views of mathematics. Therefore raising parental aspirations and confidence could have a positive impact on children's attitudes. Adults working with young children can be part of these changes, enabling parents and children to see that mathematical learning can be motivating and engaging and that children can be successful mathematical learners and thinkers.

Countries where children achieve highly on international tests such as the Programme for International Student Assessment (PISA) survey (OECD, 2010) include parts of China, South Korea, Taiwan, Singapore and Hong Kong. Husbands (2012) visited some of these countries and tried to identify factors behind this achievement. He thinks that the support of parents and the cultural status of education are vital factors. Whereas it is hard to make swift cultural changes, adults in schools and settings can work with parents to help them to support their children's learning effectively. 'But parents matter most of all, and make the biggest difference of all. The challenge is to help all parents understand the role they play' (Husbands, 2012: 49).

In England, the importance of settings and parents working together has been recognised for some time, including in the Plowden Report (CACE, 1967). The DCSF emphasised the importance of parental involvement in their children's learning in *The Children's Plan: Building Brighter Futures* (DCSF, 2007) and in the Williams Review (DCSF, 2008). Desforges and Abouchaar's (2003) research report suggests that differences in parental involvement in their child's education makes a bigger difference overall than the quality of the primary education the child receives. Pugh and De'Ath (1989) proposed a way of categorising parental involvement from 'non-participation' to 'taking control'. 'Non-participation' is sub-divided into 'active', where parents actively decide not to participate, and 'passive', where there may be factors that prevent the parents from participating. It is part of the practitioners' roles to overcome these barriers. However, Docking (1990) highlighted factors that might make this difficult for practitioners, including lack of confidence. Some schools employ a member of staff, such as a Family Liaison Officer or a Parent Support Adviser, to support teachers in communicating with parents and to support parents who may lack confidence in approaching teachers.

Pound (2006) argues that parents may not always recognize mathematical activities in early years settings as mathematics. Parents often remember their own mathematics lessons and expect to see pages of sums and other formal activities. This may apply especially to parents who were educated outside Britain (de Abreu and Cline, 2005). Practitioners therefore have a responsibility to explain how they are enabling children to learn mathematics and how parents can work with them to enhance this. Cox and Sanders (1994) suggest that adults should not only describe the mathematical experiences that children are having but also, crucially, how they will benefit and progress from these.

Home–School Knowledge Exchange Project

The Home–School Knowledge Exchange (HSKE) Project (Hughes and Pollard, 2006; Winter et al., 2004, 2009) was a funded project that took place with schools in

(Continued)

(Continued)

Bristol (England) and Cardiff (Wales) between 2001 and 2005. It aimed to find ways to enhance pupil achievement and learning dispositions by a process of knowledge exchange between parents and teachers and involving the children. There were three aspects to the project, including mathematics with children aged 7–10 years. Although the mathematics focus of this project was with older children, there are some interesting outcomes that can be applied with younger children. Based on Moll et al.'s (1992, in Hughes and Pollard, 2006) work on the notion of 'funds of knowledge', the HSKE Project proposed that exchange of knowledge between home and school would be beneficial for the children. They identified that it was helpful for the initial exchange to be school-to-home and then to develop more home-to-school activities.

Effective setting-to-home communication

In order to work together, effective communication is essential (Dunhill et al., 2009). Practitioners communicate to parents on a number of levels; while there will be general information that might be given to the parents of all of the children in a group or class, there will also be more specific information about a particular child for his or her parents.

Getting to know parents is, therefore, very important and effort should be made to do this as quickly as possible when the child joins the setting. Practitioners should introduce themselves to parents. Parents are encouraged to hear positive things about their child. It is important to highlight mathematical achievements in this way occasionally. Some staff arrange to visit a child at home before or just after they start in the setting. These visits can be helpful for staff in getting to know parents and something of the child's home life. However, these should be planned carefully because some parents will regard a home visit as stressful or even threatening.

Parent consultation evenings are a traditional aspect of setting calendars. Practitioners should prepare carefully with notes of what they want to say about the child's mathematical learning and understanding and with suggestions of activities the parents could do with their child. It is also important to ask parents about what they would like to know, about any concerns they have and about how their child uses mathematics in the home or during other activities they enjoy. Links can then be made for children within the setting, making mathematics more meaningful. Parents may also reveal expertise and interests that the setting could use to enhance learning, such as how the parent uses mathematical ideas within their interests or employment. Parent consultation evenings can also be an ideal time for setting targets for children with their parents so there is shared understanding and a shared commitment to helping a child to achieve these.

Learning journals are common across many early years settings; these are books for and about each child and are developed at home and in the setting. Photographs, drawings, captions, longer pieces of writing, tickets, leaflets and other items are stuck into the book to build up a record of the child's experiences and learning. These can be very helpful in sharing families' and practitioners' understanding of the child and in helping the child to make the vital connections between life inside and outside the setting.

General information is likely to include which aspects of mathematics are being focused upon in a particular time period with general comment about the approach being used in the setting and some ideas of activities parents could do with their children to reinforce the learning. Communication may be through:

- Face-to-face meetings and workshops
- Notes, newsletters or hand-outs (some are commercially produced)
- Text messages, emails or messages through the class or group pages on a website or Virtual Learning Environment.

CASE STUDY

Welcome to the Reception Class meeting for parents

Near the beginning of the year Sarah, a Reception Class teacher, invited the children's parents to an evening meeting in the classroom. She briefly explained what she hoped the children would learn in mathematics during the year and answered questions from parents. She talked to parents about counting, how it involves more than reciting number names in order and the type of activities undertaken in school to support children's developing counting skills. She also suggested how parents could support this in everyday situations at home. At the beginning of each half term Sarah emailed parents, outlining what was planned in the coming weeks. Additionally, at the end of some weeks she emailed parents, outlining what mathematics had been addressed during that week and one idea for an activity parents

(Continued)

(Continued)

could do with their children to encourage a dialogue between children and parents (see Figure 8.2).

This week's mathematics

This week we have been looking at money. We have played in the baker's shop we have set up in the classroom. We have been looking at coins closely and trying to recognise and identify them. It would be helpful, if you could let your child tip out the coins in your purse, wallet or pocket and sort them and if you could talk to him or her about the coins, what they are and how we tell the difference between them.

This week's mathematics

This week we have been thinking about sizes and specifically talking about things that are taller and shorter than other things. We have looked at some of the trees we can see from the playground and we have built towers. It would be helpful if you could encourage your child to build towers using wooden bricks, boxes or any construction toys at home and encourage your child to compare them using the vocabulary, 'this tower is taller than that one' and 'this tower is shorter than that one.'

Figure 8.2 *Examples of slips sent home to parents at the end of a week*

Informally, many parents said how much they valued the weekly message. One parent explained that when her son came out of school and she asked him what he had done that day, he would often say 'Nothing' or 'Played' so these updates helped her to understand what went on and she felt involved in his mathematical education. Other options might be using the class page of a website or Virtual Learning Environment. These may also be useful for gaining parents' views within the setting about aspects of children's understanding of mathematics.

At a more general level, schools and settings often hold coffee mornings, workshops for parents or information events. Parents of all children within a school or setting might be invited. Events may include a mixture of teachers giving general information (for example, explaining the school's approach to the learning and teaching of calculations) and parents 'having a go' at activities in a workshop situation. Some parents are wary of helping children with mathematics at home because they perceive that mathematics, particularly calculation, is taught differently to how they learnt it and they worry about confusing their children. These events may help parents to overcome some of their anxieties.

Inviting parents to events where their children are participating can be effective. Parents may be reluctant to attend mathematics events in school as they have negative memories of school mathematics and may lack confidence. However, if they are invited to watch a mathematics lesson taking place in their child's class or to come and see children involved in mathematics activities as part of a workshop, they are less likely to feel threatened. Some settings run family workshops, fairs, trails or challenges, where children of different ages can work with their parents on practical problem solving or puzzles. These involve parents in talking to their children about mathematical ideas and thus support their learning. They may also encourage the parents to develop positive attitudes to mathematics which may be passed on to their children. After such events, parents have reported that they wished they had been taught mathematics in this way. These ideas have been extended in some places to provision of family learning programmes.

Some working parents find it very difficult to come into school during the school day. Traditionally, settings have found it more difficult to involve fathers in children's learning (DfES, 2007a). However, with encouragement, many of them are keen to become involved. 'Fathers' interest and involvement in their children's learning is statistically associated with better educational outcomes (higher attainment as well as more positive attitudes and better behaviour) even when controlling for a wide variety of other influencing factors' (Field, 2010: 44).

The HSKE Project (Winter at al., 2004, 2009) also identified that parents for whom English is an additional language can be encouraged to take part in activities when their children are involved and can interpret for them or when interpreters are invited to a special meeting.

Video clips (Winter, 2010) of children taking part in mathematical activities in the setting may be a viable alternative for parents to watch at their convenience. This is especially useful if a way can be found for parents to comment and ask questions that arise and for practitioners to respond. Scanlan (2011) suggests that it can be effective to hold events at different venues and gives the example of a display at a local supermarket. Some parents find this more accessible in terms of timing and less threatening than going into the setting. This is also a location where other adults such as child-minders and grandparents could see the display and talk to the child about it. Sometimes, these other adults may have more time to come into the setting and might enjoy an invitation.

- Mathematics-based activities can be planned for parents and children to get involved with as they arrive in the mornings.
- Settings can lend mathematics games and story books with mathematical ideas to parents to use with their children at home, perhaps with guidance notes on mathematical activities and vocabulary.

(Continued)

(Continued)

- Provide hand-outs, displays and notices for parents about children's mathematics (see Chapter 6).
- Enable children to take their mathematical mark-making home, if this is annotated, parents can more easily understand the context of the graphics.
- Mathematics clubs and trails in a setting can be open to families.

Home-to-setting communication

Communication with parents should be two-way and parents have much to offer staff in settings about their child's mathematics. Inviting parents to tell staff about their child's previous mathematical experiences and current schemas (see Chapter 1) enables more precise planning by the staff to build on these and to use the child's abilities and interests, thus making learning more relevant. Connections between home and setting learning can be more easily made with, and by, the children. Hughes (1986) explains how hard this is for children and that especially the younger children need much help from the adults involved. The HSKE Project (Winter et al., 2004, 2009) identified that much informal mathematics goes on in home settings and that this generally falls under the two headings of games and mathematics that is embedded in family activities such as gardening and shopping. The project also describes 'cultural resources' from home that children may be able to draw on within the setting. An example of this is the way children from some cultures are taught to count on their fingers in threes or fours.

- Children and parents can be invited to take photographs of mathematical activities they are involved in outside of the setting and bring them in. This is a similar idea to the work carried out by Moss (2001) within a literacy learning context. Displays can be created to stimulate discussion.
- Families can be invited to discuss board, card or other games that they play at home and the mathematical content of these. Games may be brought into the setting to share.
- Home-school communication books can be initiated where adults and children contribute pictures, photographs, tickets and captions recording a child's learning within and outside the setting.

Summary

Parents are a child's vital first educators and have an important role to play in early mathematical experiences and learning. Effective communication with parents becomes essential as soon as a child attends a learning setting outside the home environment. Responsibility for this communication rests with the staff of the setting. The Home-School Knowledge Exchange Project (Winter at al., 2004, 2009) suggested that this should start with setting-to-home communication and evolve as the relationship matures to become home-to-setting and more balanced two-way communication.

Further reading

Tucker, K. (2010) *Mathematics Through Play in the Early Years*, 2nd edn. London: Sage.
Chapter 9 has additional, practical ideas for involving parents in their child's mathematical learning. This book is written in a very accessible style for staff in all early years settings.
Carruthers, E. and Worthington, M. (2006) *Children's Mathematics: Making Marks, Making Meaning*, 2nd edn. London: Sage.
Chapter 5, entitled 'Bridging the gap between home and school mathematics', provides helpful advice related to children representing their mathematics.

Part 2
Learning and Teaching Mathematics

Part 2

Learning and Teaching
Mathematics

Early Number, Counting and Place Value

Andrew Harris

Chapter Overview

In this chapter you can read about:

- The role of counting as a foundation for understanding number
- The principles and skills of counting children need to master to be able to count accurately and flexibly
- The purpose of place value in underpinning children's understanding of the number system
- Research findings about young children's development in understanding number.

Developing a sense for number

Adults think about and use numbers in flexible and often subconscious ways developed over a long period of time. Children learn about number by watching, listening and copying adults and their peers across a range of contexts (Anghileri, 2006). Having a sense for number involves understanding different meanings and uses of numbers, recognition of patterns, connections and relationships between numbers and number operations and an awareness of different representations of numbers and number operations. Above all, it involves developing a corresponding ability to use such understanding flexibly (McIntosh et al., 1992). Each child's mental network of number relationships and representations develops in highly individualised ways depending on the contexts the child experiences and the mental connections that are established (see Chapter 1).

Different meanings and uses of numbers

We use symbols (the numerals 1, 2, 3, …) to represent numbers in a range of contexts. Depending on the context and how they are used, numbers can have a range of different meanings. The number four, for example, could have any of the following interpretations:

- Cardinal number: the number of items in a set (for example, four monkeys, four pencils)
- Ordinal number: numerical order or position (for example, 4 on a number line comes after 3 and before 5, the 4th person in a queue, house number 4 in a row of houses)
- Nominal number: a label for identification (for example, a bus number, a telephone number) which may not correspond to the number of items present.

Children need to master these different interpretations of numbers and learn which meaning to apply in particular contexts. The cardinal and ordinal meanings of numbers are crucial in understanding counting and are also significant foundations for later work on calculation (see Chapter 10).

Early understandings of numerosity

Recognising numerical differences

Children exhibit an emerging sense for number very early in life. Six-month-old infants are able to notice numerical differences between small quantities such as two and three (Baroody, 1987; Schneider et al., 2008). Such research findings arise from experiments where infants are repeatedly shown images of a given number. After a period of time their interest appears to decline until an image of a different quantity is displayed, whereupon their interest is rekindled. This does not mean that infants can identify how many items are being shown but rather that they can perceive that a numerical difference exists. Children from about 2 years old onwards begin to use vocabulary which indicates early attempts at quantification (for example, little, much, many, lots).

Subitising

Young children can often determine the number of objects in sets of up to three or four objects rapidly without explicitly counting them (Bruce and Threlfall, 2004), a process known as subitising. When the arrangement of the items is a familiar one (for example, the arrangement of spots on dice or eggs in an egg box), children may be able to use this familiarity to recognise larger numbers of items without counting them. However, more generally, once the number of items exceeds four or five even adults resort to counting as a more reliable strategy for quantifying.

Differing views exist about how children are able to subitise. Some researchers (for example, Sophian, 1995; Dehaene, 1997) believe this is achieved through visual perception of the set as a whole without counting individual items, while others (for example Fuson, 1988; Gelman and Gallistel, 1978) suggest that a form of subliminal counting occurs. The extent to which subitising and counting may or may not be related is also still debated.

Laying the foundations for counting

A range of pre-counting experiences should be provided for young children. A key skill to develop is that of matching items, thus establishing a one-to-one correspondence between them (see Figure 9.1).

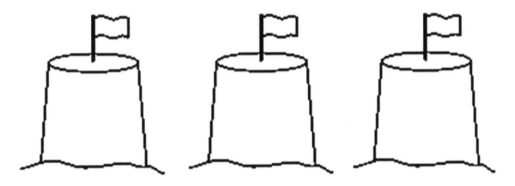

Figure 9.1 *One-to-one correspondence: matching one flag to each sandcastle*

Subsequently, children use one-to-one correspondence to determine whether sets contain the same number (the notion of 'equivalence') or differing amounts (the ideas of 'more' and 'less'). They also learn about the vocabulary used (for example, more, same, different) when comparing quantities.

Useful activities to explore one-to-one correspondence matching include:

- Pairing socks or gloves
- Putting one cup on each saucer
- Asking each child to find a partner
- Giving each teddy bear a biscuit.

When shown two equal sets of items young children often believe that one set contains more than the other because the items in one set are more spread out (Piaget, 1965; MaLT, 2005). Their judgements are informed by visual perception rather than counting. Piaget proposed that children needed to understand 'conservation of number' (knowing that the quantity of a set is unaffected by rearrangement), and to be able to correctly identify whether a subset of a set contained more items than the set (and vice versa) before they could understand number. However, contrary to Piaget's view, children's understanding of number is now widely acknowledged to be 'rooted in counting' (Maclellan, 2008) and so today emphasis is given to developing counting skills.

Learning to count

Most people believe counting involves learning a sequence of number words but counting is much more complex than this. Dowker (2008) asserts that counting requires both procedural knowledge (knowledge of the counting process and associated counting skills) and conceptual knowledge (understanding the principles which underpin counting processes).

By imitating adults, children begin to learn to recite the counting sequence as a string of words but the numbers may not be in the correct order and there may be no association of the counting sequence with actual objects. Munn (2008) reports that most children around 4 years old believe that counting is merely about saying the number words; relatively few understand that counting is about finding 'how many'. Children's experiences of counting at this stage are predominately playful rather than focused on quantifying (Munn, 2008). Children may count as far as they can to impress adults or include counting within ritualistic play (for example, counting when descending stairs). Through such experiences, children begin to learn about contexts where counting can be used (Fuson, 1988) and to mimic actions associated with the counting process.

Five principles of counting

From their research, Gelman and Gallistel (1978) identified five principles of counting:

- One-to-one correspondence principle
- Stable order principle
- Cardinal principle
- Abstraction principle
- Order-irrelevance principle.

An understanding of the first three principles is necessary in order to be able to count accurately. The final two principles enable a child to understand the breadth of contexts in which counting is possible and to count more flexibly.

One-to-one correspondence principle

This involves matching one counting word to each item to be counted. The child must co-ordinate their touching of items with their oral counting so that each item is touched and counted just once. Often children find it helpful to move each item as it is counted so that counted items are separated from those still to be counted. Children apply this principle more reliably when counting linear arrangements; non-linear arrangements are more challenging.

Stable order principle

Children who master the stable order principle know the order of the counting words and that this order is always the same. This understanding is developed through mimicking adults, repeated rehearsals of the counting sequence and application in varied contexts. Over time, children begin to relate the number words to the counted items to realise that the order of the counting sequence is always the same. Using the stable order principle requires a good understanding of ordinal number (for example, knowing that 4 comes after 3 and before 5).

Cardinal principle

When the final item in a set is counted, the final number word in the count represents the number of items in the set (known as the 'cardinal value' of the set). If a child is able

Learning and Teaching Mathematics 0–8

to consistently match one number label to each item (using the one-one correspondence principle) while reciting the number words in the correct order (applying the stable order principle) the outcome of the count should always be the same. According to Gelman and Gallistel (1978), a child who can recognise that the final number word in the count indicates how many items there are in a set understands the cardinal principle.

Some researchers (for example, Dehaene, 1997; Fuson, 1988) believe that an understanding of the cardinal principle begins to develop as children count small quantities which they have also subitised and realise that the final number in the count matches the outcome of their subitising. The final number in the count later becomes the means of determining 'how many' for sets which are too big to subitise.

Abstraction principle

This principle states that any set of items is countable, regardless of whether the items are similar or dissimilar, visible or invisible, real or imaginary. For example, a set of identical teddy bears is countable but so is a set comprising a teddy bear, a toy car and a pencil, a set consisting of a series of sounds, or a set of characters in a story. To master this principle, children must learn that when counting items only the numerosity matters and all other features should be ignored. To develop such understanding, children need experiences of counting sets containing different types of items.

Order-irrelevance principle

This principle states that the order in which items are counted is irrelevant; the cardinal value of the set will always be the same provided the one-to-one correspondence, stable order and cardinal principles are applied. In part, mastery of this principle involves learning that the use of a particular number label for each countable item is temporary, lasting only as long as the current count is in progress. For example, a doll might not always be labelled as 'two' when counting, depending on the order in which the items are counted. To understand this, children need to count a set of items in different orders. Additionally, children have to recognise that the outcome (the cardinal value) is always identical, regardless of the order in which items are counted, and experience this with a range of different sets of objects.

Debates about counting, cardinality and subitising

It is becoming evident from recent research that when considering the early stages of children's number development a distinction needs to be drawn between children knowing how to count as a procedure and understanding the underlying conceptual principles (Maclellan, 2008). While Gelman and Gallistel's (1978) counting principles are widely accepted by researchers as the principles underlying successful counting, a debate continues about whether children must understand the principles of counting before they can perform counting procedures accurately (as Gelman and Gallistel proposed) or whether, as some later researchers (for example, Bermejo et al., 2004; Sophian, 1998) believe, children learn the procedural aspects of counting first and only later acquire a conceptual understanding of the principles and purpose of counting.

Gelman and Gallistel's cardinal principle was accepted for a long time as a test of a child's understanding of cardinality. Subsequent research (Sophian, 1995) indicates that asking children to 'Give me X items' from a larger set requires deeper understanding of cardinality than tasks in which children are asked 'How many?'. This is because children cannot rely on the last word being the answer; in order to succeed, they have to understand that they must stop when their oral count reaches the requested number of items. Bruce (2000) found that children who counted were more successful than those who grabbed a handful of the requested item in such tasks. In Bruce's study of 93 3- and 4-year-old children, none of the children who used grabbing were successful for quantities larger than five. This is likely to be because, even where grabbing was supported by subitising, subitising is unreliable for more than five items. The most successful children discriminated by selecting a grabbing (supported by subitising) approach for small quantities and a counting approach for larger amounts, suggesting that developing an awareness of the limitations of the reliability of subitising may be helpful.

Numerals: representation, identification, and recognition

As children use their own invented graphics to represent quantities and numbers (see Chapter 4) they gradually acquire an understanding of conventional numerals, their names and how they relate to the cardinal, ordinal and nominal meanings of numbers in different contexts. They need many experiences of seeing and talking about these symbols in order to understand and internalise such connections.

Number identification tasks which ask a child to say the number a numeral represents (for example, knowing the symbol 4 means four) provide children with opportunities to rehearse and check their developing knowledge of written numbers. Typical adult-initiated tasks might include asking children 'What number have you landed on?' while playing a board game or asking them to read the numeral on a birthday card.

Number recognition tasks are more demanding and require the child to be able to select the correct numeral from a wider range of numerals. Possible activities include selecting a number from a set of number cards pegged on a washing line or clicking on the correct numeral on a computer programme.

Adults can also support children's developing understanding of number identification and recognition by ensuring the learning environment contains plenty of examples of written numbers with which children can interact. For example, a role-play area set up to resemble a shoe shop might include numerals in the form of telephone and calculator number key pads, shoe size labels, shelves labelled by shoe size, price labels and receipts for children to be able to write numbers on, a shop till showing a numerical display and perhaps a clock on the wall.

Supporting the development of counting

Threlfall (2008: 62) identifies three different forms of counting activity which adults should promote:

- 'Oral counting' where the child recites the counting sequence but no objects are counted (for example, in counting songs and rhymes); the focus is on ordinality.
- 'Enumeration' where the counting sequence is matched to objects but the quantity of items is not considered (for example, saying a number word as each toy is put away in the toy-box).
- Cardinality activities in which the counting words are matched to items with the purpose of finding the numerical quantity.

Clearly, enumeration is dependent on successful oral counting while cardinality requires an understanding of both oral counting and enumeration.

It is important that adults avoid over-emphasis of the cardinal aspect of number at the expense of ordinal number (Haylock and Cockburn, 2013), otherwise children's mathematical understanding of the different meanings of number may be limited. Adults can support children in exploring these different meanings of number by engaging children in rich dialogue about numbers, offering meaningful contexts to explore and selecting resources carefully.

Using resources to support counting

Children should experience a wide range of resources for exploring the cardinal aspect of number and counting. Figure 9.2 shows examples of different resources which can be used to explore cardinality with children. Each resource provides a different image of the number 'three'. Some are purely mathematical in nature while others are drawn from everyday life; both types of resource are useful in supporting children's emerging understanding.

Figure 9.2 *Modelling the cardinality of 'three'*

A range of resources exist for exploring the ordinal aspect of number and counting. Number tracks come in a wide variety of guises such as numbered floor tiles, a series of numbered birthday cards, or painted number tracks on walls or playgrounds (see Figure 9.3). Because they model the order of numbers in the counting sequence, they can also provide a good context for exploring the stable order principle (for example, re-ordering a set of number cards pegged to a washing line). A number track reflects a one-to-one correspondence between the position of each numeral and the number of squares counted so far as the child counts along it, thus connecting ordinality and cardinality. For this reason number tracks should start at 1, not 0.

A bead string (see Figures 1.2 and 9.9) provides a similar model but with the distinction that the beads are moveable, thus allowing connections to be made more easily between the ordinal and cardinal meanings of numbers.

The notion of zero is challenging for children because its cardinal meaning can only be represented by an absence of items. Rhymes and songs which involve counting back can provide an informal introduction to zero as the number that is one less than 1 (an ordinal understanding of zero). The best representation which allows the inclusion of zero is a number line (see Figure 9.4). However, using a number line involves counting intervals or 'jumps' between numbers which is much more difficult than counting squares or beads. Consequently, the number line is better introduced only when children are confident with counting using a number track.

Figure 9.3 *Examples of models for ordinal number*

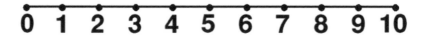

Figure 9.4 *Number line*

The following are good activities to develop children's understanding of counting:

- **Rhymes and songs:** These should provide opportunities for children to count forwards (for example, 'One, two, buckle my shoe', 'One, two, three, four, five, once I caught a fish alive') and backwards (for example, 'Ten green bottles',

'Five little ducks went swimming one day'). However, we always think that it's harder to find songs that count up rather than down so look out for songs that will assist with this such as 'One potato, two potato'! Children will need to be able to count up to 5 or 10 or so before they learn to count down (which is much harder).

- **Stories:** Many stories incorporate counting as a key focus or provide opportunities for counting items in the pictures (for example, *The Very Hungry Caterpillar* (Carle, 1969) or traditional tales such as *The Three Billy Goats Gruff*).
- **Outdoor games:** Many traditional playground games (for example, skipping games, hopscotch) involve counting.
- **Indoor games:** Traditional board games such as Snakes and Ladders and Ludo provide good opportunities to count both spots on dice and squares on a game board.

Using counting to solve problems

Exploratory tasks set in practical, meaningful contexts provide excellent opportunities for children to use and apply their counting skills to solve problems (see Chapter 1). The following case study illustrates the use of a question-based approach to posing problems which prompt the use of counting as a solution strategy.

CASE STUDY

Making gingerbread people

William, Daisy and Ahmed (aged 5) were making gingerbread people ready for snack time with Lisa (an adult).

Ahmed wanted to decorate his gingerbread people with raisins to represent buttons. Lisa asked, 'How many do you need?', thus prompting him to mentally visualise and count 'One, two, four, three'. Lisa helped Ahmed by allowing him to position the raisins and then counted them with him, 'One, two, three, four'.

When they had finished decorating the gingerbread people they placed them on baking trays ready to cook. William was counting the gingerbread people on his baking tray. Lisa asked him, 'Will there be enough for one each?' William pointed to the gingerbread people in turn as he said 'That one's for Daisy, this one's for

(Continued)

(Continued)

Ahmed and one more for me. One, two, three!' 'What about me?' asked Lisa. 'Oh, yes, I'll make you another one. That will be four altogether', said William.

When the gingerbread people were ready to eat, they put them onto plates. 'Are there the same number on each plate?' asked Lisa. The children each counted the gingerbread people on their plates. 'One, two, three, four, five. There are five,' Daisy counted, but forgetting where she had started counting. 'That's not right. It's one, two, three, four. There are four,' corrected William. 'Look, I can count them this way, too. One, two, three, four,' he said, counting them in reverse order. 'I think we all have four,' he said. 'How can you find out?' asked Lisa. They counted the gingerbread people on each plate and agreed that they each had four.

Errors in counting

Many counting errors can be attributed to an incomplete understanding (see Chapter 1) of one or more of Gelman and Gallistel's (1978) five counting principles. Thus, we can use the five counting principles to help us to analyse a child's understanding of different aspects of counting and then identify appropriate experiences which will help to support the child's developing understanding (see Chapter 7).

For example, in the case study it is evident that Ahmed is secure in applying the one-to-one correspondence principle (one number word per item) but we can identify that his knowledge of the stable order principle (consistent, accurate order of numbers) needs further reinforcement because in his initial count he reverses the order of 'three' and 'four'.

Daisy, when counting the gingerbread people on her plate, counted one of them more than once. This indicates an insecure understanding of the one-to-one correspondence principle in this particular context. This may be because the gingerbread people were positioned around the plate in a circle rather than in a straight line and so she has lost track of where she started counting (MaLT, 2005). However, her use of the stable order principle for up to five items is secure.

By contrast, William appears to have a secure knowledge of the one-to-one correspondence, stable order and cardinal principles for sets of up to four items. We can deduce this from observing that he is using one number word per item, that the order of the numbers in his counting is correct and that he concludes from his counting that there are four gingerbread people on the plate. It would seem that he is also developing some understanding of the order-irrelevance principle because he has recognised it is possible to count the gingerbread people in a different order. However, as the gingerbread people are similar in appearance it is not possible to draw

Errors in using the one-to-one correspondence principle

- Counting an item more than once (Fuson, 1988; Thompson, 2008a)
- Omitting an item when counting (Fuson, 1988)
- Oral counting and touching or moving of items not co-ordinated (Fuson, 1988; Thompson, 2008a), for example, pointing at an item without saying a number word, saying two number words for one item, touching an item for each syllable in 'seven', 'eleven', etc.
- The oral count stops before reaching the final item
- The oral count continues beyond the last item (Thompson, 2008a), for example, '1, 2, 3, 4, 5. There are 6'.

Errors in using the stable order principle

- Counting 1, 2, 3 … then a number to represent 'many' (Gelman and Gallistel, 1978)
- Using a stable sequence of numbers followed by one or more numbers which are incorrectly ordered (Bruce, 2000, in Threfall, 2008), for example, 1, 2, 3, 4, 5, 7, 6, 8, 9 …
- Using a stable sequence of numbers with some numbers omitted (Bruce, 2000, in Threfall, 2008), for example, 1, 2, 3, 4, 5, 7, 9, 10 …
- Using a stable sequence of numbers followed by a repeating cycle of numbers (Bruce, 2000, in Threfall, 2008), for example, 1, 2, 3, 4, 5, 7, 5, 7…
- Repeating a previous section of a stable sequence of numbers (Bruce, 2000, in Threfall, 2008), for example, 1, 2, 3, 4, 5, 6, 7, 8, 5, 6, 7 …
- Using a stable sequence of numbers followed by an idiosyncratic sequence (Bruce, 2000, in Threfall, 2008), for example, 1, 2, 3, 4, 5, 6, 10, 8, 20, 11…
- Using random sequences of numbers, none of which are stable, for example, 3, 1, 4, 7, 2, 5 … .

Errors in using the cardinal principle

- After counting, when asked 'How many?', the child responds by re-counting, thus indicating that the child views the counting process itself as the appropriate response rather than understanding that the final number in the count indicates how many items there are (Bermejo, 2006)
- 'Last word responding' (Fuson, 1988; Sophian, 1995): mechanically stating the final number in the count as 'the answer' to the question 'How many?' but without real understanding that this indicates how many items there are
- When asked to count out X items from a larger set, the child counts beyond the number requested (Sophian, 1995).

Errors in using the abstraction principle

- When asked to count a set of mixed items the child only counts those items which are visually similar (Lawton and Hansen, 2011)
- When asked to count a set of mixed items, the child separates the set into several subsets of similar items, each of which is then counted separately (Lawton and Hansen, 2011).

Errors in using the order-irrelevance principle

- Can count items arranged in a line starting with the item at one end of the line but when asked to start counting from a different item the child is unable to respond successfully (Gelman and Gallistel, 1978)
- Believing a valid but unusually ordered count to be incorrect (LeFevre et al., 2006)
- Having counted a set of items from left to right, the child is unable to recognise that the outcome will be the same if counted in reverse order (Cowan et al., 1996).

Figure 9.5 *Typical counting errors*

any conclusions about his understanding of the abstraction principle from the evidence in the case study.

Having a good knowledge of typical counting errors made by children is important. An adult, who can correctly diagnose a child's counting errors and determine which counting principle is not fully understood, can address the child's difficulties in a more focused manner (see Chapter 7). The list of counting errors in Figure 9.5 can be used for this purpose.

Thompson (2008a) recommends the use of a puppet or 'naughty teddy' that makes errors when counting as an approach to addressing children's own errors. By correcting the puppet's errors, children are enabled to indirectly discuss and reflect about their own counting errors with a view to refining both their procedural counting skills and their conceptual understanding of counting principles. While a child who can count accurately is deemed to have a sound procedural knowledge, a child who can identify the errors of a puppet or another child can be regarded as having a conceptual understanding of the relevant counting principles (LeFevre et al., 2006; Maclellan, 2008).

Developing skills for flexible counting

A range of skills needs to be developed for a child to be able to count successfully in a wide variety of contexts. The application of physical skills such as touching, pointing and separating counted items from items yet to be counted are important in developing the procedural aspects of keeping track when counting. Fuson (1988: 85) suggested a progression in increasing internalisation of such skills: touching, pointing at near objects, then pointing from a distance, and finally using eye fixation. However, Bruce (2000) reports that he found no significant difference in success rates between touching and pointing as a means of keeping track while counting but identified that children who only used eye movement were less successful. This suggests that adults should avoid encouraging children away from touching and pointing strategies prematurely.

It is possible for a child to be successful in applying a particular counting principle in some contexts yet fail in more challenging situations. For example, a child may apply the one-to-one correspondence principle securely when counting moveable objects positioned in a straight line but fail when counting fixed objects in other arrangements (MaLT, 2005).

Adults can support children's developing ability to apply their conceptual understanding of counting by ensuring children encounter varied counting contexts of increasing complexity. Figure 9.6 offers a suitable progression in counting contexts with examples of practical activities.

Counting Contexts (in order of difficulty)	Examples of Typical Activities
Counting moveable items arranged in a line	Counting counters, coins, buttons, shells, fruit, animals in a mini-world, building blocks, toy cars, books on a shelf
Counting fixed items arranged in a line	Counting squares on a game board, rungs on a playground ladder, stairs, parked cars, fence posts, plants planted in a row
Counting items in other arrangements	Circles and loops: Counting the beads in a necklace, children in a ring, chairs around a table Arrays: counting the eggs in an egg box, sheets of postage stamps, buns in a baking tray Other arrangements: counting motifs on wrapping paper, children in the play house, spots on a domino, shapes used to make a picture, raindrops on the window
Counting visible items which are not touchable	Counting items in a picture on the wall, people seen through a window, birds on a roof-top, chimneys on houses
Counting visible items which are transient	Counting physical actions such as jumps, hops, skips, waves breaking on the seashore, counting spoonfuls of ingredients
Counting sounds	Counting sounds from a tambourine or drum, hand claps, clock chiming, spoken words
Counting items which are mentally visualised	Counting from memory the people in my family, the number of biscuits we've eaten, how many people can fit around the table, counting imaginary items

Figure 9.6 *Progression in counting contexts*

Counting beyond 10

When the numbers up to 10 are known, children can extend their counting explorations to numbers up to 20 and then the tens numbers (20, 30, 40 …). We use a place value system for writing and saying numbers which uses a 'tens-ones' pattern (for example, sixty-two, forty-five). While children initially have no understanding of this underlying place value system, the 'tens-ones' pattern in the number words in most languages is helpful for children when learning about the order of numbers beyond 10.

However, the counting numbers in English are very idiosyncratic, particularly the numbers just beyond 10 (O'Sullivan et al., 2005). The numbers 'eleven' and 'twelve' when spoken do not fit the 'tens-ones' pattern and have to be memorised. Although the numbers 13–19 are written in a standard 'tens-ones' arrangement, they are spoken in reverse order (for example, 'four-teen' for 14 rather than 'ten-four'). Additionally, the numbers thirteen and fifteen are even more irregular because the 'ones' part of these numbers does not precisely match the corresponding single-digit numbers 'three' and 'five'. The tens numbers 'twenty', 'thirty', and 'fifty' are similarly inconsistent. Thompson (2008a) suggests this is a major reason why children learning in English take longer to appreciate the patterns in the names of numbers than children using more consistent languages. If adults are aware of these inconsistencies they can ameliorate the difficulties which ensue.

Using resources to support counting beyond 10

Number tracks, number lines and bead-strings extended to 20 provide useful models to explore how the numbers progress beyond 10. A Numicon number track (see Figure 9.7) offers the advantage that it portrays the 'tens plus ones' structure of two-digit numbers as well as their order, thus preparing for the development of place value understanding which follows.

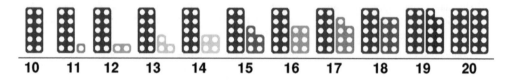

Figure 9.7   *Numicon number track showing the numbers 10–20*

A ten-division counting stick (see Figure 9.8) can be used for counting in tens to help rehearse the names of these numbers. Initially, the tens numbers can be stuck to the counting stick to support children and then gradually removed a few at a time as the numbers become more secure.

Figure 9.8   *Counting stick*

While children may be able to orally count to 50 or 100 this does not necessarily mean that they have a sense of the relative values of two-digit numbers. Inevitably, children will have limited practical experience of quantities of this magnitude so they may lack understanding that 43 is larger than 27, for example.

Developing an understanding of place value

Fundamental principles of the place value system

We identified earlier that counting is very useful for exploring small quantities. However, for numbers larger than 20, counting as a means of quantifying and of comparing quantities is relatively inefficient and prone to errors. Thus, for exploring multi-digit numbers we use a place value system. While our place value system is a very powerful tool, using it requires a sophisticated understanding of four fundamental properties identified by Ross (2002: 419):

- 'Positional': the position ('place') of a digit within the number determines its value
- 'Base-ten': working from right to left, successive positions ('places') represent increasing powers of 10 (... 10^3, 10^2, 10^1, 10^0, 10^{-1}, 10^{-2}, 10^{-3}, ...)
- 'Multiplicative': the value of a particular digit within a number is determined by multiplying the digit by its positional value (for example, in 256 the two is worth 2 x 100, the five is worth 5 x 10 and the six is worth 6 x 1)
- 'Additive': the value of the overall number is the total of the values of the individual digits (for example, 256 is worth 200 + 50 + 6).

Two consequences of the base-ten property are that only ten digits (0–9) are needed to represent numbers and that the digit zero acts as a 'place-holder' (denoting empty 'places' within numbers and thereby preserving the positional values of other digits).

Given the complexity of these properties, adults must provide a connected experience of practical representations, interpretation, discussion, and symbolic recording in order for children to achieve a full understanding of place value.

Quantity value and column value

Thompson and Bramald (2002) interviewed 144 children aged 6–8. They identified two different ways of thinking about multi-digit numbers using place value, which they called 'quantity value' and 'column value'. For example, we can think about the number 43 either as 40 + 3 (quantity value) or as 4 tens + 3 ones (column value).

Thompson and Bramald found that children were relatively successful in tasks that required understanding of quantity value (such as two-digit mental calculation

(Continued)

(Continued)

strategies). By contrast, few of the children had an understanding of column value, which is used in written calculation strategies. They concluded that initially adults should emphasise the quantity value perspective because it is more readily understood by children and because it supports understanding of mental calculation strategies which are developed earlier than written calculation strategies. Furthermore, they recommended that learning about column value be delayed until children begin to use written calculation strategies (when an understanding of column value becomes necessary).

Introducing children to place value

Children are fascinated by big numbers and will talk about them happily even if they have no real conception of their relative size. Often children will have heard adults talking about such numbers and some will have explored them, perhaps on a calculator or a computer game. Storybooks, such as *How Big is a Million?* (Milbourne, 2007) which offers visual images showing the relative sizes of one, ten, one hundred, one thousand, and one million, can provide a stimulus for discussion and an informal way to begin learning about place value.

Adults can build on such informal understandings by helping children to work on grouping items (both everyday objects and mathematical resources) as sets of ten, and subsequently sets of ten plus some additional 'ones'. This can be introduced as a speedier form of counting initially but it is important to make explicit

Figure 9.9 *Representing 43 (using Multilink, Numicon, Dienes' Base 10 materials and a bead string)*

the connections between the physical representations and the digits used to write the numbers. When discussing such representations, adults should refer to the tens quantities using quantity value (ten, twenty, etc.) rather than column value referents (1 ten, 2 tens, etc.). Through experiences of reading, writing and representing numbers and associated mathematical talk, children begin to connect the value of each digit in a number with the position of the digit as well as the digit itself. Figure 9.9 shows possible resources which might be used.

Typical activities to support this development might include:

- Using 0–9 digit cards to make numbers, talking about how the value of each digit changes when their positions are changed and then discussing the impact of the changes on the size of the numbers
- Using a 0–9 dice, base-boards marked with tens and ones columns and a predetermined target (for example, making the largest number or the number closest to 50), children take it in turns to roll the dice and place the digit obtained in either the tens or ones position on their base-board with the winner being the child whose number is closest to the target when everyone has made a two-digit number.

Partitioning numbers and combining digit values

Partitioning numbers involves splitting numbers into separate positional components based on the value of each digit (for example, 143 is partitioned as 100 + 40 + 3) and combining is the reverse of this process. Both make use of the 'quantity value' aspect of place value and Ross' (2002) additive property. To be able to partition numbers into tens and ones (and later hundreds, tens and ones) children need to appreciate how the value of any digit is determined by its position within a number (Ross' (2002) positional property). Arrow cards and Gattegno place value charts (see Figure 9.10) are useful resources for supporting both partitioning and combining activities (Anghileri, 2006).

The partitioned form 100 + 40 + 3 indicates how the number is spoken (one hundred and forty three) whereas the combined form 143 indicates how the number is written. Later, it becomes important for children to explore alternative partitionings of numbers because this will support flexibility when calculating (Anghileri, 2006) (see Chapter 10). For example, 59 can be considered as 40 + 19 or 60 − 1 as well as 50 + 9.

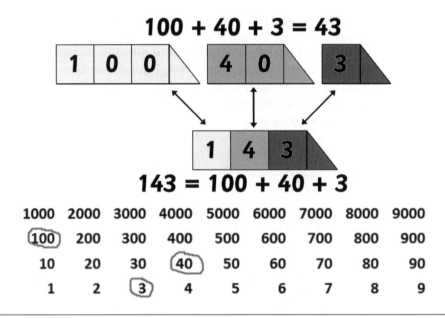

Figure 9.10 *Using arrow cards and Gattegno chart to model partitioning and combining*

- When do you use the 'quantity value' and 'column value' perspectives in everyday life? Which were you taught at school?
- Which of the place value resources discussed in this chapter reflect the quantity value perspective of 43? Which are better used to model the column value interpretation?

Learning to use place value

There are several key applications of place value which children encounter, namely:

- Ordering numbers
- Rounding numbers
- Supporting calculation with multi-digit numbers (discussed in Chapter 10).

Ordering numbers

Initially, memory of the counting sequence is used for ordering numbers. Later, children can be helped to perceive the patterns that exist in our number system and to then make use of these patterns when ordering numbers. The arrangement of the numbers in a hundred square makes the patterns in the written numbers up to 100 more apparent (see case study in Chapter 1, pp. 8–9). Within each row the recurring ones-digit pattern advances in 1s while the tens digit remains constant until it changes at the end of the row. Within each column the tens digit advances in 1s while the ones digit remains constant. A hundred-square jigsaw provides a good opportunity for children to use these patterns to reconstruct the hundred square.

For bigger numbers more sophisticated strategies are needed. Children need to learn that to order numbers they must compare the values of digits of equal significance (hundreds digits with hundreds digits, tens digits with tens digits, etc.) in turn starting with the most significant digits (so hundreds digits are compared before tens digits and tens digits before ones digits). For example, for the numbers 128 and 135 the hundreds digits are both worth 100 (and so are equal in value) but the tens digit 3 (worth 30) in 135 is larger than the corresponding tens digit 2 (worth 20) in 128, so 135 is larger than 128. Children need to be familiar with the order of 10s and 100s numbers to enable them to compare the values of corresponding digits.

- What developing strategies for ordering numbers are being used by each of the children in the following case study?
- Identify the nature of the children's misconceptions and uncertainties about place value which become evident in their discussion.
- How could you help the children overcome their difficulties?

CASE STUDY

Ordering numbers on a washing line

Tony, an adult, was listening to three children, Megan, Yassim, and Carlos (all age 6), who were trying to reorder some number cards pegged on a washing line (see Figure 9.11).

(Continued)

(Continued)

Figure 9.11 *Number cards on a washing line*

Carlos: This number [he picks up the 7] is bigger than that one [points to 64] 'cos it has a 7. Seven is bigger than six.

Yassim: No, it can't be because it only has one number. It's the only card with one number so it has to be the smallest [she repositions the 7 at the left end of the line].

Megan: I think the sixteen is next [she places the 61 to the right of the 7].

Yassim: Silly, it's sixty-one, not sixteen 'cos it starts with a 6.

Megan: Oh, OK. I think this one [she points at 54] must come after 7.

Carlos: And the 6 [he points to 60] comes before the 7 because 6 is less than 7.

Megan: No, it has a zero in it so it can't be just 6. It must be sixty-something.

Yassim: It's 60, like we did in counting earlier: 10, 20, 30, 40, 50, 60. So it's bigger than 54 'cos 60 comes after 50 [she moves the 60 to the right of the 54].

Carlos: What about the 26 [he picks up the 206 card]?

Megan: It's not 26. It's really big 'cos it has three numbers.

Yassim: Yes, it must be the biggest. I don't know which of these is bigger, though [she points to the 61 and 64 cards]. They both start with 6 ... .

Rounding numbers

To be able to round whole numbers to the nearest ten or hundred successfully children need to know the order of the tens and hundreds numbers. Additionally, they need to learn the convention that, should the number to be rounded be equidistant from the previous and the next tens or hundreds numbers, the number should be rounded up and not down. A number line provides a good representation to support children in determining which tens or hundreds number is nearest to the number to be rounded.

Place value errors and misconceptions

In the earlier case study the children exhibited a number of common place value misconceptions and errors:

- Reversing digits when reading or writing teen numbers (Lawton and Hansen, 2011; MaLT, 2005; Thompson, 2008a). For example, in the case study Megan knew that sixteen is written with a 1 and a 6 but was unsure about the order in which the digits are written and so mistakenly read 61 as sixteen. Children also commonly write sixteen as 61. This is a particular issue with teen numbers (and their corresponding reversals) because of the way in which we say the 'teen' numbers in English.
- Not understanding the role of 'zero as a placeholder' which maintains the values of other digits (Lawton and Hansen, 2011). In the case study, Carlos read 206 as 26 (a 20 followed by 6) and 60 as 6. Similar errors are made by children when writing numbers, for example 26 is written as 206.
- Believing that numbers with more digits are larger (MaLT, 2005). For example, Megan and Yassim believed 206 was the biggest number because it had three digits. While it is true that whole numbers with more digits are larger, it is not necessarily true for decimal numbers which the children will experience later. At this stage in development, adults can accept this as prototypical reasoning which will later be refined.
- Comparing values of digits of unequal significance when ordering numbers. In the case study, Carlos compared the values of the initial digits of the numbers 7 and 64 rather than comparing the values of digits of equal significance.

You might also have noticed in the case study that Yassim and Megan both use the word 'number' when the term 'digit' would have been more accurate (Lawton and Hansen, 2011).

Some further common place value errors include:

- Decade transition errors when counting (Thompson, 2008a), for example, '... thirty-eight, thirty-nine, thirty-ten ... '. Similar counting errors occur when reaching the next hundreds number.
- Not understanding that the position of digits determines their value, for example, 2 tens + 7 ones is interpreted as 9 items (MaLT, 2005)
- Putting more than 9 items in a particular position or 'place' within a number when representing numbers or when performing number calculations
- Recording each ten as a separate digit, for example, writing 24 as 114.

Summary

In this chapter we have identified the different meanings of numbers which children encounter. We have considered the principles which underpin successful counting, the errors which children make and ways in which adults can offer supportive learning experiences. In addition, we have noted the significant features of place value which young children must learn, resources which can support such learning and some of the difficulties children experience. In the next chapter we consider how counting provides a foundation for understanding number operations and learning number facts and how place value understanding is applied in different calculation strategies.

Further reading

Anghileri, J. (2006) *Teaching Number Sense*, 2nd edn. London: Continuum.

Chapters 1–3 provide a clear overview of progression in children's learning of number.

Haylock, D. and Cockburn, A. (2013) *Understanding Mathematics for Young Children*, 4th edn. London: Sage.

In Chapter 2 Haylock and Cockburn provide a detailed discussion of key ideas about number, counting and the number system.

Montague-Smith, A. and Price, A. J. (2012) *Mathematics in Early Years Education,* 3rd edn. Abingdon: Routledge.

In Chapter 2 the authors offer useful guidance on planning practical number and counting activities and experiences for young children.

Thompson, I. (ed.) (2008) *Teaching and Learning Early Number*, 2nd edn. Maidenhead: Open University Press.

In Chapters 2, 5 and 6 respectively, Munn, Threlfall and Maclellan discuss the issues and research associated with the development of children's counting skills in more detail.

10

Calculation

Andrew Harris

 Chapter Overview

In this chapter you can read about:

- Different forms of addition, subtraction, multiplication and division
- How children progress from counting to calculating
- The different mental and written calculation strategies used by children
- Resources and models for supporting understanding of calculation
- The importance of understanding, reliability, efficiency and fluency in calculation.

Different forms of addition and subtraction

To appreciate the complexities of addition and subtraction we need to recognise that there are different forms of each which children experience. Carpenter and Moser (1983) identified four different types of addition and subtraction contexts: combine, change, compare and equalise (see Figure 10.1). Models and typical word problems are provided to illustrate each form.

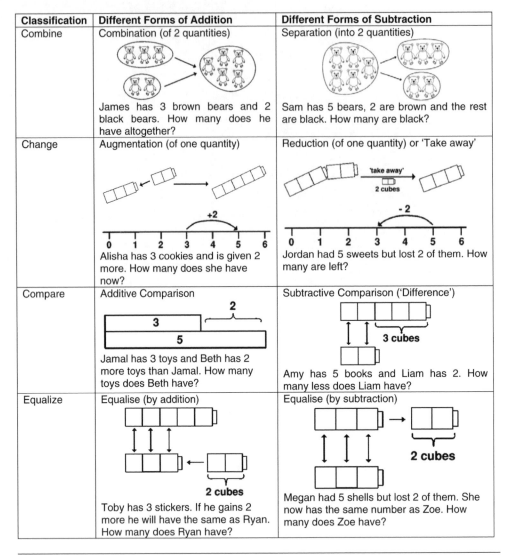

Classification	Different Forms of Addition	Different Forms of Subtraction
Combine	**Combination (of 2 quantities)** James has 3 brown bears and 2 black bears. How many does he have altogether?	**Separation (into 2 quantities)** Sam has 5 bears, 2 are brown and the rest are black. How many are black?
Change	**Augmentation (of one quantity)** +2 0 1 2 3 4 5 6 Alisha has 3 cookies and is given 2 more. How many does she have now?	**Reduction (of one quantity) or 'Take away'** 'take away' 2 cubes - 2 0 1 2 3 4 5 6 Jordan had 5 sweets but lost 2 of them. How many are left?
Compare	**Additive Comparison** 2 3 5 Jamal has 3 toys and Beth has 2 more toys than Jamal. How many toys does Beth have?	**Subtractive Comparison ('Difference')** 3 cubes Amy has 5 books and Liam has 2. How many less does Liam have?
Equalize	**Equalise (by addition)** 2 cubes Toby has 3 stickers. If he gains 2 more he will have the same as Ryan. How many does Ryan have?	**Equalise (by subtraction)** 2 cubes Megan had 5 shells but lost 2 of them. She now has the same number as Zoe. How many does Zoe have?

Figure 10.1 *Forms of addition and subtraction (for 3 + 2 = 5 and 5 – 2 = 3)*

The form of addition or subtraction to be used is determined by the context (if any) and by the child's interpretation. Additionally, the position of the unknown quantity in the corresponding equation or 'number sentence' may influence which operation is used. For example, a context corresponding to 3 + 2 = ☐ (e.g. 'Alisha has 3 cookies and is given 2 more. How many does she have now?') will be interpreted as addition, whereas a similar context corresponding to $\square + 2 = 5$ (for example 'Jon was given two extra biscuits and now has five. How many did he have originally?') is more likely to be interpreted as subtraction.

The comparative form is more difficult for children to appreciate because it is passive in nature (nothing is changing) whereas the other forms are active (one or more quantities are changing). Additionally, the answer in a compare context is a relationship (the 'difference') between the two quantities rather than a quantity in its own right (Maclellan, 2012). It is worth noting that the term 'take away' only refers to one form of subtraction, not subtraction in general.

- Think of some different addition and subtraction contexts and identify which form of addition or subtraction is applicable.
- What mathematical vocabulary would be needed to discuss them?

From counting towards early addition

The roots of addition and subtraction lie in the understanding of counting and are developed by establishing two key ideas:

- 'one more' or 'one less' than a number
- 'counting on' or 'counting back' from a number.

The notion of 'one more or less' should be explored with children through a range of contexts. Counting songs and story books (for example, *Mr Magnolia*, in Chapter 1) which have an increase or decrease on each page can be used for this purpose.

CASE STUDY

The bus journey

Jo had set up a bus route in the outdoor play area to enable a group of children (aged 4) to explore the idea of one more or less. The children used a large play vehicle as the bus and teddy bears as passengers getting on or off the bus at different bus stops along the route. Jo engaged them in conversations about the varying number of passengers on the bus, modelling the use of mathematical language (one more/less, how many, how many more/less).

Once the idea of 'one more than' is secure, this can be extended to introduce addition of single digit numbers. Carpenter and Moser (1984) established the following progression for children's developing knowledge of early addition, exemplified here for $2 + 5 = 7$:

- Count all: $2 + 5$ calculated by counting the first set (1, 2), counting the second set (1, 2, 3, 4, 5), combining the two sets and then counting this (1, 2, 3, 4, 5, 6, 7)
- Count on from the first number: count the first number (1, 2) and then 'count on' by the amount indicated by the second number (3, 4, 5, 6, 7)
- Count on from the larger number: recognise that counting on from the larger number involves less counting
- Count on from either number: realising that the outcome will be the same (using the commutative law for addition)
- Known fact: $2 + 5 = 7$ becomes internalised as a known fact which the child no longer needs to consciously calculate
- Using known facts to derive related number facts: calculating $3 + 5$ by deducing that it must be one more than $2 + 5$.

The transition from 'count all' to 'count on' is a major leap (Nunes et al., 2009b). It involves recognising that a count can be continued from a number other than one, learning to treat the number names themselves as countable items and using a parallel count to keep track, often using fingers, as the main count is continued. Additionally, the starting cardinal number has to be reinterpreted as an ordinal number (see Chapter 9) to allow the counting-on to proceed and the final ordinal number in the count has to be reinterpreted as the corresponding cardinal value (Thompson, 2008b). Many children are about 6 years old by the time they can count on confidently, although some will acquire this understanding before starting school.

Over time, and through engagement with a range of practical calculation contexts, the pool of known number facts acquired by a child should expand, thus also increasing the range of related number facts which potentially can be derived. Having a bank of known, recallable facts reduces cognitive demand when tackling harder questions. Research suggests that children who can make connections between recalled and derived facts make better progress than those who rely on lower-level counting procedures and physical resources (Askew et al., 2001).

From counting towards early subtraction

A similar progression from counting towards early subtraction has been identified by Thompson (2010), exemplified here for $7 - 2 = 5$:

- Count out: count out 7 items (1, 2, 3, 4, 5, 6, 7), count and remove two (1, 2) and count the remnant (1, 2, 3, 4, 5)

- Count back from: start from 7 and count back 2 numbers (6, 5)
- Count back to: start from 7 and count back to 2 (6, 5, 4, 3, 2), tallying the five numbers (perhaps using fingers)
- Count up: start from 2 and count upwards to 7 (3, 4, 5, 6, 7), tallying the five numbers
- Known fact: 7 − 2 = 5 is internalised as a known, recallable fact
- Using known facts to derive related number facts: calculating 7 − 3 by deducing it must be one less than 7 − 2.

'Counting back' is much harder than 'counting on' because it involves synchronous counts in opposite directions; the child's main count is backwards but the parallel 'tracking' count is a forwards count.

Learning early addition and subtraction facts

Hughes (1986) identified that 3-year-old children could do addition and subtraction calculations for very small numbers, provided that they were presented in familiar, meaningful and practical contexts which allowed them to develop mental imagery. Such mental imagery developed over time will support calculation later in more abstract contexts. Thus, it is important that children are given opportunities to calculate using both mathematical and non-mathematical resources in a wide variety of practical contexts to help them acquire knowledge of addition of numbers with totals up to 10 and then 20 and the corresponding subtractions. Figure 10.2 provides some examples of resources which can be used to model these basic facts.

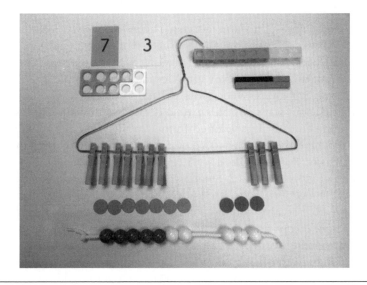

Figure 10.2 *Models for 7 + 3 = 10 and 10 − 3 = 7*

However, it is important that such experiences are not treated as mere practice or memorisation of number facts but rather enriched by explicitly enabling children to understand underlying mathematical structures and patterns (for example, different ways of making 10, the inverse relationship between addition and subtraction, the commutative law for addition: $2 + 3 = 3 + 2$), otherwise flexibility and fluency in using such facts may be impaired (Baroody et al., 2009).

Promoting children's recognition of particularly useful facts such as doubles (for example, $7 + 7 = 14$) and numbers which pair to make 10, and of numbers as being '5 and a bit' (for example, 7 is 5 and 2 more) is helpful because this also supports more efficient calculating approaches. Resources such as Numicon (see Figure 9.7) and bead strings with beads grouped in 5s (see Figure 10.2) can be used to model these ideas.

Recording using number sentences should be modelled by adults during teacher-directed activities to support the transition from children's own invented representations to conventional use of symbols (see Chapter 4). Introducing the idea of an unknown value represented by an empty box or similar symbol within a number sentence (for example, $7 + \square = 9$) lays a foundation for work on algebra (compare with $7 + x = 9$) much later in a child's development. The idea of an unknown value can be introduced practically through activities such as adding or subtracting objects from a bag or box whose contents are concealed from the children. It is important that children are presented with contexts where the unknown value is in different positions within the number sentence (for example, $\square - 2 = 9$ or even $4 + \square = 7 - 2$) to expose overly narrow interpretations (for example, 'makes', 'leaves') of the equals sign.

Mental addition and subtraction strategies

When some addition and subtraction facts have been learned (typically, additions with totals 0–20 and the corresponding subtractions), work can begin on extending the 'counting on and back' strategies for calculations with larger numbers. Initially, the additions and subtractions should be within decades (for example $25 + 4$, $38 - 6$), but then extended to calculations which cross decade boundaries. The key idea here is using known facts about ways of making 10 to decide what to add or subtract to reach the next tens number. This is developed further in the strategy of 'bridging through multiples of 10' where the number to be added or subtracted is partitioned to make the calculation easier. For example, $17 + 5$ can be reconfigured as $(17 + 3) + 2$ where the 5 has been partitioned as $3 + 2$. Similarly, $32 - 8$ can be calculated as $(32 - 2) - 6$. Children should be encouraged to use known facts to add on or subtract back rather than persisting with primitive counting-based strategies. A bead string with every 10 beads in a different colour provides a good model because it supports the identification of the complement needed to reach the next tens number. Later, a number line can be used alongside the bead string to help children make connections between cardinal and ordinal forms. Children should also be taught to add on or subtract back in 10s from a given number (e.g. 32 + 20, 45 – 30). The hundred square, 100-bead string and the number line can be used to support these strategies.

Mental addition and subtraction of two-digit numbers

Thompson (2000) identified five principal mental calculation strategies used by children for both addition and subtraction of a pair of two-digit numbers (see Figure 10.3), all of which require understanding of the 'quantity value' form of place value (see Chapter 9). They can be classified as 'Split Number' methods, where both numbers are split (partitioned) into tens and ones, and 'Complete Number' (also referred to as 'Jump' or 'Sequential') methods, where one of the numbers is retained as a complete number and the tens and ones of the second number are added or subtracted sequentially (Foxman and Beishuizen, 2002).

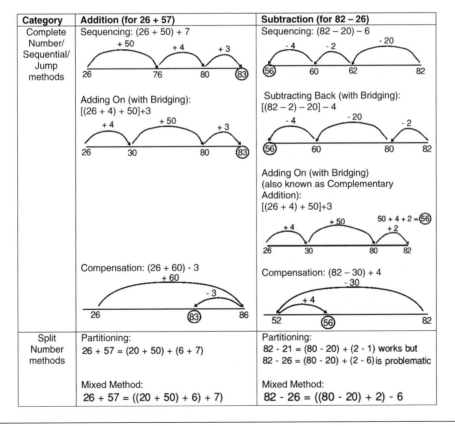

Figure 10.3 *Principal mental strategies for two-digit addition and subtraction*

The compensation method is a variant of the sequencing method used for special cases (where one number is just below a multiple of 10 or 100) while the mixed method is a mixture of the partitioning and sequencing methods. Complete Number methods have the advantage that children can use 'empty number line' (ENL) jottings (as shown in Figure 10.3) to note intermediate answers if they find it difficult to retain these mentally, while also supporting their mental calculations with visual imagery. However, the Split Number methods cannot be represented in this way because the start number is 'lost' when it is partitioned.

The partitioning strategy has an added complexity for children in some subtraction calculations where the ones digit in the second number is larger than the corresponding digit in the first number (for example, 82 − 26). Because they lack understanding of negative numbers, most children reach an impasse in such cases and are prone to making the common 'smaller from larger' (2 − 6 = 4) error (Ryan and Williams, 2007). Those who do recognise the impasse are forced to adapt the partitioning strategy (for example by reordering: 82 − 26 = [(80 − 20) − 6] + 2). As a result, children who prefer the partitioning strategy for subtraction cannot use the same strategy for all pairs of numbers, leading to errors and confusion (Thompson, 2000).

Children's success in using particular strategies

Foxman and Beishuizen's (2002) research indicates that 11-year-old children are much more likely to be successful and fluent using Complete Number strategies than Split Number methods. This is likely to be because Split Number methods involve working with four parts of the original numbers rather than the three parts found in Complete Number methods, thus requiring children to remember more intermediate answers before reaching an answer. Also, besides being more efficient, Complete Number strategies use a 'running total' approach, enabling children to keep track of the calculation process more easily. For both reasons, the demand on working memory is believed to be lower for Complete Number strategies. Foxman and Beishuizen (2002) found that higher achieving pupils favour Complete Number strategies while lower achieving pupils prefer Split Number methods which they perceive as easier. Higher achievers were also much more likely to recognise opportunities for using the compensation strategy.

Threlfall (2002) stresses the importance of helping children to notice characteristics of numbers that will permit them to adopt a flexible approach when choosing calculation strategies. Factors that influence strategy selection include the size of the numbers, the distance between the numbers, their proximity to tens or hundreds numbers, recognition of special cases (for example doubles numbers) and personal preferences.

- What are the implications of Foxman and Beishuizen's findings for supporting children's learning?
- Try some mental two-digit additions and subtractions yourself. What factors influence your personal choices of calculation strategies?

CASE STUDY

Progression within a calculation strategy

Zoe was planning a series of lessons for the 6- and 7-year-old children in her class who are at different stages in understanding the 'adding on with bridging' strategy for subtraction. To support her planning, she identified the best progression for learning this strategy (see Figure 10.4).

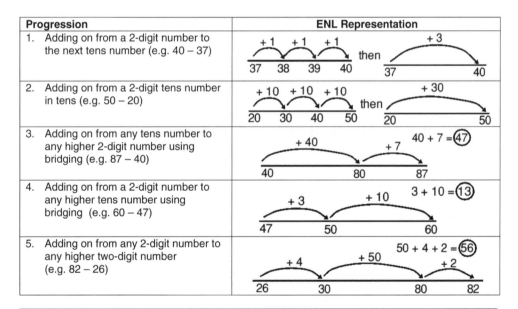

Progression	ENL Representation
1. Adding on from a 2-digit number to the next tens number (e.g. 40 – 37)	
2. Adding on from a 2-digit tens number in tens (e.g. 50 – 20)	
3. Adding on from any tens number to any higher 2-digit number using bridging (e.g. 87 – 40)	
4. Adding on from a 2-digit number to any higher tens number using bridging (e.g. 60 – 47)	
5. Adding on from any 2-digit number to any higher two-digit number (e.g. 82 – 26)	

Figure 10.4 *Progression in 'adding on with bridging' strategy*

The case study illustrates how mental strategies should be developed via a carefully considered progression. Figure 10.4 provides an example of building such a strategy. Within such progression children may initially use jumps of an ad-hoc size on ENLs but should gradually be expected to recognise more efficient choices of jumps.

Written addition and subtraction strategies

The written methods for addition and subtraction (see Figure 10.5) are derived from the corresponding mental partitioning strategy described earlier. Unlike mental methods which are presented horizontally and rely on understanding of the 'quantity value' aspect of place value, written methods for addition and subtraction are presented vertically and require an understanding of the 'column value' aspect of place value (see Chapter 9). Efficient, written methods have the disadvantage that children can lose sight of the value of the different parts of the numbers involved unless adults make these explicit, resulting in procedural learning without understanding. It is important that children are fluent in partitioning numbers as a tens number plus a teen number (for example $67 = 50 + 17$) before encountering the written subtraction method.

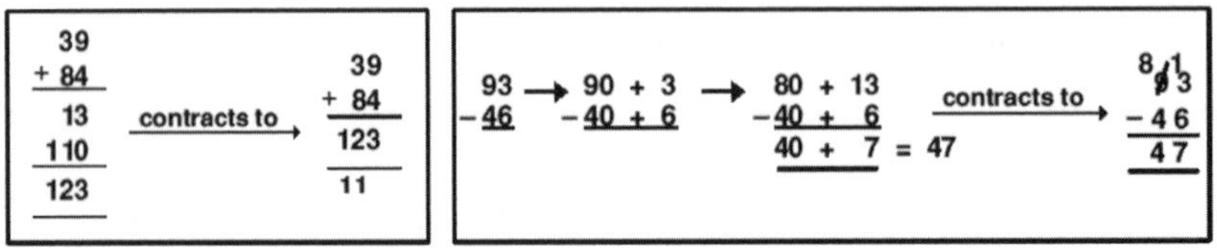

Figure 10.5 *Expanded and standard written methods for addition and subtraction*

Different forms of multiplication and division

The principal forms of multiplication and division (Fischbein et al., 1985; Greer, 1992; Kouba, 1989) are shown in Figure 10.6. The form to be used is determined by the context (if any) and by the child's interpretation.

The equal sharing form of division only makes sense in contexts where the divisor is a whole number. While the repeated addition and equal sharing models are easier to understand and commonly used by children (Kouba, 1989), children should experience other forms of multiplication and division to ensure that their understanding is sufficiently flexible. Barmby et al. (2009) propose that the array model, while more challenging to appreciate, provides a more versatile basis for understanding some of the properties of multiplication such as the commutative and distributive laws.

Where there is no obvious context specifying the form of multiplication or division, the mathematical language used to interpret the x and ÷ symbols influences how children visualise and represent multiplication and division calculations. For example, the multiplication $3 \times 2 = \square$ can be read as '3 multiplied by 2', '3 times 2', '3 lots/sets of 2' or '3 twos'. These interpretations each correspond to one of two structurally different representations (see Figure 10.7).

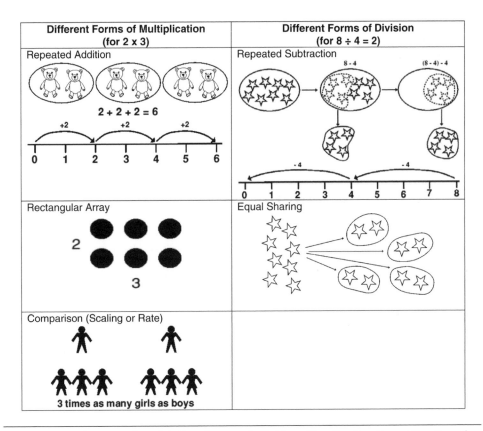

Figure 10.6 *Forms of multiplication and division (for 2 x 3 = 6 and 8 ÷ 2 = 4)*

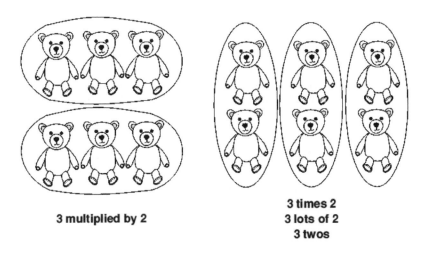

Figure 10.7 *Two different representations of 3 x 2 = 6*

This ambiguity in interpretation of the x symbol causes much confusion for children until the commutative law for multiplication (3 x 2 = 2 x 3) is understood. A similar confusion in language and associated representations exists for the division 6 ÷ 2, with '6 divided/shared by/between 2' and '6 divided/shared into 2s' corresponding to two different representations. However, as division is not commutative (6 ÷ 2 ≠ 2 ÷ 6), this issue is less easily resolved for division. Additionally, 6 ÷ 2 can also be interpreted as 'how many twos in 6?' (i.e. in terms of multiplication).

From counting to multiplication

As for addition and subtraction, the roots of multiplication and division lie in counting. Children first begin to engage with multiplication when they explore groups containing equal numbers of items (and associated language). Often these will be inherent groupings such as pairs of hands, feet, socks or shoes (for 2s), sets of knives, forks and spoons (for 3s), wheels on toy cars (for 4s) and fingers on a hand (for 5s) or two hands (for 10s). To complement these familiar groupings, children can also experience collections where the groupings are not inherent and so less obvious (for example, threading sets of three beads in different colours, pairing each child with a friend).

Mulligan and Mitchelmore (1997: 316) offer the following progression in learning about multiplication, illustrated here for 2 x 4:

- 'Unitary counting': items are just counted (1, 2, 3, 4, 5, 6, 7, 8) with no recognition of groupings
- 'Rhythmic counting': emphasising the sub-totals (1, 2, 3, 4, 5, 6, 7, 8) as each group is counted
- 'Skip counting': saying the sub-total numbers (2, 4, 6, 8) for each group, with intervening numbers suppressed or internalised
- 'Repeated addition': adding on 2s sequentially (2 + 2 = 4; 4 + 2 = 6; 6 + 2 = 8)
- 'Known multiplicative fact': being able to recall 2 x 4 = 8 which has been internalised as a known fact
- Using known facts to derive related number facts: deriving 2 x 5 = 10 by knowing the answer will be two more than 2 x 4 = 8.

The progression here is from counting strategies supported by resources, towards addition-based strategies and ultimately, multiplicative strategies. Anghileri (2008) indicates that, when rhythmic counting, children must use the cardinal principle (see Chapter 9) to recognise the last number in the ordinal count of each group as the cardinal value of the groups counted so far before recommencing the ordinal count for the next group. To extend this into skip counting requires two concurrent counts (counting the items and counting the 'beat', corresponding to the number of items in each group, as the counting of each group is completed). Adults can help children develop the skills of counting in multiples through a process of gradual internalisation: by counting in ones and emphasising the multiples (for example, by clapping, by drum beat, etc.), then suppressing the intervening numbers by whispering them, and later thinking, but not saying, the intervening numbers but keeping track of the unspoken numbers, perhaps by nodding the head or other gestures. A third layer of concurrent counting is required to tally the number of groups counted so far. When the child is able to switch from counting on to adding on, this can be formalised as the notion of repeated addition. A subsequent transition from additive to multiplicative thinking is shown in the knowledge and use of multiplication facts.

From counting to division

Early learning about division centres around informal experiences of equal sharing using counting-based strategies and the development of associated vocabulary (for example, equal, fair, each) often developed in home contexts such as sharing food at mealtimes. There is a subtle difference between equal sharing in real contexts (where the child is usually a recipient as well as the distributor) and mathematical contexts (where the child is a distributor but not necessarily a recipient). Children should be given experiences of sharing both discrete and continuous quantities.

Sharing discrete items could include:

- Sharing toy animals between fields in small-world play
- Sharing people between teams to play games
- Holding a teddy bears' picnic and sharing food items among the bears.

Sharing continuous quantities could include:

- Sharing fabric or paper (by folding and cutting)
- Sharing fruit juice by pouring between containers until the level in each is the same or sharing play dough using a two-pan balance (using direct comparison).

Mulligan and Mitchelmore (1997: 316) provide the following progression for early division, illustrated here for 8 ÷ 2 = 4:

- Equal sharing: dealing out items one at a time, then more than one at a time
- 'Trial-and-error grouping': roughly grouping the items (e.g. 5 and 3) and then equalizing the group sizes (as 4 and 4).
- 'Rhythmic counting': counting back (7, 6, 5, 4, 3, 2, 1, 0) and tallying the number of 2s
- 'Skip counting': counting back in multiples (6, 4, 2, 0) and tallying the number of 2s.
- 'Repeated subtraction': subtracting 2s sequentially (8 − 2 = 6; 6 − 2 = 4; 4 − 2 = 2; 2 − 2 = 0) and counting the number of 2s subtracted
- Using 'known multiplication facts': deriving 8 ÷ 2 = 4 from knowing 2 x 4 = 8.

Learning multiplication and division facts

Children generally learn the 2x and 10x tables first, quickly followed by the 5x table. The range of facts is then expanded to include the 3x and 4x tables. The last to be learned are the 6x, 7x, 8x and 9x tables. Most children need a varied approach to learning these key number facts. Providing experiences which support conceptual understanding as well as procedural learning through a combination of auditory, oral, visual and kinaesthetic approaches is helpful.

Some possible approaches include:

- Identifying patterns within a particular multiplication table, such as final-digit patterns in the 2x, 5x, 9x and 10x tables
- Exploring relationships between multiplication tables (for example, circling multiples of 2 and 4 in different colours on a hundred square or number line helps to show that the 4x table is double the 2x table)
- Using song versions of multiplication tables
- Using a counting stick with numbers attached for counting in multiples, noting relationships between different multiples and gradually removing the numbers a few at a time. Mansergh (2009) provides an example of this at http://www.youtube.com/watch?v=yXdHGBfoqfw
- Exploring multiple patterns using the constant function on a calculator (for example, pressing the keys 0, +, +, 3, =, =, = ... to generate the 3x table).

CASE STUDY

Exploring multiplication facts

Tessa used the story *One is a Snail, Ten is a Crab* (Pulley-Sayre and Sayre, 2003) for exploring multiplication facts with a group of 7 year olds. In the story animals' feet are used as images of equal groupings which can be used to make different numbers. For example, the number 20 can be made using 10 people (10 x 2 feet), 20 snails (20 x 1 foot) or 5 dogs (5 x 4 feet). After discussing the different multiplications in the story, the children chose their own numbers and similarly found different ways to make them. The next day, Tessa developed their understanding further during a mathematical investigation in which they had to find all the possible combinations of people (2 feet), dogs (4 feet) and insects (6 feet) which would make 48 feet in total.

The commutative, associative and distributive laws for multiplication

It is helpful to introduce the commutative law for multiplication (for example, 2 x 3 = 3 x 2) as soon as children have learned some multiplication facts. It reduces the number of multiplication facts children have to learn; if a child knows 7 x 3 = 21 there is no need to also learn 3 x 7 = 21. Children often mistakenly believe that division is commutative also. The commutative law can be demonstrated on a number line (as repeated addition) or using rectangular arrays (see Figure 10.8).

The associative law which allows the order of multiplication operations to be switched (for example, 2 x (3 x 4) = (2 x 3) x 4) underpins mental strategies where numbers are factorised and then reordered before multiplying them (see Figure 10.10). It is particularly used in multiplications involving multiples of powers of ten (for example, 20 x 50, 3 x 400).

The distributive law for multiplication is best modelled using a rectangular array, first for single-digit numbers and then for two-digit numbers (see Figure 10.9). The distributive mental strategies in Figure 10.10 rely on understanding this law.

Mental strategies for multiplication and division

Figure 10.10 provides a synthesis of strategies identified in research literature (for example, Anghileri, 2001; Downton, 2010; Ell et al., 2004; Foxman and Beishuizen, 2002;

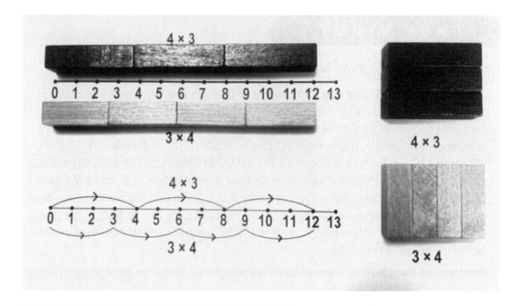

Figure 10.8 *Modelling the commutative law for multiplication*

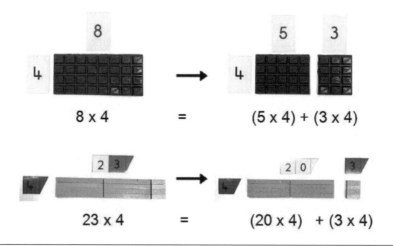

Figure 10.9 *Modelling the distributive law using chocolate bars and Cuisenaire rods*

Heirdsfield et al., 1999). All of the strategies other than basic repeated addition and subtraction rely on children having a good knowledge of multiplication facts up to 10 x 10, and most also require knowledge of how to multiply and divide by 10, 100 and 1000 (and thus of place value). To multiply a number by 10, children should shift each digit in the number one place to the left and fill any empty places with zeros (using zero as a 'placeholder', see Chapter 9). Conversely, to divide by 10, digits are shifted one place to the right.

	Multiplication Strategies	**Division Strategies**
Repetitive Grouping and Chunking Strategies	Repeated Addition so 6 x 4 = 6 + 6 + 6 + 6 = 24	Repeated Subtraction so 24 ÷ 6 = 4 because 24 - 6 - 6 - 6 - 6 = 0
	Additive Chunking (adding multiples of the multiplier) so 4 x 23 = (4 x 10) + (4 x 10) + (4 x 3) = 92	Subtractive Chunking (subtracting multiples of the divisor) 94 ÷ 5 = 18 r4
		Additive Chunking (adding multiples of the divisor) 94 ÷ 5 = 18 r4
Distributive Strategies	Partitioning e.g. 15 x 3 = (10 + 5) x 3 = (10 x 3) + (5 x 3) This can be represented as an array or as the Grid Method:	Partitioning e.g. 128 ÷ 4 = (100 + 20 + 8) ÷ 4 = 25 + 5 + 2 = 32 This strategy is often used to halve numbers (e.g. ½ of 36 = ½ of 30 + ½ of 6).
	Compensation e.g. 19 x 5 = (20 x 5) − (1 x 5) ('20 lots of 5 is 100, so 19 lots of 5 must be 5 less than 100, which is 95')	Compensation e.g. 72 ÷ 8 = (80 ÷ 8) − (8 ÷ 8) (' 80 is 10 lots of 8 and 72 is 8 less so it must be 9 lots of 8')
Factor-based Strategies	Factorising (with reordering) e.g. 16 x 25 = 2 x 8 x 5 x 5 = 8 x 5 x 2 x 5 (reordering) = 40 x 10 = 400	Factorising (with sequential division) e.g. for 324 ÷ 18 we note that 18 = 3 x 6 So 324 ÷ 18 = (324 ÷ 3) ÷ 6 = 108 ÷ 6 = 18

(Continued)

(Continued)

Factorising (using powers of 10)	Factorising (using powers of 10)
e.g. 30 x 400 = (3 x 10) x (4 x 100) = (3 x 4) x (10 x 100) = 12 x 1000 = 12000	e.g. 350 ÷ 7 = (35 x 10) ÷ 7 = (35 ÷ 7) x 10 = 50 ÷ 10 = 5
Repeated operations	Repeated operations
e.g. 23 x 8 calculated by repeated doubling (the 8 is factorised as 2 x 2 x 2) 23 x 2 = 46; 46 x 2 = 96; 96 x 2 = 192	e.g. 96 ÷ 4 calculated by repeated halving (the 4 is factorised as 2 x 2) 96 ÷ 2 = 48; 48 ÷ 2 = 24
Double one number and halve the other e.g. 15 x 6 = 30 x 3 = 90 (the 6 is factorised as 2 x 3 so the calculation becomes 15 x 2 x 3 = 30 x 3)	

Figure 10.10 *Mental strategies for multiplication and division*

Children do not consistently use the most sophisticated strategies they know (Ell et al., 2004; Heirdsfield et al., 1999). Downton (2010) indicates the size of the numbers, the multiples involved and teaching approaches influence children's choices of strategies.

Written multiplication and division methods

The expanded written method for multiplication is usually developed from the grid method because the partial products correspond to those inside the grid squares. The expanded written division method is based on the 'chunking' form of repeated

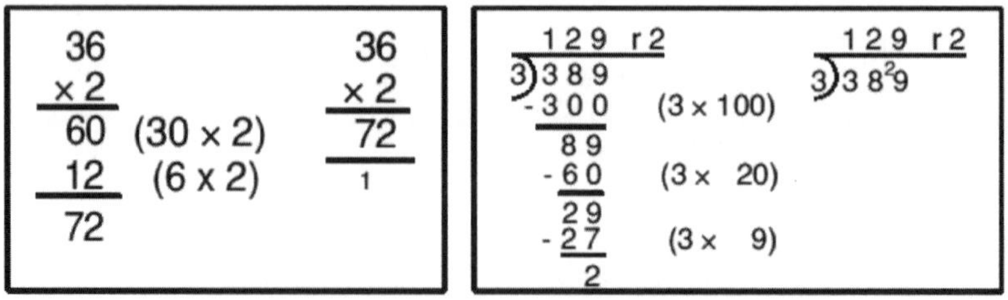

Figure 10.11 *Expanded and standard written methods for multiplication and division by a single-digit number*

subtraction (with the chunks being the largest possible hundreds, tens and ones multiples of the divisor respectively which are less than the remnant from the previous subtraction).

Summary

Within the chapter we have identified that understanding of the four number operations is rooted in counting and that there is a gradual transition from counting-based strategies towards addition, subtraction, multiplication and division. For addition and subtraction, complete number strategies are more successful for children but require more flexibility in understanding. For multiplication and division, repeated addition and equal sharing are accessible early strategies, but developing more flexible and sophisticated strategies is important. Teaching approaches must support increasing efficiency and reliability in children's strategies while ensuring understanding and promoting fluency in calculation.

Further reading

Thompson, I. (ed.) (2008) *Teaching and Learning Early Number*, 2nd edn. Maidenhead: Open University Press.
In Chapters 8 and 9, Thompson and Anghileri provide a helpful overview of progression in learning about addition, subtraction, multiplication and division.
Barmby, P., Bilsborough, L., Harries, T. and Higgins, S. (2009) *Primary Mathematics: Teaching for Understanding*. Maidenhead: Open University Press.
In Chapter 4 Barmby et al. provide a detailed consideration of the use of the array as a model for multiplication and division.

11

Fractions and Decimals

Jon Wild

 Chapter Overview

In this chapter you can read about:

- The key ideas about fractions which children need to understand
- How children's understanding of fractions and decimals develops, often in informal contexts at an early age and then progresses to more formal understanding
- Practical ideas for exploring fractions with children.

Early experiences of fractions

At the simplest level, fractions are highly practical and encountered informally by young children. Sharing a chocolate bar with someone else, serving up a pudding into portions and making sure that everyone gets a piece of birthday cake are typical experiences for young children. They introduce notions of fairness and equality as well as early fraction ideas based on the principle of equal sharing. Typical conversations between parents and children might include 'One for you, one for me', 'Let's share this together' or 'Some for teddy, some for you and some for me' and later progress to 'Half for you, half for me'. As children get older, you often hear them exclaim 'I want the biggest half!' as Mum or Dad slices the cake, pizza or pie (see Figure 11.1). These informal, everyday situations allow young children to explore simple fractions and associated vocabulary (for example, equal, part, half, not half).

Figure 11.1 *'The biggest half'*

CASE STUDY

Fractions at the dinner table

Serena (age 3) went out for dinner with her mum to a friend's. She enjoyed eating out with the grown-ups because it made her feel important. She liked being asked how much pizza she wanted. The conversation proceeded as follows:

'Can I have a big bit, please?'

'How big?'

'Ooh, that much!' spreading her arms wide.

'Maybe not. How about a quarter?'

'I'm hungry! That's not enough!'

'How about half of the pepperoni then?'

> - What early fractions-based ideas are implicit within such experiences?
> - Consider how such everyday contexts provide rich opportunities for informal exploration of an understanding of fractions.

The importance of fractional language

As in much of mathematics, language is crucial in ensuring that children develop understanding (Bottle et al., 2005; O'Sullivan et al., 2005). As noted previously, early language about fractions centres around the notions of equal sharing and fairness. Young children are eagle-eyed in their quest to make sure that Cesc doesn't have a bigger slice than Jan, or that Djamila has the same number of sweets as Chelsea. Children need plenty of opportunities to practise this language within corresponding practical contexts.

However, sometimes the everyday language that adults use when discussing fractions is slightly confusing for children. We often informally use fractional language imprecisely in everyday life. For example, an adult sharing a biscuit between two children might break the biscuit in two pieces and say 'You can have half each' even though the two pieces might not be exactly equal in size.

When formal language about fractions is introduced, such as references to splitting the 'whole' into parts and then naming the parts, this can also be confusing for the child. The naming conventions for denominators do not follow the naming pattern for whole numbers in all cases so children often use unconventional terms such as 'threeths' instead of 'thirds'. There is also some research evidence to suggest that some lower attaining children may interpret terms such as 'quarters' as meaning 'pieces' rather than the more precise 'four equal parts' (Keijzer and Terwel, 2004). Additionally, the term 'whole' can be confused with the homophone 'hole' (Haylock, 2010: 208). Using slightly longer forms of words that make more sense to children can be helpful. So, instead of asking 'What fraction of the whole have we eaten?' we might ask 'What fraction of the whole pie have we eaten?'

> - Review the mathematical language you use when discussing fractions with children. What would you alter?
> - How can support staff be best prepared to promote appropriate use and understanding of fractions vocabulary?

Fraction notation

Very young children sometimes invent their own symbols for simple fractions to represent contexts that are meaningful to them (see Figure 4.4 in Chapter 4) and some may even learn the conventional notation for writing $1/2$, albeit without understanding it fully. However, learning to interpret and use fraction notation with understanding is much more complex than for whole number notation. Nunes et al. (2009b) argue that this is because writing fractions requires the use of two numerals rather than just one and because the fractional quantity is represented by a relationship between the values of the two numerals rather than their separate values. Stafylidou and Vosniadou (2004) found that 38% of 10 year olds treated the numerator and denominator as independent numbers and 22% were unable to explain how to interpret them, suggesting that understanding the relationship involved is challenging for children. Also, the 'line' between the two numerical values 2 and 3 in $2/3$ can be interpreted as 2 'out of' 3 parts or as 2 'divided by' 3 in different contexts. It is also quite common for children to confuse the numerator and denominator (for example, writing $3/1$ instead of $1/3$).

Children need to develop a sound understanding of the connections between the written form of the fraction and the associated practical context, as well as an understanding of the symbols. This involves understanding the vocabulary numerator and denominator as well as identifying the aspects of the context to which they refer (Suggate et al., 2010). It is important to ensure that as children encounter this formal, and rather abstract, notation of fractions, they also have opportunities to discuss what they are recording and its associated meaning.

As children's understanding of writing fractions develops, they are introduced to fractions where the numerator is larger than 1 (for example, $3/4$, $2/5$ or $7/8$) but the overall fraction is less than 1, and subsequently to fractions greater than 1 which can be written either as improper fractions (for example, $9/8$, $10/4$) or as mixed numbers (for example, $1\,1/8$, $2\,2/4$).

Conceptual understanding of fractions

Initially, children need to recognise the possibility and the need to be able to quantify a part of an item, an idea which develops after the age of 2 (Piaget et al., 1960). Experiences such as the discussion over dinner in the case study above provide good, informal contexts for this. The understanding gained from such informal experiences can then be refined more formally as a set of fundamental ideas about fractions. When specifying a fraction we need to recognise:

- that we are describing a number of parts
- that parts must be equal

- that each part is a proportion of 'the whole'
- what constitutes 'the whole'.

It is important that children learn to identify the whole correctly. It is not enough to only identify the fractional part. For example, half of a large cake and half of a small cake are not the same amount of cake.

These key ideas will need to be explored in a range of different types of fraction contexts to ensure that children have a full understanding of the use of fractions to describe quantities. Dickson et al. (1984), Haylock (2010) and Mooney et al. (2012b) offer the following set of contexts where fractions are used:

- Part of a single entity (or 'whole'), for example cutting a quarter of a pie, finding half of a shape
- Numbers on a number line (such as $4\,^1/_2$ or $7\,^3/_4$) which lie between two whole numbers, for example Harley proudly declared 'I was four and a half but now I'm five' to his best friend and wrote the numbers $4\,^1/_2$ and 5 next to a picture of himself (see Figure 4.4 in Chapter 4).
- Comparing part of a set with the whole set, for example if I have a packet of 12 sweets and 6 of them are blue, $^6/_{12}$ or $^1/_2$ of the sweets are blue.
- Comparing two separate quantities (or sets) to illustrate a relationship, for example if there are 4 girls and 3 boys sitting at a table, the number of boys is $^3/_4$ of the number of girls. Haylock (2010) describes this as a ratio between boys and girls.
- Comparing the sizes of two measurements, for example on sports day if Cecile jumps 100cm and Djoma jumps 50cm, Djoma's jump is $^1/_2$ of Cecile's.
- The outcome of a division, for example if a group of 8 children divides 5 chocolate bars between them each child receives $^5/_8$ of a chocolate bar.

Nunes et al. (2009b) have summarized these different fractions contexts as belonging to two broader categories:

- Measurement situations where the quantity that is measured cannot be represented using only whole units of measurement. In these instances, it might be that the quantity involved is smaller than the unit of measurement (for example $^1/_2$ of a jug, $^1/_4$ kg of sugar) or that it involves a mixture of whole units and parts of a unit (for example $2\,^3/_4$ apples, $7\,^1/_2$ cm of string).
- Division situations where, 'if the dividend is smaller than the divisor, the result of the division is represented by a fraction' (Nunes et al., 2009b: 3) (for example, sharing 2 cakes among 5 children so each child receives $^2/_5$ of a cake).

Sometimes children find fraction ideas easier in one context than another, for example the sharing of a pizza rather than diluting orange squash. This means that children need plenty of experience in different contexts (Nunes et al., 2006). Additionally,

Nunes et al. (2009b) indicate that children do not readily transfer understanding of fractions acquired in one situation to others, so it is crucial that they experience the breadth of contexts in which fractions can be used.

There are different ways of finding fractions depending on the context and it is important that children experience a wide range of strategies. Useful strategies include:

- **Cutting:** cutting cakes, pizzas, fruit and other food items
- **Folding:** folding paper shapes, paper strips or string into halves or quarters
- **Comparing:** putting counters or number rods into rows of equal number using one-to-one correspondence, using a two-pan balance to find equal quantities of play dough, pouring between two containers until the water level is the same in each
- **Equal sharing:** sharing one by one sweets, counters or playing cards for a game
- **Counting:** counting marbles or shells into equal piles
- **Measuring:** using measuring devices to halve a quantity of flour or an amount of water.

Some of the above strategies such as folding are relatively easy for halves and quarters but more difficult for other fractions.

Part of a single whole

The 'part–whole' model for fractions is traditionally used to introduce fractions formally in schools and is probably the predominant image of fractions for both adults and children, perhaps because it is used often in everyday life and because it dominates many published mathematics schemes used in schools. However, while the 'part–whole' model is a valuable image to support children's understanding of fractions, it should not be used exclusively. Children should not be restricted to colouring pre-partitioned shapes otherwise they may not realise that all parts have to be equal (Pepperell et al., 2009).

Children make a range of common errors in 'part–whole' contexts, such as dividing the whole into unequal parts, dividing the whole into the wrong number of parts (for example, interpreting $1/2$ as meaning 'make 2 cuts' or 'draw two partitioning lines') or comparing the specified parts with the remaining parts rather than with the whole (MaLT, 2005) (see Figure 11.2). These errors all stem from the misunderstanding of one or more of the fundamental ideas about fractions outlined earlier. Additionally, many children find it difficult to recognise and interpret 'part of a single whole' contexts where the parts are not contiguous or are visually dissimilar but nonetheless equal (see Figure 11.2).

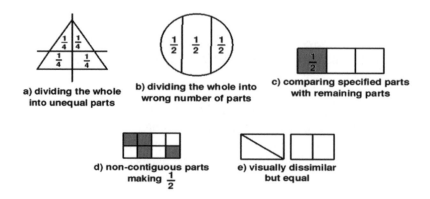

a) dividing the whole into unequal parts

b) dividing the whole into wrong number of parts

c) comparing specified parts with remaining parts

d) non-contiguous parts making $\frac{1}{2}$

e) visually dissimilar but equal

Figure 11.2 *'Part–whole' misconceptions*

In situations where the whole is pre-divided into a number of parts equal to a multiple of the denominator, children's facility to identify a specified part of the whole reduces markedly. The MaLT (2005) project identified that while 81% of 8 year olds could identify $1/4$ of a cake if there are four portions visible, only 39% were able to do this if the cake was subdivided into eight portions. Of the remaining children, 43% selected one of the eight portions instead (a 'unit-fraction' prototypical misconception).

Children's strategies in 'part–whole' contexts

Nunes et al. (2009b: 9) indicate that research suggests that children employ a partitioning strategy in 'part–whole situations'. For example, when they need 3/4 of a pie, they split it into 4 equal parts and take 3 of these parts. In this situation, a key idea is for children to see that the more parts into which the whole is partitioned, the smaller each part is going to be.

Piaget et al. (1960) found that children younger than 6 years old struggle to partition a whole correctly. However, the success rate for subdividing a single whole depends on the shape of the whole and the number of parts. For example, rectangles are easier than circles to subdivide. In many contexts, children often use the strategy of repeated halving to subdivide a single whole, and so find it much easier to subdivide into quarters and eights than into thirds or fifths, for example (Boulet, 1998).

Finding fractions of a quantity

Sometimes this is referred to as using a fraction as an 'operator'. Children often have difficulty with finding fractions of a quantity. As the 'whole' in this context is a set of items rather than a single item such tasks require numerical thinking rather than just visual perception. Finding $1/4$ of 12 requires an understanding of division (to find one quarter by dividing by 4). Children may initially use sharing strategies to do this but should then progress to using knowledge of multiplication facts and, if needed, mental or written division methods (see Chapter 10). Where the fraction involved is non-unitary (for example $3/4$ of 12), a subsequent multiplication (in the form of repeated addition, use of known multiplication facts, or mental or multiplication strategies) is also needed. Consequently, this is a more difficult proposition than finding a fraction of a shape.

Fractions (also known as rational numbers) are quite different from the counting numbers. In particular, fractions are relative quantities; the specification of the whole of which the fraction is part is critical. For example, $1/2$ of 6 and $1/2$ of 4 are different even though we represent both with the notation $1/2$ because the whole in each case is different. Nunes et al. (2006) indicate that the relative nature of fractions is a source of difficulty for children.

Comparing a subset with a set

Typical examples for exploring this type of fraction context might be comparing the number of girls with the overall number of children in a team or finding what fraction of a 1–10 set of cards shows even numbers. In this type of context, children often mistakenly compare the subset with the rest of the set rather than with the whole set. In the MaLT (2005) project, 7-year-old children were shown four oranges on a plate and a further four oranges not on the plate. When asked 'What fraction of these oranges are on the plate?', 38% of the children responded $4/4$, indicating that they had identified the 'whole' incorrectly and viewed this as a ratio context (4 on:4 off). A further 7% selected $1/4$ as the required fraction, indicating the presence of a prototypical 'unit fraction' misconception.

A common classroom activity is to analyse the contents of a small packet of sweets (see Figure 11.3):

- How many sweets are there?
- How many different colours are there?
- How many of each colour is there?

(Continued)

(Continued)

Figure 11.3 *Composition of a packet of sweets*

The adult might ask the children various question about the packet of sweets, such as:

- What fraction of the sweets is red?
- What fraction of the sweets is green?
- If my friend ate the yellow sweets what fraction would this be?
- If my friend ate the green and orange sweets how many are left? What fraction of the sweets is this?

Fractions as numbers on a number line

We can introduce children to the idea of fractions being numbers in their own right by counting in multiples of simple fractions both forwards and backwards, perhaps using a counting stick to support this, for example $1/4$, $1/2$, $3/4$, 1, 1 $1/4$, 1 $1/2$ ... . Counting in fractions requires children to use simple equivalences between fractions such as $2/4 = 1/2$. It also introduces the idea of mixed numbers for fractions greater than 1.

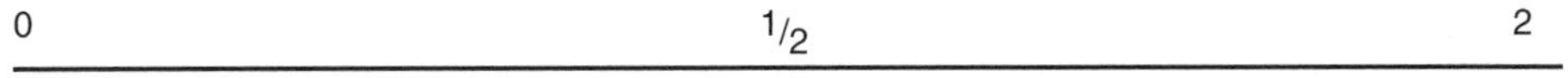

0	¹/₂	2

Figure 11.4 *Incorrectly marking 1/₂ on a number line*

In this context, the whole is the length of the interval between 0 and 1. However, children often think that half on a number line is halfway along it (see Figure 11.4). A child with this misconception needs to understand fractions as numbers, not just as the result of a division (Nunes et al., 2006).

Fractions as the outcome of division

This fraction context builds on children's intuitive understanding of division and, in contrast to the part–whole contexts considered earlier, it involves two quantities. When dividing 3 chocolate bars between 4 people, the fraction ³/₄ represents both the division operation 3 ÷ 4 and the amount received by each person (Nunes et al., 2009b).

Children's strategies in division contexts

Within division contexts children 'use correspondences between the units in the numerator and the units in the denominator' (Nunes et al., 2009b: 3). This is quite different from the partitioning strategy which children often adopt for 'part–whole' contexts. For example, if 4 children decide to share 3 cupcakes they consider how the number of cakes and the number of people correspond and identify that each child can have ¹/₄ of each cake or, alternatively, ³/₄ of one cake. Nunes et al. (2009b) report that children as young as 5 or 6 years old are capable of using such correspondences to ensure that equal shares are obtained.

The division model of fractions is more versatile than the 'part–whole model'. Children often implicitly restrict the part–whole model to fractions less than 1 because they believe that the sum of the parts cannot be larger than the whole, whereas for the division model there is no relation between the amount to be divided and the number of recipients, allowing a greater range of fractions to be modelled. Additionally, children recognise that as long as the correspondences between the two quantities in the division model are 'fair' the distribution method is not significant.

Nunes et al. (2009b) propose that the division context supports the introduction of the notion that there is an inverse relationship between the number we are dividing by and the outcome. For example, the more people sharing a chocolate bar, the less each person will receive. Additionally, Nunes et al. suggest that children find it easier to reason about equivalence ideas in division contexts. For example, if we double the number of chocolate bars to share and also double the number of recipients, the shares will be still be the same (i.e. equivalent).

Equivalence

As their familiarity with fractions develops, children learn to make connections between common fractions. For example, they might notice that two quarters of a cake is the same as a half of the cake or three-thirds of the cake is the same as the whole cake. Sometimes children do not recognise when the parts can be recombined to make a whole. Using resources such as fraction walls, sections of circles, squares or other shapes can help with this as children try to fit pieces back together.

CASE STUDY

After the party

A group of children (aged 8) were clearing up the classroom following a special celebration. There had been party food such as crisps, pizza and cake. Petr put 4 slices of left-over pizza onto a plate and realised he had created a whole pizza. Celia noticed something different, yet similar. She had picked up two plates, each with half a pizza left over. On one plate there were 4 slices of pizza, on the other there were 3 slices of pizza.

- What questions could an adult ask to help these children develop their understanding of equivalent fractions?
- In what other contexts could this kind of discussion take place?

Children will gradually extend their understanding of equivalence within families of related fractions such as halves, quarters and eighths or thirds, sixths and twelfths. Knowledge of multiples will help when identifying and recognising equivalent fractions (Turner and McCullough, 2004). Ryan and Williams (2007) noticed that some children found it difficult to shade $1/4$ of a circle that was partitioned into 8 equal parts. This may have been due to lack of experience where previously they had only shaded $1/4$ of shapes partitioned into four.

- Pairs, dominoes or 'Happy Families' type games where children collect equivalent fractions could be used to reinforce the ideas.
- Barmby et al. (2009) suggest an activity where children are encouraged to design flag patterns using quarters in as many ways as they can.
- Use of a washing line where children can peg fractions in order, including hanging some in the same position, will help children to understand equivalence.
- Fraction walls provide a visual support for children's understanding of equivalence (see Figure 11.5). Children could construct fraction walls using Cuisenaire rods or lengths of paper or card. Similar representations could also be constructed using circles, regular hexagons or other shapes.

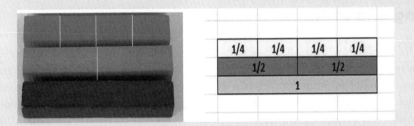

Figure 11.5 *Fraction walls*

Simplifying fractions

As children become more familiar with the ideas of equivalence they will need to be able to express fractions in their simplest form, for example $4/8$ can be expressed as $1/2$ (see Figure 11.6). In this context children can be encouraged to see the relationship between the numerator and the denominator and then see how this could be recorded more simply using an equivalent fraction. Haylock (2010) identifies this as a way of indicating that the ratio between the two elements of the fraction, the numerator and the denominator, remains constant. Just as knowledge of multiples helps children in identifying equivalent fractions, knowledge of factors can help when simplifying (Turner and McCullough, 2004).

Figure 11.6 *Modelling 4/8 = 1/2*

Comparing and ordering fractions

In order to compare and order fractions, children will need to understand fractions as numbers that can be placed on a number line. Hopkins et al. (2004) suggest that one of three approaches can be used when attempting to order fractions. Using the example of ordering $3/4$ and $2/3$, they suggest that $1/4$ is needed to add to $3/4$ to make one whole and $1/3$ is needed to add to $2/3$ to make a whole and as $1/3$ is larger than $1/4$, $3/4$ must be larger than $2/3$. They call this approach an intuitive sense of size. The next approach is using a visual image of the size of the fraction. The final approach is to order fractions by changing them to fractions with the same denominator. To start with, children will order fractions with the same denominator such as $1/4, 2/4, 3/4, 4/4$. Then they can progress to ordering unitary fractions (those with a numerator of 1) for example, $1/2, 1/3, 1/4$ and $1/5$. Children may be tempted to order them as we have here, not recognising the inverse relationship between the denominator and the quantity (Nunes et al., 2006). Relating the fractions to a visual image or considering the fractions in the context of sharing may be helpful. Once they are familiar with these they can order different sets of related fractions, then find common denominators. For example, ordering $2/3$ and $3/4$ by recognising that $2/3 = 8/12$ and $3/4 = 9/12$. Later, they can include mixed numbers such as $1\,1/2$ and improper or 'top-heavy' fractions such as $3/2$.

Simple operations

By age 8, children will start to add and subtract using fractions. This will probably start with adding fractions with the same denominator totalling 1, for example,

$2/5 + 3/5 = 5/5 = 1$. They can then progress to adding fractions with the same denominator within one, such as $1/6 + 3/6 = 4/6$. Similarly, they will subtract fractions such as $5/7 - 3/7 = 2/7$. Building on their understanding of equivalence and simplifying fractions, they can then progress to adding and subtracting fractions within one whole by finding a common denominator.

A common error is to add the numerators and the denominators independently, for example $1/4 + 1/4 = 2/8$. To address this, children would need to be encouraged to use a visual image to add two quarters and realise using equivalence that $2/8$ is not correct (Hopkins et al., 2004).

Introducing decimals

Decimals are an extension of the whole-number place value system (Hansen, 2011) (see Chapter 9) and will be introduced to children formally towards the top of the age band covered by this book, but they are likely to have encountered decimal ideas informally at an earlier age, perhaps at the petrol pump or on the car trip meter. Although we use decimal notation to represent amounts of money, because of the differences in the way amounts of money and decimals more generally are articulated, this might not be a helpful starting point for young children (Dickson et al., 1984). For example, £8.15 is read as 'eight pounds fifteen', whereas 8.15 should be articulated as 'eight point one five'. The decimal point needs to be introduced to children as a marker between the whole and decimal part of a number (Frobisher et al., 1999).

A starting point for young children could therefore be through making connections (Askew et al., 1997) to their fraction knowledge of tenths. Pagni (2004) advises that fractions and decimals should be taught together because they are just different representations of the same numbers. Thus, children might find four-tenths of a chocolate bar and label it $4/10$ and 0.4 (see Figure 11.7) and place equivalent decimals and fractions together on number lines. Rapid recall of some common equivalents is useful, such as $1/2$ and 0.5. However, sometimes children find it difficult to convert between fractions and decimals, for example they might write $1/4$ as 1.4 or $1/6$ as 0.6. This means that plenty of practical experience alongside effective classroom talk to confront misconceptions is necessary (see Chapter 7).

Children can also be encouraged to count in steps of 0.1, going through the 1 boundary from 0.9 to 1 then to 1.1. Once children are familiar with talking about, reading and writing tenths in this way, they can move on to numbers with two decimal places, tenths and hundredths. Care should be taken to enunciate the words 'tenths' and 'hundredths' clearly as they are easy to mishear as 'tens' and 'hundreds' which could cause confusion (Frobisher et al., 1999). Using a blank 10 x 10 grid as a whole is helpful here, where smaller squares can be coloured and children can identify how much of the larger square is coloured (see Figure 11.8). Counting will be helpful, especially through tenth and whole number boundaries such as 0.09, 0.1, 0.11 and

Figure 11.7 *A bar of chocolate showing 4/10 or 0.4*

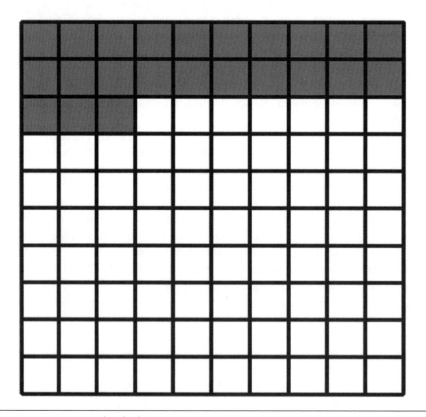

Figure 11.8 *Square shaded to represent 0.23*

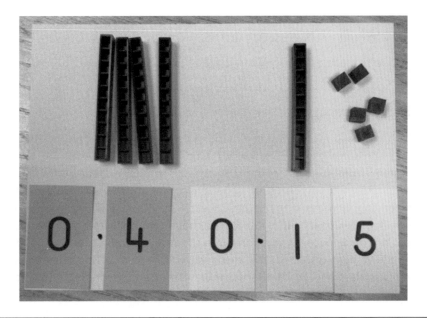

Figure 11.9 *Representations of 0.4 and 0.15*

2.99, 3, 3.01. Once again, if children are able to recall some common equivalents such as 0.25 = $^1/_4$ it can help with later mathematics.

Ordering numbers with one and two decimal places can be difficult and may expose misconceptions. For example, a child may think 0.15 is larger than 0.4 because they know that 15 is larger than 4. Resnick et al. (1989) called this the 'whole number rule' because the children appear to ignore the decimal point. Barmby et al. (2009) identify that other children believe 0.15 is larger than 0.4 because it has more digits and indicate that this 'longer is larger' error becomes less prevalent with age. Using base ten resources helps children to understand the relative size of decimal numbers. The number 0.15 would be represented by one 'long' and 5 small cubes and 0.4 by four 'longs' (see Figure 11.9).

Children will also need to learn about dividing single-digit numbers by 10 (for example 5 ÷ 10 = 0.5) and progress to dividing two-digit numbers by 10 and 100. Connections should be made to their familiarity with multiplying by ten (see Chapter 10). It is important for adults to model the correct language when explaining this idea, talking about moving the digits one column to the right when dividing by ten, rather than moving the decimal point, as this could cause difficulties later.

Connections between measures and decimals are useful in making this area of mathematics meaningful for children (see Chapter 13). When children are learning about numbers with one decimal place, they can record measurements of length in centimetres, for example 9.5 cm. On progressing to two decimal places, they can record measurements of length in metres such as 1.24 m. At this stage, connections with money should be discussed. Later, they will progress to using more decimal places.

Summary

In this chapter we have identified a range of contexts in which children encounter fractions and some of the complexities which cause children difficulty. Many of these stem from children continuing to use whole-number-based thinking inappropriately or from confusions about the nature of the whole. The importance of embedding learning within practical experiences and modelling ideas using visual images has been highlighted. The challenges of learning about the key concept of equivalence for fractions are acknowledged and ways of supporting learning have been discussed. The introduction of fractions and decimals extends children's understanding of the number system and we have indicated the importance of making connections between them explicit for children.

Further reading

Barmby, P., Bilsborough, L., Harries, T. and Higgins, S. (2009) *Primary Mathematics: Teaching for Understanding*. Maidenhead: Open University Press.
Chapters 5 and 6 provide a good overview of the key issues and ideas associated with learning about fractions and decimals.
Frobisher, L., Monaghan, J., Orton, A., Orton, J., Roper, T. and Threlfall, J. (1999) *Learning to Teach Number: A Handbook for Students and Teachers in the Primary School*. Cheltenham: Stanley Thornes.
Modules 5 and 6 give a detailed account of the teaching of fractions and decimals with relevant research findings and activities for the classroom.

12

Pattern

Gina Donaldson

Chapter Overview

In this chapter you can read about:

- The importance of pattern in mathematics, particularly in investigative thinking, number and calculations
- Key mathematical concepts of pattern
- Progression in the way children understand and use pattern in their thinking
- Practical ways in which adults can explore pattern with children.

CASE STUDY

Investigating stars

Susan, the adult working with of a class of 7 and 8 year olds, set the children in her class a challenge just before Christmas. She showed them a star shape made

(Continued)

(Continued)

out of interlocking cubes and told them it was the first in a series of stars which would get larger each time. The first star was made of 5 cubes (see Figure 12.1).

Figure 12.1 *The first star*

Then she showed them the second star in the series (see Figure 12.2). The children were asked to talk about how this star had been made and how the two stars were the same and how they were different.

Figure 12.2 *The second star*

She asked them to say how many cubes she used to make this second star. Then the children were asked to make the next star in the series and count how many cubes they used. Susan asked them to describe how to make the stars in as many different ways as they can. For example, one child, Oliver, said that the first star was made up of one cube along each arm and one in the middle. The second star was made up of two cubes along each arm, and one in the middle. The third star was made up of three cubes along each arm and one in the middle. Other children had different ways of talking about what they saw. Susan listened to each one and asked them to compare how they perceived the pattern developing.

Then Susan set the children the challenge of working out how many cubes they would need to make the fourth star, before they made it. They talked about this in small groups and tried to predict how many cubes they would need. After they had made their predictions, they made the fourth star to test them. They decided that they needed 13 cubes and they talked again about how they saw the stars grow and how they described how to make each one.

The next challenge from Susan was to work out in groups how many cubes they would need to make the tenth star, before they actually made it. The children talked about this for some time. They decided that they would need to use what they knew to work out how many cubes they would need.

One group of children drew up a table of what they had found out already (see Figure 12.3).

Star number	How many cubes we used
1	5
2	9
3	13
4	17

Figure 12.3 *Recording cubes used for each star*

They noticed that the number of cubes increased by four each time and the whole class talked about what they had found. Susan asked them to explain why the number of cubes increased by four for each new star and the children talked about the new star having an extra cube along each of four arms. Now they

(Continued)

(Continued)

realised that they could continue this pattern to see how many cubes they would need for the tenth star, by adding four to each total of cubes (see Figure 12.4).

Star number	How many cubes we used
1	5
2	9
3	13
4	17
5	21
6	25
7	29
8	33
9	37
10	41

Figure 12.4 *Predicting cubes needed for larger stars*

One child, Ellen, said that she had guessed there would be 41 cubes by looking at the shape of the stars. If the fourth star was made of four cubes along each arm and one in the middle, then the tenth star would be made up of 10 cubes along each arm and one in the middle. The children made the tenth star to see if Ellen's thinking was correct. Then Susan asked them to say how many cubes for the hundredth star! And then any star in the series.

- How were the children using patterns in the shape of the stars and in the number of cubes to predict the number of cubes for the tenth star?
- How did Susan help them to do this?
- What were the children learning?

Pattern as a key idea of mathematics

In the star investigation above, the children used a spatial and a numerical pattern to make sense of the activity. They were guided into noticing how the shapes of the stars changed each time, and how the number of cubes changed. They were asked to try to use the spatial pattern to show why the numbers of cubes increased by four each time. In this way the adult was linking the patterns. Instead of presenting the children with an abstract series of numbers, 5, 9, 13, 17 and asking them to provide the next number in the series, she asked them to see why in this case the numbers were increasing by four. She might have made some of the stars again, showing the middle cube, in fact the constant, in a different colour to the arms of the star, which change in each case and are therefore a variable. This provides both a numerical and spatial context for the pattern. By asking the children to predict the number of cubes before making the star, the children had to use the pattern they had begun to describe and start to use what they knew to visualise the next star. There was a focus on talk in the activity. The children were asked to discuss the pattern and their predictions at several points in the lesson. They described both sorts of patterns using informal language, but nevertheless they were able to use these formulations of the pattern to make predictions. They were, in fact, moving towards a general statement: the number of cubes you need to make a certain star in the series is that certain number multiplied by four, for each arm, plus one for the cube in the middle. This could be expressed algebraically but there is no need for young children to do this, it will occur later on in the curriculum. They have nevertheless shown their understanding of the general rule.

This example demonstrates the role of pattern as key in children's responses to investigative mathematics, where they are challenged to find some sort of relationship, in this case between the star in the series and the number of cubes used to make it. You will find that many investigations ask children to find such relationships based on patterns (see later examples).

Mason et al. (2010) found that pattern is an important part of the thinking we undertake when we investigate mathematics and other areas of the curriculum. They identified a loop of thinking where children begin by manipulating, perhaps physically exploring, something which forms a pattern. They then get a sense of pattern, seeing the pattern in the objects. They might continue to explore this physically, copying it and extending it, and talking informally about it, saying the pattern to themselves and checking what they say against the physical representation. This can move on to articulating the pattern more symbolically. This could take the form of recording it in some way or describing the pattern in general terms. The case study above included some of these stages.

Such investigative activities challenge children to explain their thinking:

- 'I have noticed this pattern'
- 'I can explain it using everyday language or pictures'
- 'I can use the pattern to make a prediction about what will happen next, and then test it'
- 'I can think about why my pattern works and how it might work for any example in my series, expressing it more formally and generally'.

Exploration of pattern therefore is a key opportunity to develop mathematical reasoning or thinking. The importance of mathematical reasoning has been emphasised by the research findings of Nunes et al. (2009a).

Pattern is also significant in children's understanding of the number system. Consider how our number system works, using base ten (see Chapter 9). As they learn about number, children negotiate pattern in several ways. Children will engage with, for example, odd and even numbers. They will learn to appreciate that the natural numbers, or positive whole numbers, are arranged in the pattern odd, even, odd, even, odd, even … . They might be introduced to this idea by adults through rhythmic counting activities. For example, they might count on in ones, whispering and then shouting every second number (see Chapter 10). Real contexts such as house numbers, or locker numbers at their local swimming pool arranged in odd and even numbers help children to recognise each set. They learn that each odd number is one less than an even number, and that a set of two consecutive natural numbers, numbers next to each other in the counting sequence, will have one odd and one even number. A set of three consecutive natural numbers will include either two odds and one even, or two evens and one odd. This knowledge of the patterns in the number system will help them to reason about numbers. For example, they might notice that when we add two even numbers, we get an even total, and when we add an odd and an even number, we get an odd total, and start to think about why this might happen. When they count in steps of five, they will notice the pattern of the multiples of five and their units digits, and look for similar patterns when they count in tens and twos. Later they might realise that when they start with a one-digit number, and add five to make a series of numbers they will get a similar repeating pattern. In fact, the multiples of most whole numbers fall into some sort of pattern, and an appreciation of these patterns can make the multiplication facts much easier to learn. Later, they will develop these patterns. They will recognise that the multiples of even numbers are always even, the multiples of odd numbers have a pattern of even, odd, even, odd … .They will notice, for example, that the common multiples of 2 and 3 are, in fact, the multiples of 6.

Anghileri (2006) argues that children should be helped to develop number sense, or a feel for number. She says that children with number sense are able to work flexibly with number, solve problems and make generalisations based on the pattern of number. Certainly, when a learner becomes attuned to noticing patterns in number, it can help them to appreciate interconnections, rather than seeing mathematics as chaotic and confusing.

For example, appreciation of the pattern of number can support children's understanding of how to calculate. For example, consider the patterns in the set of calculations:

$$0 + 5 = 5$$

$$1 + 4 = 5$$

$2 + 3 = 5$

$3 + 2 = 5$

$4 + 1 = 5$

$5 + 0 = 5$

This pattern might be displayed visually, with interlocking cubes, pictures or coloured pegs (see Figure 12.5).

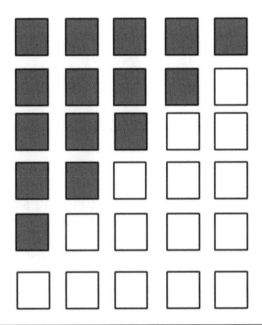

Figure 12.5 *Visual pattern of number bonds to 5*

Connecting number facts like this can help children to spot patterns and discuss them, even if to start with they talk about the patterns in a simple way. Instead of just completing this set of number facts and them moving on to another activity, an adult can ask children to look at them again and talk about what they notice. Displaying the pattern in a methodical way, such as in Figure 12.5, can support the children's reasoning. The recording of results in a methodical way is a key investigative skill. Going beyond the patterns in each column of numbers, the first and the second number, they might be guided to consider how each number sentence connects to the one before it and after it, thus supporting learning and recall of number facts. This is an example of making connections, which the researchers Askew et al. (1997) found to be a feature of the effective teaching of mathematics (see Chapter 1).

Other patterns could be identified in number sentences such as:

$2 \times 10 = 20$

$10 \times 2 = 20$

and also in number sentences such as

$2 + 3 = 5$

$2 + 2 + 1 = 5$

and

$2 + 4 = 6$

$20 + 40 = 60$

$200 + 400 = 600.$

Identifying patterns

Mulligan and Mitchelmore's (2009) research with 5 and 6 year olds found that children's ability to identify pattern was consistent across areas of mathematics. Children could generally recognise both number and shape patterns equally well. Awareness of pattern was a good indicator of mathematical achievement. Mulligan and Mitchelmore suggested this was because children who are aware of pattern work well with models, such as arrays, which are used for the learning of ideas such as multiplication. When learning new concepts, such children identify important features through pattern recognition, discard irrelevant features and focus on similarity and difference, all of which are key mathematical ideas.

We have argued that our number system is based on pattern and that an appreciation of pattern can support children's understanding of number, calculation and the investigation of number. Mathematics is ordered. There is a feeling of regularity in mathematical facts and the way they are expressed. By recognising patterns, children are actually engaging with the structures of mathematics, the way it works. An adult who recognises the patterns of mathematics themselves can support children in exploring them. They can challenge children to expect pattern in mathematics (Mason et al., 2010). This can not only increase children's understanding but also build their confidence, as well as help to lessen the burden on their memory. For example, a child who realises that a multiple of five can end in only a zero or a five can use this to help them memorise the five times table.

Children can use the patterns of mathematics to make sense of it, to make predictions and to connect mathematical ideas. Furthermore, an appreciation of the pattern, beauty and elegance of mathematics can develop children's sense of awe and wonder and satisfaction in, and fascination for, the subject itself.

- Can you identify some of the patterns in number?
- How do you use the patterns of number in your everyday life?

Key mathematical concepts in pattern

Linear repeating patterns

Children will see repeating patterns in the world around them, including patterns based on colour, shape, size and number. For example, a bracelet made of beads arranged in the pattern blue, white, white, blue, white, white has a repeating motif. The simplest motif is the set of beads which are blue, white, white, but children could also notice a longer motif of blue, white, white, blue, white, white. Such motifs are repeated in a linear way along the bracelet string. Other patterns might have a simple motif repeated in more than one direction. For example, a piece of birthday wrapping paper might have a set of pictures which are repeated horizontally and vertically (by translation) across the paper (see Chapter 14). When working with repeating patterns children need to be able to identify and describe the motif, ideally in its simplest form as this is the shortest way to remember it. This enables them to predict, visualise and make the next item in the pattern.

Errors and misconceptions can occur when children are not able to 'see' the motif correctly, including more or fewer items. Identifying a motif with more items is harder than identifying one with a smaller number of items. Children can be encouraged initially to copy a provided, simple pattern (for example a motif of two elements) and then progress towards describing the motif and pattern to themselves and checking with the visual clues to ensure they are correct. When the pattern is multi-linear, such as in wrapping paper designs, highlighting different instances of the motif makes it easier to appreciate how the pattern progresses.

'Growing' patterns

Other patterns do not repeat the same motif identically, but follow a rule in the way they replicate. For example, consider making a set of steps using interlocking cubes (see Figure 12.6).

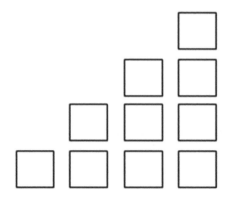

Figure 12.6 *Step pattern*

Here the pattern follows the rule 'for every new step we need to have the same number of cubes as before and one extra'. Initially, children need to notice and describe the progression within the pattern. Familiarity with this can help them to predict the next step before making it, as they can imagine or visualise what it will look like. Explaining the pattern in different ways can help children to form a generalisation which describes each element in terms of its position within the pattern. In this case, children could generalise that the number of cubes needed to make an extra step is the number of the step itself. Furthermore, in this case, the total number of cubes needed to make a set of steps up to any given number is the total of all the whole numbers up to and including that number.

CASE STUDY

Making patterns

In a nursery, James, an adult, noticed Milly (aged 4) making a row of coloured train carriages. The carriages already positioned were in a repeating pattern: red, green, red, green. Milly was hunting through the box of carriages to find some more.

James sat with Milly and talked about the pattern in the line of carriages. He asked her to tell him which colour carriage she was looking for so he could help her. The next colour in the pattern was red and she was indeed looking for a red carriage. James asked Milly why she needed a red one and she told him about the pattern of red, green, red, green carriages. They found a red carriage together and she added it to the line. James asked which one she would need next and she said a green carriage. After they had found another green carriage and added it, Milly said, 'Now I need red, and then green, and then red.'

Later that day, James showed Milly some other repeating patterns in the paving slabs outside the classroom and in a picture book which they had been looking at together.

- How was James encouraging Milly to focus on pattern?
- How could James extend Milly's ability to manipulate items, get a sense of pattern and describe the pattern more symbolically or generally, as suggested by Mason et al. (2010)?
- How will this activity and others considered in this chapter lay the foundations for her later use of patterns in mathematics?

Progression in recognising and using pattern in mathematical thinking

We have seen that pattern is a key idea in mathematics and in the mathematical thinking which children use when investigating. How then does children's understanding of pattern progress, and how can they be supported in using it in their thinking? Although it is recognised that progression in learning is not easily predicted, the section below offers a guide for consideration.

Children's earliest experiences are often rhythmic. Consider how adults rock small babies, with a gentle rhythm. This is both comforting and soothing for the baby. In fact, parents of small babies can be seen to rock even when their children are not in their arms! As they get older, children enjoy more complex but still rhythmic play. An adult might engage with a toddler on their knee, repeatedly giving them three small bounces and then a big bounce. The toddler giggles with anticipation of the big bounce. The songs and rhymes which adults traditionally sing with young children are repetitious in nature, with simple repeating rhythms and sometimes repeated actions. Children bang drums and follow simple patterns with real musical instruments or bang their hands on surfaces and stamp with their feet.

From their babyhood, pattern is embedded in their interactions with adults. The toys and practical experiences they encounter can build on their awareness of pattern. Stacking cups or coloured building bricks lend themselves to patterned arrangements. Sometimes children themselves might arrange them in a pattern, or an adult playing with a child might naturally arrange items in a pattern which the child might notice, even if they choose to dismantle the arrangement for fun.

Children might begin to create their own repeating patterns as part of child-initiated activity, or with other children or an adult, or they might choose to copy a pattern they can see has already been made, using a one-to-one matching. The simplest pattern might be a repeating pattern with a motif of two items. This might progress to a motif of three items and then more items. With support and questioning children might use the following words, reinforcing their understanding of these terms:

- same
- different
- next
- after
- before
- first, second, third … .

The children might describe the pattern, predict the next item and test it by continuing the pattern and then progress to giving instructions to make a repeating pattern. They might be supported in recording such a pattern informally in their own way by copying it, drawing the actual pattern, and then perhaps by inventing a short-hand representation, say a coloured dot, for elements within the pattern (see Chapter 4).

This development might progress to being able to spot a pattern and use it to answer a question about what comes next; for example, 'If the bricks are arranged in a tower of cube, cylinder, cube, cylinder … which shape will be next?' They then might progress to answer questions about later items beyond the next one; for example, 'In the tower if you carry on adding bricks which shape will be the third one you add?' They can also be challenged to identify the repeating motif or the rule the pattern follows. This development will be supported by sustained shared thinking (Siraj-Blatchford et al., 2002: 9) about pattern. Adults can create opportunities for this through recognising and talking about patterns in the environment (decorations in places of worship, floor tiles, brickwork patterns, musical patterns, patterns in art and designs, patterns in nature) and different types of patterns (linear repeating patterns, symmetrical patterns, 'growing' patterns). Key questions should focus on what is being repeated, explaining the pattern sequence and predicting what will come next.

We have seen that more complex patterns involve following a rule (for example, the star and making steps activities discussed earlier). Here children will need support to describe the pattern, and say the rule, predict the next item and then test their prediction by continuing the pattern to see if it follows the visual pattern. Again they might progress to recording the pattern informally by making it, then drawing it, and perhaps representing it using invented short-hand. They could devise instructions to make such a pattern and follow pictorial or written instructions to make similar patterns. Adults can ask questions which encourage children to spot a rule-based pattern, state the rule and predict next and subsequent elements.

When they become more confident with talking about pattern, children will be able to use the pattern to predict future elements within the pattern without constructing intermediate elements, for example, asking children to describe the tenth or hundredth item. Because it would be tedious to consider all the intervening elements this creates the need to think deeply about the pattern and make a prediction based on it instead. Children are likely to be familiar with multiples of 10 and 100, so asking for the tenth and hundredth elements may help to make the pattern more transparent. Consider the first case study of the series of stars. The tenth star needed 41 cubes and the hundredth needed 401 cubes. The rule of the pattern, multiply the number of the star in the series by four for each arm and add one for the middle cube, is made more transparent in these examples.

The aim is for children to explore why patterns occur and how they can be used, rather than simply spotting patterns (Askew, 2012). When patterns are set in realistic contexts, and are linked to real visual examples then children can start to explain why a particular repeating pattern occurs, or why it follows a particular rule. Again, in our first case study, the children might say that the number of cubes needed for each new star grows by four each time because each of the four arms has to have an extra cube. Here the pattern is provoking more complex thinking. The pattern is not simply accepted as a given, but something which can be reasoned about. Children can be challenged to say why it occurs, and therefore begin to reason about, and to convince others of, the truth of a conjecture or prediction. The next step in the line of reasoning is to construct general statements about the pattern and verify them. In the case of the beads threaded on the bracelet in the repeating pattern blue, white, white, an example of a general statement might be every third bead is blue.

- Think of a child you have observed exploring patterns. Use the above outline of progression to identify the next steps in their learning about pattern.
- What sort of questions would support further progression in the child's thinking and understanding?

In this section, contexts for children's exploration and discussion of pattern will be identified.

- Exploring pattern in colour, shape, size, texture, position and quantity as recommended by Montague-Smith and Price (2012) in and around the school, home or nursery setting, or in outside areas

(Continued)

(Continued)

- Exploring patterns with ICT using 'copy and paste' or stamps
- Patterns in musical rhythms and dance routines
- Rhythmic counting, with actions
- Decorating shapes such as crowns or castle shapes which are composed of repeating shapes
- Looking closely at pictures, artefacts, symbols and patterns from buildings such as castles, churches, temples and other places of worship, fabric, wrapping paper, wallpaper, or wallpaper borders
- Time for child-initiated activity with a range of resources which might lend themselves to arrangement in pattern such as coloured building bricks, coloured beads, sets of coloured plates, cups and bowls, coloured paper, or fabric cut into triangular shapes to make bunting
- Investigation activities which generate pattern and can be used for methodical recording of pattern such as:

  o How many different ice creams can you make if you choose one scoop of either chocolate or strawberry ice cream with a plain or chocolate cone?
  o How many different football strips could you make choosing from 2 T-shirts and 2 pairs of shorts?
  o A ladybird has seven spots. How many different ways can these spots be arranged on the two sides of her body? How do you know you have found them all?

Summary

In this chapter we have argued that pattern is a key mathematical idea and that when children engage with patterns such as those within our number system, they are in fact engaging with key mathematical concepts. Furthermore, the use of pattern is an important process in the thinking used to undertake investigations in mathematics.

Children engage with pattern from their very earliest experiences and naturally explore it as part of their environment. Adults can help children to understand pattern and to talk about it. Articulating a pattern, even informally, is a key part of understanding it, and this supports later, more sophisticated thinking such as making predictions about further items in the pattern, stating generalisations and beginning to reason about why these generalisations might be true. In this way not only is pattern a key mathematical idea in its own right, but exploring patterns promotes the development of mathematical thinking skills. Recognising and making sense of patterns enables children to appreciate mathematics as a connected and beautiful subject. Adults who realise this themselves can support and challenge children's mathematical understanding.

Further reading

Orton, A. (ed.) (2005) *Pattern in the Teaching and Learning of Mathematics*. London: Cassell. This book provides an in-depth review of children's learning of pattern.

Montague-Smith, A. and Price, A. (2012) *Mathematics in Early Years Education*, 3rd edn. London: Routledge.

Chapter 4 of this book discusses other key research relating to children's learning of pattern and provides practical activity ideas.

13

Measures

Louise O'Sullivan

Chapter Overview

In this chapter you can read about:

- Progression in learning in measures including length, mass and capacity
- Common misconceptions and areas of difficulty
- Key concepts of conservation and transitivity
- Difficulties children encounter when learning to tell the time
- Recommendations for effective, interesting and engaging activities.

Key ideas about measures and measurement

Measurement is a means of quantifying the relative amount of a given feature (for example, mass, length) of an object (Barmby et al., 2009). It also serves as a way of comparing such quantifications for different objects. Measures are, by definition, exact. For example, every object has a precise length, mass and volume and, at any moment in time, a person will have lived for a precise length of time.

However, the act of measurement is imprecise. Whatever is chosen as a method of measuring, and whatever device (if any) is used for measuring, the numerical value assigned to the measurement can only ever be approximate because of the inherent imprecision of the method and measuring device (Dickson et al., 1984; Montague-Smith and Price, 2012). Thus, the methodology and the device used for any measurement are important because they determine the degree of accuracy of the measurement.

In addition, all measures are continuous (Barmby et al., 2009); that is, between any two measurement values there are always other values.

Transitivity is a key concept in a child's understanding of measures (Piaget et al., 1960). The concept is one of understanding indirect comparison. Imagine a child is thinking about three items and they want to know which one is longest. They know that the first item is longer than the second item and they know that the second item is longer than the third item. A child who understands the concept of transitivity would be able to deduce that the first item must therefore be longer than the third item without having to directly compare the third and first items. This concept applies to all forms of measures, including length, capacity and mass.

Conservation is another key concept in understanding measures. Conservation is a key idea that was first identified by Piaget et al. (1960) and applies to many areas of mathematics (see Chapter 9 about number). In relation to measures, it is the idea that, for example, the mass of an object does not change when the shape changes, as long as material is not added or taken away from the original item. To illustrate this, think of a child playing with a ball of modelling clay. The child needs to develop the understanding that if they roll that ball into a long, thin sausage shape it will still have the same mass. If they understand this then they have grasped the concept of conservation of mass.

Early experiences of measures

Babies appear to be aware of quantities related to visual measures such as length and area and begin to develop ideas about weight through handling objects (Montague-Smith and Price, 2012). As their understanding grows, children begin to use informal language such as big and little to describe objects. This can arise through practical informal contexts such as filling the bath or seeing an elephant at the zoo. They then need to extend their vocabulary and come to differentiate between attributes (for example, length, mass or volume) of objects.

Montague-Smith and Price (2012) suggest that children around 3–4 years old use one of three referents for judging size: perceptual (based on the appearance of objects), normative (comparing with a mental image of what they deem to be normal) and functional (deciding if it is appropriate for its intended use). Children sometimes select a referent which is inappropriate for the context (for example, judging age based on a person's height).

Opportunities for children to explore skills and understanding associated with measures can be incorporated into role-play areas, for example, providing scales in the greengrocers or baby clinic, including watering cans of different capacities and pots of different sizes in a garden centre.

Developing an understanding of units of measurement

Comparing and ordering objects

Very young children begin to develop an understanding of measures by comparing and ordering objects. They are very interested in all aspects of the size of items and will happily discuss, whilst playing, which is the biggest of any range of items. They are interested in who in their family is biggest, which of their friends is biggest, which meal is biggest, and so on.

Young children will use the words big, bigger and biggest for almost anything. In order to develop their mathematical understanding and vocabulary adults who are engaging with the children should begin to encourage more accurate language. Children need to begin to consider the various aspects of measures more accurately and this can be developed using more specific language such as long, longer, longest or heavy, heavier and heaviest. Research by Piaget et al. (1960) suggests that young children find this comparative language challenging. They are generally able to accurately identify the longest or heaviest, etc. as an absolute, but are less likely to use associated terms such as shortest or lightest. Later, they begin to use vocabulary for comparing two objects such as longer and heavier. Copley (2000, in Montague-Smith and Price, 2012) suggests the importance of using language for estimation and approximation such as 'almost', 'nearly' and 'about'. Providing opportunities for this will help the child's understanding develop. Stories such as *Goldilocks and the Three Bears* can be used to help to develop the idea of comparing items and looking at their relative sizes.

When we use the term length sometimes we are referring to the height of an object but at other times we might be referring to width or depth. Children need to learn through practical experiences which interpretation is appropriate in different contexts. Additionally, the multiplicity of vocabulary for length is confusing for children. A potential misconception can occur when children are directly comparing the lengths of two items. Care needs to be taken to ensure that the items are compared at the same starting points, as illustrated in Figure 13.1.

In order to develop this idea of comparison for mass, experiences such as holding items in each hand in order to decide which is heavier or lighter are helpful (see Chapter 5) (Montague-Smith and Price, 2012). Later, young children will experience using balance scales, on which the mass of two items is compared. Initially, activity

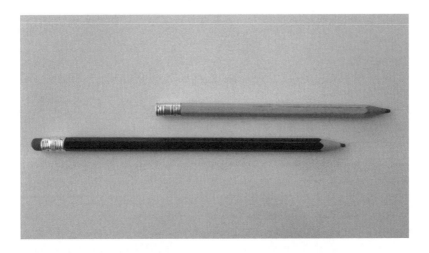

Figure 13.1 *Incorrectly comparing the length of two items*

will focus on putting an item on each side of the scale and the child deciding which they think is the heavier. This can then progress to children trying to find items that they think are lighter or heavier than a particular item. They can test their predictions by comparing them on the balance scales. Subsequently, children can compare more than two items by comparing them in pairs and then trying to order them in terms of their mass. Young children (and some older ones) will often think that larger boxes will weigh more than smaller ones (Dudgeon and Hansen, 2011). Consequently, small heavy parcels and large light ones in role-play shops, post offices and so on can help overcome this misconception.

At home, and in early years settings, children can explore much of this comparison and ordering through play-based activities. For example, when playing in sand and water trays they can explore the comparative capacities of containers as they pour liquid or sand from one to the other and watch one overflow. Development of the vocabulary 'holds more/less' can be promoted through such play.

A very common misconception held by many children is that a taller container will have a bigger capacity (Dudgeon and Hansen, 2011). A good choice of containers in the play area and judicious questioning and discussion can help children to explore and overcome this misconception. Providing a selection of shallow, wide containers that have the same or greater capacity as tall, narrow ones and encouraging children to pour sand or water from one to the other to see which holds more can develop this understanding.

Later, children can compare more than two containers by indirect comparison using the transitivity principle, pouring from one container into a second container and then from the second container into a third.

- Explore making beds for the three bears in the story *Goldilocks and the Three Bears.*
- Use microworlds such as a train set to explore lengths of trains with different numbers of carriages.
- Present children with a range of mystery parcels of different shapes and sizes. Using balance scales only, children can be asked to order the parcels from lightest to heaviest.
- Brown and Leibling (2007: 126) suggest using extracts from traditional stories about 'Giants and Tiny People' such as *Jack and the Beanstalk* as a stimulus for comparing the sizes of objects and discussing their uses (for example, an eating fork for a giant may also be a garden fork for a person). They recommend using a washing line as 'a size line' and order items along it according to size.
- Present children with 'concept cartoons' (Dabell, 2008) showing misconceptions (see Chapter 2) such as 'Bigger objects weigh more'.

Measuring using arbitrary, non-standard and standard units

Once the ideas of direct and indirect comparison are secure, children can progress to assigning numerical values to measurements through the use of arbitrary units and subsequently non-standard units. Arbitrary units are reference items which may not be identical such as hand-spans, pencils and pebbles. Non-standard units are identical reference items used as 'units' for measuring (Mooney et al., 2012a). Examples include 2p coins, cotton reels, playing cards, sheets of A4 paper and Cuisenaire rods. Measuring with arbitrary and non-standard units enables children to quantify measurements by counting objects (rather than reading scales) and they are more convenient for young children to handle than standard units. The approach illustrated in the following case study can be used to help children perceive the benefits of non-standard units over arbitrary units.

CASE STUDY

Transition from arbitrary to non-standard units

A group of children, aged 5 and 6, are asked to explore the question 'How big is the playground?' The children set about this activity and can be seen measuring in foot lengths and paces, running and walking. The children come up with a large range of answers. The adult working with the children questions them and asks them to explain how all these answers can be correct. The children explain that different people's feet are different lengths and that similarly their paces might be different lengths too. Some children suggest that the distance across the play-ground will be shorter if the children measuring it are running.

- Why might the children think that running will make the distance shorter?
- Before reading further, consider how this exploration can help develop children's understanding of the benefits of non-standard units?

You may have identified that using non-standard rather than arbitrary units would allow children to obtain the same measurements repeatedly and thus to compare measurements with each other.

Progression towards standard units

The developmental approach (progressing from comparison to non-standard units and then to standard units) is based on Piaget et al.'s (1960) research. More recent research (Boulton-Lewis, 1987; Nunes et al., 1993; Stephan and Clements, 2003) suggested that some children are unsuccessful with this approach for length and area but were successful if introduced directly to standard units and measuring devices after gaining experience with comparison.

Imperial units and metric units are the two commonly used types of standard units of measurement. While children will experience imperial units in everyday life (for example, recipes in ounces or reading distances in miles on road signs), formal learning focuses on metric units. The SI (Système Internationale) metric units of measure are internationally agreed. Initial learning focuses around using a standard unit as a reference item. For example, children might search for items which are longer or shorter than a metre ruler or find containers which hold more or less than a litre. Children can then begin to use subsidiary units such as grams and centimetres to measure items and attach a numerical value to these. As some of these subsidiary units are relatively small, the numerical values often extend into numbers beyond 100 and such numbers may be beyond their current facility with number.

Children will begin to use these units in their learning and begin to measure with increasing accuracy as they practise. They need to develop understanding of which unit of measure is most appropriate to the task in hand. This developing knowledge is two-fold. Firstly, an understanding of which units belong to which measure is needed. For example, length can be measured in centimetres, metres or kilometres but not grams and kilograms. After this children then need to develop an idea of the relative size of each unit and when it is appropriate to use which. This understanding can be developed by actually measuring a range of items or considering which units you would use for the capacity of an egg cup, empty bottle or sink. Ultimately, as the accuracy of the measuring equipment being used increases, so does the accuracy of the measurement and older children will need to understand that all measurement is approximate.

- Measuring the distances travelled by each toy car
- Designing and constructing a tent for children to play in
- Investigating whether tall people have the biggest feet/longest arm span/ biggest circumference of the head
- Using digital cameras children can go on a hunt looking for things longer than 1 metre and record them by taking a photo. These can then be shared and discussed with a larger group and could form part of a mathematical display.

Reading scales

Clearly, one of the key skills involved in the study of measurement is the ability for children, as they develop, to be able to measure accurately. One particular aspect of this is to be able to read a scale. The most common and earliest scale for measuring that children will encounter is a ruler.

CASE STUDY

A common misconception when measuring

Using a ruler to measure a straight line seems a very simple activity to adults who are able to do this. Consider the case of Zoe, a 5 year old, who was learning to measure lines with her ruler. The adult working with her noticed that each one of her answers was a centimetre shorter than the actual length of the line. The adult sat next to Zoe and watched her measuring. She noticed that instead of measuring from the zero marked on the ruler Zoe was measuring from the end of the ruler itself.

- Consider why this occurred. Think about the range of rulers and tape measures (see Figure 13.2) that are available to young children.
- What are the appropriate rulers to use for a child of this age?
- What issues arise when we move from one type of ruler to another? It might be useful to refer to Chapter 9 about number lines and number tracks.

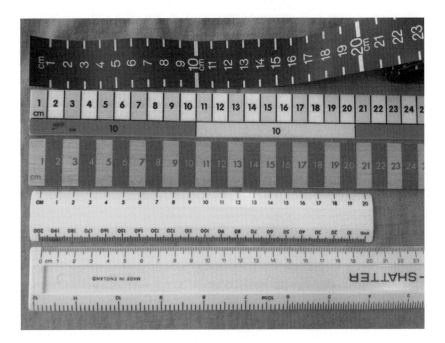

Figure 13.2 *Rulers and tape measures*

When measuring, children will encounter many scales to read on rulers, tape measures, trundle wheels, weighing scales, measuring cylinders and jugs and many more devices. Children's experience of this equipment needs to be built in an incremental way. The child also needs to be able to understand the use of a scale, from a simple scale progressing in ones on a ruler, through to complicated scales where each division might represent more than one unit, such as the circular scales often found on kitchen balance scales.

Prototypical errors

Ryan and Williams (2007) explore this point in their research. Throughout their research they discuss what they call 'prototypical errors' (see Chapter 7). They suggest that children's usual experience, and thus the prototype they expect, is that scales will increase in ones. In their research they presented children of a range of ages with scales where each division represented more than a single unit. They found that only 32% of 8 year olds were able to correctly identify a measurement illustrated on a ruler with divisions greater than one and older children faced similar issues, particularly with scales on measuring cylinders. Of the 8 year olds answering the ruler question Ryan and Williams found that 17% of them used a 'unit scale prototype' and 27% estimated the reading.

- What does this research suggest about the range of scales adults provide for children to use?
- How can adults expose and help children to address such 'prototypical understanding' (Ryan and Williams, 2007)?

As children become confident with rulers where each division represents one unit they will then need to experience measuring devices with a range of non-unitary scales. For example, on different kitchen scales the individual divisions may represent 25 grams or 50 grams. Consequently, to measure the mass of ingredients the child needs to identify the value of each interval on the scale and then count up, from the last numbered division, in chunks for each subsequent interval. Circular scales (as on kitchen scales) are more challenging to read than linear scales (as on a ruler).

Measuring cylinders need to be placed on a flat surface to ensure the liquid is level at the measuring point. However, children often hold measuring cylinders at eye level instead (Dudgeon and Hansen, 2011). When measuring the width of the door, children often fail to keep the tape measure straight or measure diagonally across the door rather than along one edge (the shortest possible distance).

Estimation

Estimation is a key skill used frequently in everyday life, for example:

- Will we be able to fit our car into the empty car park space?
- Have we got enough time to go shopping before our favourite television programme begins?
- Will we be able to empty all of the remaining drink into this glass?

It is a well recognised issue that when encouraged to estimate, children are, understandably, keen to get their estimation as close to the actual measurement of the item as possible. The result of this can be that children actually change their estimation after the actual measurement in order to appear more accurate.

One way to overcome this can be to encourage children to estimate within a range. This reflects what adults do in real life. So, when being asked to estimate the mass of an object, for example, the children give a range, rather than a single estimation. Games can be developed whereby children, or teams of children, gain points if the actual mass of the object falls within their estimated range. As their skills develop, children can be encouraged to narrow the range of their estimates. After all, it is easy to estimate that the height of a cupboard is between 50 cm and 5 metres and this does not really help with the skill of estimation at all!

Another practical approach when developing the skill of estimation is to identify a range of familiar reference objects that children can use for comparison. One gram is a very small measure and can be very hard for children to understand. They will almost certainly be familiar with bags of crisps and probably consider that these are very light. If they know that a bag of crisps usually weighs 25–30 grams then developing the idea of one gram being very light indeed becomes more understandable. They can then use such items to help them estimate: 'Is this lighter or heavier than a bag of crisps?'

- Ask children to close their eyes and start a timer. Children are asked to open their eyes when they estimate a specific amount of time has passed, for example, 30 seconds. Use of a timer on an interactive whiteboard or on a smart phone can enable children to see how near the target time they were.
- Children can estimate how far they want a floor robot to move and then programme it to travel that distance.

Mass and weight

There is a difference between our common use of these terms and the specific uses within mathematics and science (Mooney et al., 2012a). For young children it is usually regarded as acceptable for them to use the terms weight and weighing to refer to finding the mass of an object but the distinction will be made when children refine their understanding of forces in science. Mass is the measure of the quantity of matter in an object and the SI Unit to measure mass is kilograms. Weight is the force exerted on an object by gravity and the SI unit to measure weight is Newtons. So, an object that was taken to the moon would maintain the same mass but would have a lower weight than the same object on the Earth.

Developing an understanding of time

Children need to master both 'telling the time' and understanding the measurement of the passage of time (Dickson et al., 1984; Dudgeon and Hansen, 2011). Telling the time is a necessary life skill for children as well as adults. However, learning to tell the time is particularly challenging for many children, not least because of the range of time formats and clocks (analogue, digital 12-hour and digital 24-hour clocks).

Sequencing and ordering

The beginning of developing an understanding of time for the very youngest children is for them to begin to sequence events. With the very youngest children this understanding begins with children becoming aware of routines and times such as dinnertime and bedtime (Montague-Smith and Price, 2012). They will ask repeatedly about when these times are, initially with very little concept of the passage of time. So just after they have had breakfast they may well begin to ask if it is nearly lunchtime. An activity that can develop the understanding of the sequence of events is the use of pictorial timetables. These help young children to map out the events during the day and understand their fixed order.

Commonly included in this aspect of the mathematics curriculum are the elements of time that are related to knowing the days of the week, months of the year and being able to use and read calendars and timetables and calculate the duration of events. For very young children nursery rhymes and songs are very helpful when learning the names and order of the days of the week and months of the year. Children need to grasp the idea that these day and month names recur in a cyclical order. A well-known traditional rhyme to help children remember how many days there are in each month is 'Thirty days hath September'.

Later, children need to develop an understanding of chronology. The youngest children will often say that all events in the past happened 'yesterday'. Adults will be familiar with the confusion children have about events in the past. For example, they may ask grandparents if they are Victorians. The idea of chronology is, of course, explored in history-based activities once the children are in school. Activities that help children to order and sequence events are essential at this stage. These can be ordering activities around personally significant events, such as themselves being born, siblings being born, significant holidays, or beginning school (Montague-Smith and Price, 2012).

The passage of time

There are differences between the informal use of measurement vocabulary in everyday life and its precise use in mathematics. For example, we often ask children to 'wait a minute' when the actual length of the wait may be more or less than a minute (Mooney et al., 2012a). Similarly, the response to the question 'Are we nearly there?' is seldom answered accurately! These inaccurate responses in everyday life can make it difficult for children to develop an understanding of the passing of time.

To help with sequencing:

- Present children with a range of pictures, perhaps from a familiar story, that they can sequence to develop their understanding of events.
- Children can take photographs of activities at various times of day (for example, assembly, lunchtime, snack time) to sequence later.

To help children develop understanding of the passage of time try the following activities:

- How many things can you do in a minute? For example, use an egg or sand timer to find out how many times you can write your name or jump on the spot in a minute.
- Use stopwatches to time how long it takes to undertake specific activities, for example, walking to a certain place, eating a meal, etc.

Telling the time

We have discussed the difficulties in reading scales earlier and this is a key difficulty with clocks. Because they are circular, it is difficult for children to identify the beginning and end of the scale. In addition, the numbering on the scale is challenging. There are, in effect, two scales superimposed on each other; the numbers 1 to 12 not only represent the hours but they also 'count' each set of 5 minutes.

To address these challenges, Catterall (2008) proposes a strategy where children become familiar with the clock and clock face initially. She then suggests children are introduced to the hands on the clock one at a time, starting by adding the hour hand to the clock face. Once familiar with the hour hand, she suggests the hour hand be removed and the minute hand introduced. Only when children understand the purpose of both hands individually should they be combined.

We commonly use the language of 'quarter past', 'half past', and 'quarter to' when reading an analogue clock. Children commonly confuse 'quarter past' and 'quarter to' (MaLT, 2005). Children, therefore, need an understanding of simple fractions and of half- and quarter-turns (see Chapters 11 and 14). One of the common difficulties children encounter when telling the time on an analogue clock is that they muddle the minute and hour hands on the clock (for example, reading quarter to six as half-past nine). It is very important here that the adults think about the models and images they are offering when teaching this aspect. The best practice here would be to use geared clocks wherever possible so that the hands move in synchronisation with each other and point to the correct places on the clock face. It does not help children to understand if the examples that are used to teach them have the hour hand always pointing exactly at the 'hour number' (see Figure 13.3). This is not what happens on real clocks as the hour hand moves incrementally towards the next hour as time passes.

Figure 13.3 *Incorrect and correct positioning of hands on clock faces*

It is best practice when demonstrating time if the adult moving the clock hands always ensures that they move the hands in a clockwise direction. If the hands are moved forwards on a geared clock from 1.10 to 12.20 the children can see this takes a lot longer than, for example, moving from 1.10 to 2.20, and this will help reinforce the idea that some times are close together and others further apart.

Children frequently see digital clocks (for example video timers, microwave and oven displays) in the home environment. Therefore, children should be introduced to digital clocks alongside analogue clocks to help establish the connections between them. Children need to learn that the 'dots' separate the hours from the minutes and are not to be confused with decimal points. For digital times, the hour is stated before the minutes, whereas for analogue times we often say the minutes before the hour. Thus, children may incorrectly read 12:10 as '12 minutes past 10' (Dudgeon and Hansen, 2011). An awareness of Roman numerals will help children to read a wider range of analogue clocks.

- What range of clocks (analogue, geared analogue, digital, 24-hour, 12-hour, Roman numerals) do you have for children to learn to tell the time?
- Do these aid their understanding or add to their confusion?

Similarly the use of language contributes to the difficulty of learning to read the clock and tell the time when we consider all the ways that we might actually say a time such as 2.35p.m.

We might say:

- Two thirty-five,
- Two thirty-five in the afternoon,
- Twenty-five to three,
- Five and twenty to three,
- Thirty-five minutes past two … .

and you can probably think of more. There is also potential for confusion between a.m. and p.m. times (Barmby et al., 2009). Later, children will learn about 24-hour clock times.

Time intervals

When finding differences in time by counting on, children find it difficult to 'bridge' through the hours, for example, 9.59, 9.60, 9.61… . Bridging through midnight and midday is especially challenging because both hours and minutes change (Barmby et al., 2009). A further confusion is that, unlike number which is in base 10, time works in a base of 60 (60 seconds in a minute, 60 minutes in an hour). Other bases are encountered later when children consider the number of hours in a day, the number of days in a week, and the number of days in a year. As children get older, the non-decimal nature of time causes further issues when they begin to work on using addition and subtraction to find time intervals, because many methods, including the standard written methods (see Chapter 10), simply will not work with these calculations (MaLT, 2005).

Summary

In this chapter we have explored the progression in measurement from children's earliest experiences of describing measures, using associated vocabulary, direct and indirect comparison of objects, and moving on to use of arbitrary, non-standard and standard units of measurement. The importance of estimation was highlighted. We have looked at common misconceptions and areas of difficulty and have considered particularly the difficulties encountered in learning to tell the time and how these might be overcome. When exploring this area of mathematics children should be involved in a range of practical activities. Principally, children need to acquire a conceptual understanding of measures and not just learn how to measure (Castle and Needham, 2007).

Further reading

Catterall, R. (2008) 'Doing time', *Mathematics Teaching*, 209: 37 – 39. Available at: http://www.atm.org.uk/mt/archive/mt209.html (accessed14 February 2013).

You can read more about Catterall's idea for another way to teach about time in this article. Catterall has tried her ideas with her class and reports here on the issues that arose and the impact of her ideas on the children's learning. Catterall also explores some of the issues that arise when children learn to tell the time.

Montague-Smith, A. and Price, A.J. (2012) *Mathematics in Early Years Education*, 3rd edn. Abingdon: Routledge.

Chapter 6 contains many ideas for developing understanding for children through practical experiences, discussion and more direct intervention.

Hansen, A. and Vaukins, D. (2012) *Primary Mathematics across the Curriculum*, 2nd edn. London: Sage.

In Chapter 4, the authors provide many helpful examples of cross-curricular activities for learning about measures.

14

Shape, Position and Movement

Paula Stone

 Chapter Overview

In this chapter you can read about:

- Why learning about shape, position and movement is important
- The key theories that have underpinned the learning and teaching of shape, position and movement
- Early understanding of shape, position and movement
- Open-ended starting points for learning in shape, position and movement.

The importance of shape, position and movement

Shape, position and movement involves learning about two-dimensional and three-dimensional shapes and their properties, ways of describing the positions of objects in space and of giving directions, and different kinds of mathematical movements or transformations such as reflections, rotations and translations. Frobisher et al. (2007) suggest that learning about shape, position and movement is often under-appreciated and claim that it is fundamental to other aspects of mathematics beyond the spatial. Exploration of shape, position and movement is a part of human activity that is performed by even the youngest children as they begin to explore the area around them, and it is through the development of children's understanding of shape, position and movement that they can have a better understanding of the world. It starts with the concrete, that is, what young children can see and touch, and develops to more abstract spatial reasoning. Our knowledge and understanding of shape, position and movement enables us to create and use representational systems to describe locations, transform shapes in a mathematical manner and use a spatial approach to solve problems. It has a significant influence on how we go about our daily lives, from planning our garden, building flat-packed furniture to finding our way to a party or train station.

De Moor (2005) suggests that learning about shape, position and movement has three functions: a practical value, a preparatory value and a personal value as it is an area of mathematics in which a curiosity about geometrical ideas and a fascination with spatial patterns can be fostered. Frobisher et al. (2007) add that learning about shape, position and movement not only provides children with a non-numerical perspective of the world, but can also support number and algebraic concepts. They use the example of a number track or a number line which they say are geometrical representations of the number system along which children can move backwards and forwards. They also argue that spatial concepts and skills contribute to problem-solving activities by enabling children to use diagrams to represent data.

One of the key issues that make the learning of shape, position and movement challenging for children is the complexity of the language. Not only is there a vast range of vocabulary to learn, but also many words have a mathematical use and a common everyday use (for example face, space and regular) that could confuse children as they develop their understanding.

Early understanding of shape, position and movement

Progression in understanding shape, position and movement

Much of the existing research is rooted in the theories expounded by Piaget and Inhelder (1956). They proposed progressive stages of development in spatial thinking dependent on age which follow a definite logical order, beginning with spatial relationships such as enclosure (one shape inside another) and continuity (joining shapes and lines), progressing towards understanding different perspectives, and moving later to formal study of common two- and three-dimensional shapes.

In contrast, van Hiele (1986) offers a learning sequence which starts with two- and three-dimensional shapes, progresses to understanding perspective, and ends with more abstract spatial ideas such as topology. Van Hiele (1986) argues that children's understanding of shape develops through a fixed, ordered sequence of spatial concepts. He offers five stages but only three are shared here, as stages four and five are beyond the scope of this book. At the first level, the 'visualisation' stage, shapes are judged by their appearance and generally viewed as 'a whole', rather than by distinguishing parts; for example, a child might say, 'It's a circle because it looks like the clock'. At the second 'descriptive' level children can identify and describe the properties of shapes; for example, an equilateral triangle can be distinguished from other triangles because of its three equal sides, equal angles and symmetries. Most children up to the age of 8 will be working within level one or two. Later, they will begin to make progress towards the third 'abstract' level. At level three, children will be able to identify relationships between classes of shapes and can deduce one property from another. At this stage, children need to refine their existing understanding of shapes as being distinct to accommodate a more sophisticated understanding in which some shapes are viewed as special cases of others. For example, a square is a special case of a rectangle with all sides equal.

Both models are based on social constructivist approaches to teaching and learning which propose that the social environment, and particularly social interaction with other people, is an important aspect of the teaching and learning process. In contrast to Piaget and Inhelder, van Hiele (1986) suggests that progress is dependent on educational experiences rather than on age or maturation and that, despite some natural development of spatial thinking, deliberate instruction is needed to move children through the levels of geometric understanding and an individual child's level may vary from concept to concept.

Many children come to school with a great deal of intuitive knowledge of shape, position and movement. Piaget and Inhelder (1956) suggest that spatial concepts begin to develop as the infant becomes aware of the four basic topological concepts:

- Proximity – being aware of the relative nearness of an object or event to any other object or event
- Order – having an awareness of the sequence of objects or events (in time) according to size, colour or some other attribute
- Separation – being able to distinguish between objects and parts of objects
- Enclosure – knowing an object or event is surrounded by other objects or events.

At first, the location of objects in space is seen in relation to the infant's own body. Later, as the infant begins to move around, the position of each object in space is referenced to its surroundings. As they explore the space around them, the baby will begin to develop an implicit understanding of concepts like 'near', 'far', 'up', 'down', 'big' and 'little'. As the infant becomes more mobile and begins to explore further afield they begin to develop their understanding of new spatial ideas such as 'here', 'there', 'in', 'out', 'under' and 'over'. The placement of features or objects in relation to each other and taking account of vertical and horizontal relationships becomes part of the child's way of viewing the world.

Piaget and Inhelder (1956) argue that just as children start formal schooling they begin to use geometric ideas such as distinguishing between straight and curved lines and between specific shapes (like squares and circles). They will begin to name and describe two- and three-dimensional shapes and some of their properties, such as the length and number of sides and corners. They are also developing an emergent awareness of symmetry. According to Bryant (2009), it is informal early experience that prepares young children for the more formal aspects of shape, position and movement that they will learn in school, but he argues that, at this stage, understanding is largely non-numerical and implicit. Bryant also argues that it is important that adults in early years settings are aware of the kinds of spatial relationships that young children recognise and are familiar with, such as the use of a stable background to help remember the position and orientation of objects. They should use these to prepare children for learning about shape, position and movement in a more formal context that will enable them to develop more abstract spatial reasoning. Frobisher et al. (2007) suggest that many mathematicians believe that young children are unable to attain abstract thought with regards to shape, position and movement, but argue that teachers and practitioners should be aiming for this.

Supporting the development of shape, position and movement

The rest of this chapter will present ideas about how to support the development of each area of shape, position and movement through the use of talk to support learning. Two pedagogical approaches will be discussed here which seem to encapsulate many of the theories suggested by other mathematics educationalists. One is the use of variance and invariance (Johnston-Wilder and Mason, 2005) or equivalence and transformation, that is, what is the same about mathematical objects and what is different or has been changed (Frobisher et al., 2007; Haylock and Cockburn, 2013). This strategy enables children to make connections between and within shapes and identify how they have been transformed using mathematical skills like predicting, hypothesising, testing and generalising. It also supports children's developing understanding of the inclusivity and exclusivity of definitions (for example that a cube is a special sort of cuboid). A second pedagogical approach is the use of instruction or explanation; this is explained in more detail below.

Van Hiele's (1986) Theory of Instruction

As indicated earlier, van Hiele (1986) maintains that deliberate instruction is needed to move children through the levels of geometric understanding, suggesting adults should plan sequences of lessons that scaffold children's learning through exploration and talk. Van Hiele presents a sequence of five phases of activity types that are designed to promote the progression of children's thinking from one level to the next. These phases may be spread over one activity or many, and may vary in length.

- **Phase 1: Inquiry.** Children are encouraged to explore the resources in the environment and discover some properties and structures for themselves through play.
- **Phase 2: Direct Orientation.** Activities are presented in such a way that children's attention is focused on particular characteristics of the shapes or puzzle pieces.
- **Phase 3: Explication.** This involves tasks and games that deliberately develop the vocabulary associated with the ideas that have been encountered so far, while continuing to explore the properties of the shapes.
- **Phase 4: Free Orientation.** The children engage in activities and problem-solving tasks that are open-ended or can be completed in different ways.
- **Phase 5: Integration.** Opportunities are given for the children to summarise and integrate what they have learned, developing a new network of objects and relations. This would be the perfect opportunity to ask children to discuss variance and invariance (Johnston-Wilder and Mason, 2005): what is the same about the mathematical objects, what is different, or has been changed?

Van den Heuvel-Panhuizen and Buys (2005) offer a similar model to that presented by van Hiele (1986). They suggest that there are just three learning and teaching phases in developing children's understanding of shape, position and movement: experiencing, explaining and connecting. This model, advocated by de Moor (2005), argues that the development of the cognitive abilities of young children connected with shape, position and movement does not take place in isolation, but in fact occurs alongside their social-emotional development, so learning in this area of mathematics should be integrated into the other areas of the curriculum whenever possible.

CASE STUDY

Bethan playing with wooden blocks

Bethan (aged 4 years) is playing with wooden blocks (see Figure 14.1). She is quietly exploring the resources independently, working out how shapes fit together or how some roll and others do not. She piles some up and screams in delight when they tumble down. As the adult approaches she picks up a cube and exclaims, 'Look, a red square'.

Figure 14.1 *Bethan playing with wooden blocks*

Bethan is working within the inquiry stage of van Hiele's (1986) phase model of activity, or de Moor's (2005) experiencing phase, and at this point the adult should focus Bethan's attention on the particular characteristics of the shape (i.e. it can be picked up so it must be three-dimensional) to address the misconception (believing it is a square). This is an ideal opportunity to extend Bethan's learning by showing her that the six faces are all squares. This is the direct orientation phase of van Hiele's (1986) model. As Bethan's understanding develops in this phase, the adult could start to introduce some mathematical vocabulary related to two- and three-dimensional shapes such as 'corners', 'faces' and 'edges'.

The adult then picks up a sphere and rolls it to Bethan and asks her to describe what is happening. At this point Bethan could be given a cuboid or a prism and asked to roll this, too. The adult could then draw on the concept of invariance by asking Bethan what is the same or what is different about the shapes. Other examples of questions could include 'Why can some shapes be put on top of one another and others cannot?'

According to van Hiele (1986), the next phase of activity to develop Bethan's understanding of both two- and three-dimensional shapes involves explication. At this stage, the adult would provide more opportunities for Bethan to sort and categorise objects and shapes while continuing to support the development of vocabulary and concepts, thus enabling Bethan to build connections between the mathematical concepts (de Moor, 2005). For example, Bethan could be asked to sort the shapes into those with straight edges and those with curved edges or, using paint, to print with the different faces of the shape. In the free orientation phase Bethan could be asked to draw on the knowledge and skills she has previously learnt to build a tower six shapes high or to build a house. As she builds, it is the adult's role to ask questions about the choices she is making: 'Why have you put that shape there?' or 'What would happen if I swapped … ?'. The final activity phase, integration, is an opportunity for Bethan to synthesise all her knowledge about three-dimensional shapes. With an adult, or another child, she could play 'guess my shape' using a feely bag.

Through engaging in these activities, Bethan will have developed her understanding from simply recognising some shapes to being able to discuss the shapes in terms of specific geometric properties and perhaps make some comparisons between shapes. She will have moved from visual thinking to descriptive thinking in regards to these particular shapes (van Hiele, 1986).

Two- and three-dimensional shapes

Young children should be encouraged to explore both natural and man-made objects through touch, sight, smell and sound. With the support of adults they should be encouraged to use new vocabulary to describe their texture, colour, size and shape and begin to describe features that are the same or different when sorting and classifying objects. As young children develop their understanding of shape and space they should be given opportunities to explore objects that fit together and/or come apart through construction activities, use of clay, paper folding (Montague-Smith and Price, 2012). Dialogue alongside these activities will enable children to develop their own informal description of shapes. Later, children can be supported to describe shapes and their properties using more precise mathematical terms (see Chapter 2).

When engaging in activities involving two-dimensional shapes, adults should remember that commercially-produced 'two-dimensional shapes' are technically three-dimensional and this may lead to confusion for some children. Drawing around these solid shapes will produce shapes which are truly two-dimensional.

- How do van Hiele's (1986) five phases of instruction or van den Heuvel-Panhuizen and Buys' (2005) three-phase model apply to each of the activities and case studies which follow?
- How can the adult best support the learning of the mathematical concepts involved?

Figure 14.2 offers examples of interesting activities to help children develop sound understanding of two- and three-dimensional shapes.

Key Spatial Ideas	Resources and Activities	Role of Adult
Shape vocabulary (names and properties of shapes)	Free play with junk boxes, outdoor play equipment, building bricks; exploring spaces using large cardboard boxes, play houses, dens Look for shapes in the natural and built world outside (see Chapter 5)	Encourage mathematical talk about the shapes and spaces explored Expanding shape vocabulary, discussing shape properties
Constructing shapes	Making and drawing shapes, pictures with shapes, and patterns using: • play dough, • gummed paper, foam or felt shapes • sand Construction kits Floor robots and LOGO software	

Key Spatial Ideas	Resources and Activities	Role of Adult
Links between two- and three-dimensional shapes	Printing with the painted faces of three-dimensional shapes, shape posting boxes, drawing round three-dimensional shapes	Enable children to recognise the two-dimensional shapes that form the faces of three-dimensional shapes
Similarity and difference Sorting shapes	• Ask children to look at their two- or three-dimensional shapes and talk about what is the same and what is different (Figure 14.3). Ask them to find a partner who has a matching shape • Use a story, for example, *Captain Invincible and the Space Shapes* by Stuart Murphy (2001) • Present children with pictures or ICT-based images of a wide selection of two-dimensional polygons and non-polygons to sort in different ways	Guide children towards a one-criterion Venn diagram (Figure 14.4) or one-criterion Carroll diagram (see Chapter 15)
Visualisation	• In pairs children sit back-to-back. One child describes a shape pattern (see Figure 14.5) to a partner so that they can draw it. They may use the name of the two-dimensional shapes or describe them instead • Play 'Peek-a-Boo' (Figure 14.6). This could be completed using an interactive whiteboard or a selection of two-dimensional shapes behind a screen	Refining children's precision in using shape vocabulary, developing children's mental images of shapes Ask questions such as: • What shapes could/couldn't it be? Why? • Is that angle greater or less than or equal to a right angle? • Is the shape symmetrical? How many lines of symmetry does it have? Challenge prototypical views of shapes (for example triangles always having a side on the horizontal).

(Continued)

(Continued)

Key Spatial Ideas	Resources and Activities	Role of Adult
Investigating the properties of shapes	Investigate: • All triangles have three sides • If you cut off the corner of a square you will always get a pentagon • A prism always has five faces	Encourage children to summarise and develop new networks of ideas

Figure 14.2   *Developing children's understanding of two- and three-dimensional shapes*

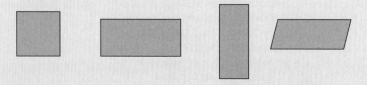

Figure 14.3   *What is the same and what is different?*

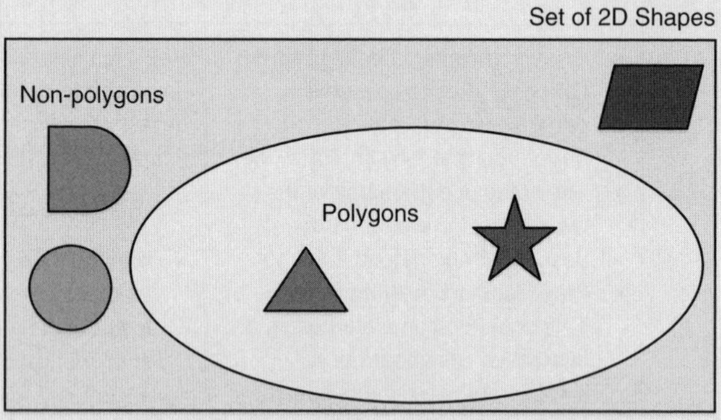

Set of 2D Shapes

Non-polygons

Polygons

Figure 14.4   *Single criterion Venn diagram*

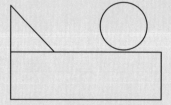

Figure 14.5   *Mathematical visualisation activity*

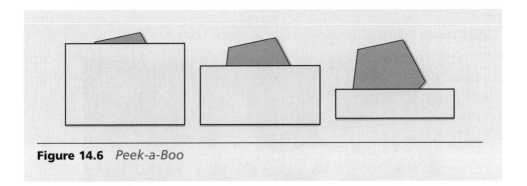

Figure 14.6 *Peek-a-Boo*

Position and direction

Learning about position and direction enables children to describe the position of an object in relation to the location of other objects in space using direction, angle, distance, and co-ordinates. De Moor (2005) identifies two distinct aspects of position and movement:

- Localising – locating where something is
- Taking a point of view – being able to say what can be seen from a certain point and what cannot.

Understanding perspective

Based on a 'three-mountain' task in which children were asked to draw how the mountains would look from a doll's point of view, Piaget and Inhelder (1956) argued that young children (around 4 years) were unable to adopt another person's perspective because of their age or stage of development. However, research since the 1970s – for example, Hughes (1975) – has shown young children's perspective-taking ability to be affected by a variety of situational variables.

CASE STUDY

Freddie and the train set

Freddie, 3 years old, is engrossed in playing with the wooden train set (Figure 14.6). As he moves the train around the track the adult asks him 'Where is the train?',

(Continued)

(Continued)

Figure 14.7 *Freddie playing with the train set*

'Where has it stopped?' and 'Can you find somewhere different for the train to stop?'. The adult then suggests that Freddie places the bridge over the track, the conductor next to the signal box, etc. Using prompting and probing questions the adult is developing Freddie's ability to localise through describing the relative positions or locations of objects.

- How could you use the train set context to develop Freddie's ability to adopt another point of view?

Figure 14.8 provides examples of activities which can support the development of children's understanding and use of positional language and directions.

Key Positional Ideas	Resources and Activities	Role of Adult
Developing positional vocabulary	• Play 'Who is it?' Children sit in a grid arrangement. Provide clues such as 'The child I am thinking of is sitting between/behind/to the left of Jack and Joseph'. Ask the children to identify who you are describing • Using an interactive whiteboard or a shelving unit, place items in different locations on the shelves (Figure 14.9). Ask children to describe the position of objects and move objects to new positions on the shelves. • Tidying up (for example, put the book on the shelf above the toy truck) • Discussing positions of jigsaw puzzle pieces • I Spy games in which children have to find out where something is, for example 'I spy something beginning with C'. The children ask is it on the floor? Is it on the wall?	Check for understanding of positional vocabulary such as behind, in front of, between Adults can vary the number of items on the shelves and even vary the number of shelves to suit the level of understanding
Developing positional and directional vocabulary, sequencing directions	• Planning a series of directions to help a storybook character find their way. Represent the route by drawing maps • Work in pairs to plan a route from one end of the hall or playground to another through a series of obstacles • Input directions using floor robots or LOGO software	• Refining precision in the use of positional and directional vocabulary • Helping children to understand the relative nature of positional and directional terms (for example left and right depend on which way you are facing) • Using sequences of directions rather than just a series of single instructions
Using co-ordinates to specify location	• Using a large grid marked on the floor or playground, ask children to follow instructions such as 'Start in square (B, 1). Move two squares forwards, turn right, move backwards one square. Where are you now?' • Plotting points on a treasure island map to locate the treasure	• Ensuring children understand the order of co-ordinate pairs (letter, number) or (number, number), • Checking for understanding of co-ordinates as specifying the intersection of a row and column or, later, the intersection of two perpendicular lines • Check for difficulties with zero co-ordinates

Figure 14.8 *Developing children's understanding of position and direction*

(Continued)

(Continued)

Figure 14.9 *Shelving unit*

Mathematical movements

There are three types of mathematical movement or transformations that 0–8 year olds will encounter: reflection, translation and rotation. Children learn about these movements through informal activities such as:

- Finding objects which turn (for example windmills, wheels, door-handle)
- Turning on the spot through whole-, half- and quarter-turns

- Exploring reflective symmetry through folding, experimenting with mirrors, building symmetrical patterns with bricks
- Sliding beads on a bar, drawing curtains and running along a straight track.

Later, children will meet a fourth kind of transformation, namely, enlargement. Children will extend their understanding developed through practical experiences of transformations to include paper-based activities.

- Wrapping paper and wallpaper motifs (see Figure 14.10) provide opportunities to talk about translation, reflection and rotation. Adults should ask the children to describe what has happened to the motif, encouraging them to use and extend mathematical vocabulary. Children could then make their own repeating pattern wallpaper using shape translations and reflections.

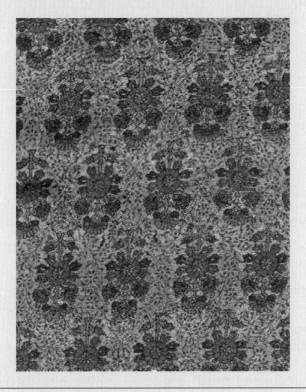

Figure 14.10 *Translating patterns*

(Continued)

(Continued)

- Johnston-Wilder and Mason (2005) and Haylock and Cockburn (2013) both recommend a discussion of similarities and differences in shapes once they have been transformed. They suggest presenting children with a variety of shapes that have been transformed (Figure 14.11) and asking questions such as 'What is the same and what is different about these shapes?' or 'Which is the odd one out?'.

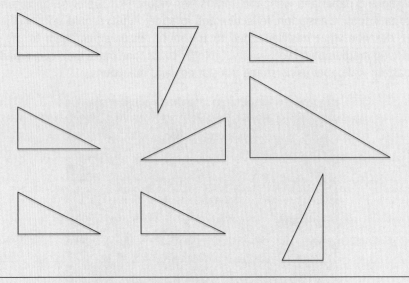

Figure 14.11 *Different transformations of a triangle*

Summary

Understanding of shape, position and movement is significant in children's mathematical development. It supports logical thinking and is necessary for the general spatial awareness needed for everyday life. Young children engage with shape, position and movement activities long before they come to school and adults in early years settings and schools should be aware of previous learning including the possible misconceptions that children bring with them into the formal learning environment. Research, by van Hiele (1986) and de Moor (2005) among others, has presented us with strategies to move children's understanding of shape, position and movement forward. Central to both of these pedagogical approaches is the provision of opportunities for exploration in which adults scaffold learning through effective interaction.

Further reading

Blinko, J. (2000) *Shape, Space and Measure*. London: A and C Black.
This book includes a range of activities that can be used to investigate a range of shape and space concepts.

Frobisher, L., Frobisher, A., Orton, A. and Orton, J. (2007) *Learning to Teach Shape and Space: A Handbook for Students and Teachers in the Primary School*. Cheltenham: Nelson Thornes.
This is a comprehensive text to support teachers' and student teachers' understanding of concepts surrounding all aspects of shape, position and movement.

Montague-Smith, A. and Price, A.J. (2012) *Mathematics in Early Years Education*, 3rd edn. Abingdon: Routledge.
Chapter 5 of this practical book contains lots of ideas for further activities.

Van den Heuvel-Panhuizen, M. and Buys, K. (eds) (2005) *Young Children Learn Measurement and Geometry: A Learning-teaching Trajectory with Intermediate Attainment Targets for the Lower Grades in Primary School*. Utrecht: Freudenthal Institute, Utrecht University.
The text provides a comprehensive list of developmentally scheduled lessons. The learning activities are structured to promote connections between mathematics and daily environments.

Handling Data

Gina Donaldson

Chapter Overview

In this chapter you can read about:

- What handling data involves, and the key ideas which children will need to understand to become confident in handling data
- How children's learning of data handling progresses, particularly their skills of sorting, recording and representing data, and the ways in which they can interpret data to solve problems
- Practical ideas for exploring data with children.

Early experiences of data

Children live in a world full of data, which is another word for information. This is presented to them as pictures, music, spoken words, objects, written words and numerals. They think and talk about this information to help them to make sense of their world. Children engage with toys, everyday items and natural objects, playing with these and exploring them. Young children might find that spoons are cold and hard, and that they make a noise when banged on the table. This will be different to the feel of soft toys and the sound these make on the table. Children group items together if they seem to be similar. For example, cars and lorries might all be grouped together as cars initially, but later differentiated as cars and lorries, two similar but distinct groups. They then refine these categories as they become more experienced. At home and in nursery settings they learn to recognise and interpret signs and symbols such as those which tell them where to put their toys when tidying up. Early experiences of data might include:

- Exploring properties of real objects and using these to select what they want. Young children do this as soon as they can pick up and physically handle items
- Understanding what is said to them, interpreting the words and phrases, discarding what is not important and focusing on what is important. Young children often repeat what has been said to them to help them to do this
- Interpreting information shown as a picture, for example, putting their snack into a box with a picture of fruit on it in their nursery setting or finding their own peg in the cloakroom which is labelled with their picture.

The purpose and nature of data handling

Children and adults live in a world where they are required to know, understand and solve problems based on information represented in charts, graphs and tables. Consider the amount of information presented this way in timetables, in the television programme schedule, and during the news and weather forecast each day. Certainly, at the time of a general election adults are presented with data which is aimed at persuading them towards certain arguments and viewpoints. Being able to sort and interpret data is a life skill. It allows us to take control of issues and make informed decisions. For example, it enables us to make judgements about global issues such as our impact on the environment, or to make sense of a gas or electricity bill. Pound and Lee (2011) argue that handling data involves communication. Children develop both the ability to interpret data presented to them and to use data to communicate to others. When we teach children to handle data, therefore, we are equipping them with a valuable set of skills.

Data handling is about asking and answering questions to solve problems. It is useful then to consider data handling as a cycle of:

- Asking a question
- Deciding on the data which would best answer the question
- Gathering, recording and organising that data
- Representing the data
- Interpreting the data to answer the question.

Children need to recognise that data handling is a key tool for solving problems. Therefore, data-handling activities should be designed to address questions which matter to children, thus making them meaningful and purposeful (Barmby et al., 2009; Haylock, 2010). Adults can model looking at tables, graphs and charts and search for answers to questions.

- What sort of question would be meaningful for a pre-school child and could be answered by an exploration of data?
- What about a 5 year old, 6 year old, 7 year old?

Suggested activities for data handling:

- Set up a bird table and record the number of birds visiting for an hour in the morning, taking it in turns to watch the table. Change the food and see what happens.
- On how many days has it rained this week? What is the best way to record this information? What would the information be like if we repeated the activity in a few weeks' time?
- How many children walked to school today? Will it be the same tomorrow? What if it rains tomorrow?
- How many supermarket coupons has each class collected?
- How many birthdays in each month of the year?
- Do all packets of the same sort of sweets contain the same number of sweets?
- How many house points have been awarded this week?

Representing data can be time-consuming when done by hand, although it is important for children to engage with the process on some occasions. Adults and children can use ICT packages to represent data quickly and efficiently, allowing time for interpretation and problem solving. ICT can also be used in the gathering of data, for example with temperature sensors and digital cameras.

- Consider the learning involved in drawing graphs by hand as opposed to manipulating them using ICT. How often should children draw graphs themselves and how often should they use ICT for this process?

Progression in learning about data handling

We can trace the progression in children's learning about data handling in a number of ways, considering distinct, but linked skills and concepts. This section will consider progression in children's skills of sorting, their understanding of recording and representation of data, and their interpretation of data to answer questions.

CASE STUDY

Sorting cars

Alex (aged 5) took a box of cars to play with on the carpet of her Reception classroom. The adult, Jenny sat with her. Alex was looking for red cars, saying that they were like her Mum's car. She sorted through the whole box and carefully separated the red cars from the other cars. She lined up the red cars, and Jenny began to line up the other cars too. Jenny asked Alex what was special about her line of cars. Alex explained that they were all red like her Mum's car. They looked at Jenny's line of cars. Jenny asked Alex why these cars were not in her line. She said it was because they were all different colours and not red. Jenny asked her which line held most cars. Alex did not want to count them, so they put their lines of cars close together, carefully matching them side by side. Alex could see that there were more cars which were not red and they talked about how she knew this.

- What were the important things Jenny asked Alex to talk about?
- To what extent do the lines of cars resemble a more formal mathematical graph or chart?

Progression in sorting

Providing children with a good range of items to sort, including everyday items (both natural and man-made), as well as more structured resources designed for sorting, will help them to develop understanding of sorting in different contexts. In the case study we saw how young children quite naturally sort items within child-initiated play. Sorting is a way of making sense of information. By handling objects and exploring their properties, they begin to notice differences and similarities.

Initially, young children use these similarities to group objects and then label the collection. Later, children are able to decide on sorting labels or criteria before commencing the sort. For example, pre-school children might sort toys to match their favourite colour. They might look for toys with features which match a particular theme or character from a film or television programme. When they are playing cafés, they will look for plates and cups. When they are copying someone doing some DIY, they will select toy saws and hammers. In this process, they are focusing on certain attributes or properties of the toys. They check these attributes against a criterion, perhaps the colour, or the shape, or the link to recognised characters which are important in their play. When questioned by an adult, they will probably be able to say what is 'special' about the items they have selected, or the property which is significant. This is a valuable question for adults to ask, as it demands that children clarify the property they have focused on, and the criterion they applied. It could involve some self-checking, 'Do all these items really have this property?' Although not using the word, the child is discussing the criterion they used for the sorting. For example, Alex in the case study had focused on the property of colour, and her criterion for the way she sorted the cars was that she wanted to sort out the cars that were red.

As they progress in their sorting, children will begin to consider the properties of items not selected, or not meeting the criteria. For example, if a child sorts out the buses from a pile of vehicles, with support from an adult, he can begin to describe the discarded vehicles. What property do they share? They might include cars, lorries, aeroplanes and vans, and therefore be a diverse group, but what is important in this sort is that they are all 'not buses'. This language of not having a property is important for children's later sorting and their solving of logic problems. For example, later children in schools may come across problems such as 'Which whole numbers less than 10 are not multiples of three?'. It is as important to ask questions about the items disregarded as well as the selected group of items. Adults can help young children in their understanding of negative labels (for example, 'not buses', 'does not float') by careful questioning about their sortings.

Sorting by one property (for example, toys which are red/not red) is known as a 'one criterion sort'. With support, children then progress to sorting using more than one property, a 'two (or more) criteria sort'.

Young children sort their toys informally, taking out the toys they want from a box and leaving the rest inside, or choosing what they need and leaving the other items where they were. It is much easier for children to see the properties of the items they group and disregard if they are laid out more clearly. An adult might help the child to separate the items selected and disregarded, and therefore make talking about them easier. As they progress, distinct groups of items could be placed on separate pieces of paper, or in plastic hoops. This is the beginning of a progression towards the more formal recording of sorting in Venn and Carroll diagrams.

A Venn diagram should show all the data or items, called the universal set, in an enclosed rectangle (as in Figure 15.1). The property, or the criterion, which characterises the sort is used to label the circle inside.

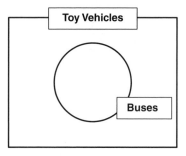

Figure 15.1 *Venn diagram for a one criterion sort*

A Venn diagram can also be used to show more than one criterion, which might or might not be intersecting. For example, children might sort the vehicles to make a group of buses and a group of lorries, and leave the other vehicles aside. There probably won't be a vehicle which is deemed to be both a bus and a lorry, so here the groups will not intersect (see Figure 15.2).

Alternatively, they might decide to look for all the red vehicles as well as choosing the buses. Some of the buses might be red, so in this case the groups will intersect (see Figure 15.3). Sometimes, one set might be part of another. For example, if children separate the cars from the other vehicles, they could then make a subset of blue cars, which would be part of the wider set of cars (see Figure 15.4).

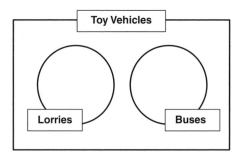

Figure 15.2 *Venn diagram for a non-intersecting two criteria sort*

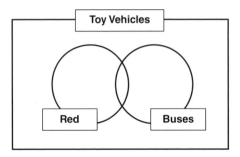

Figure 15.3   *Venn diagram for an intersecting two criteria sort*

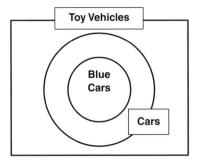

Figure 15.4   *Venn diagram for a two criteria sort involving a subset*

- What criteria might children use to sort numbers or shapes using an intersecting two criteria sort?

A Carroll diagram, named after Lewis Carroll, can also be used to record sorting. In a Carroll diagram, labels are given to each area to show whether the items inside the area meet or do not meet the criterion. An understanding of the language of not meeting the criterion is necessary for the Carroll diagram (see Figure 15.5).

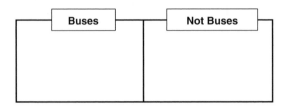

Figure 15.5   *Carroll diagram for a one criterion sort*

A Carroll diagram can be used to show items which are sorted according to two criteria (see Figure 15.6), which might be intersecting or non-intersecting.

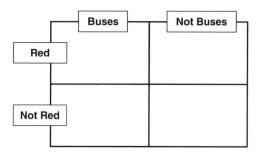

Figure 15.6 *Carroll diagram for a two criteria sort*

Sorting is a key skill in data handling and we have seen how it develops from early play to more complex sorting. When they collect themed cards, with information about characters or sports teams, children often sort these according to quite complex properties. Adults sort books and music collections, and their files and folders on computers in a similar way. Data handling is underpinned by an understanding of the properties which data share, and do not share.

Furthermore, sorting underpins children's understanding of the language of logic. Piaget (1953) claimed logic is important in structuring children's thinking, and argued that this develops during the concrete operation stage of development. Although his ideas of when logic first develops in children's thinking might be disputed, mathematics itself is certainly underpinned by logical ideas. Logic is used to prove whether mathematical ideas are true or false. As they sort, children begin to use the language and thinking of logic.

Sorting is also a key process which children use to understand other areas of mathematics. They explore properties of shapes and numbers, sorting these and using increasingly complex properties in their problem solving. For example, they might be asked to find all the even numbers which are multiples of 3. This develops their number sense (Anghileri, 2006) or general understanding of number. They might use the properties of cubes and cuboids to build stable towers. They will also learn about classification in science.

Sorting requires children to be methodical, checking each item against a criterion, and this methodical way of thinking is a key feature of mathematical investigation and problem solving. It is a valuable skill and one which adults can support in their questioning, even from an early age.

Progression in recording and representation of data

Young children often invent their own representations of data (see Figure 4.5 in Chapter 4). While these may not be conventional, children are still conveying meaning through these emergent representations. Adults can engage in meaningful discussions with children to explore their representations.

CASE STUDY

Pancake Day

A group of children are excitedly anticipating Pancake Day. The adult working with them, Tom, asks them to help him to gather information about their favourite toppings for pancakes. This will help him to buy the correct items for when they make pancake batter and eat pancakes together. The children are asked to choose between chocolate sauce, lemon and orange.

At the earliest stages of their understanding of recording and representing data, children will use the data itself as a representation. For example, young children use themselves to show their choice of pancake topping. Tom might arrange bottles of chocolate, lemon and orange sauce in different places in the room and ask the children to sit next to their favourite topping. In effect, the children constitute a frequency table, with each area of the room showing how many children prefer each topping, or the frequency of votes for each topping. Tom and the children counted those choosing each topping. This type of activity can be done in several ways. Circles or rectangles can be marked in chalk on the playground or with tape on the carpet and children asked to sit in a particular area according to the sorting they are doing as a class. Or they might be sorting toys, shoes or pencil cases, say, according to colour or type and the children put the actual toy, shoe or pencil case in the correct area. This is the simplest form of recording data because the items represent themselves.

The next step in the progression is to use a pictorial representation of the data. For example, the children might have pictures or photographs of themselves. When selecting their topping they place their picture next to it. They can see that their picture represents them. The children might count the pictures where they lie or discuss with Tom how the pictures might be counted more easily if they were arranged in lines. Sticking the pictures in three lines, one for each topping, creates a simple pictogram (see Figure 15.7). It is important for ease of comparison that the pictures are all the same size and are lined up carefully side by side.

Pictures can be replaced with blocks when children can cope with the increased level of abstraction involved. To develop children's understanding of block graphs, Tom might begin by giving each child an interlocking cube. Then the children would be invited to add their cube to make towers to show how many children prefer each topping. This forms a three-dimensional block graph, which is more usually drawn as a two-dimensional version. In a two-dimensional block graph, the number of people

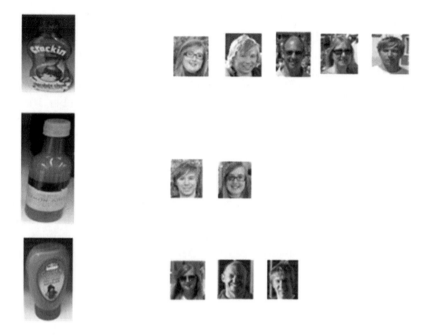

Figure 15.7 *Pictogram showing children's choices of toppings for pancakes*

choosing each topping is shown by colouring or sticking squares, or blocks, in adjacent lines (see Figure 15.8). The number of children choosing each topping is calculated by counting the blocks.

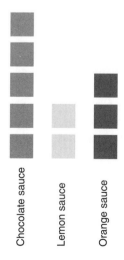

Figure 15.8 *Block graph showing children's choices of toppings for pancakes*

For most block graphs and pictograms, it is not necessary to have a vertical axis, as the information is found by counting the blocks or pictures. The horizontal axis is necessary to keep each line of blocks or pictures level, to aid comparison. Where the vertical axis of the pictogram or block graph is drawn and labelled with numbers, it is important to place the numbers next to the blocks or pictures, and in this way the vertical axes resembles the number track (see Chapter 9). The number 1 should be level with the first block, and therefore the counting begins from one rather than zero. There is a one-to-one correspondence (see Chapter 9) between each piece of data and each block or picture.

Another form of showing the data in a one-to-one correspondence is the tally chart (see Figure 15.9). Here, each piece of data is represented with a single mark in a frequency table showing how many times each data category occurs. These marks are arranged in fives in such a way that each group of five is easily identifiable. It is useful for counting larger numbers, where counting in fives rather than in ones is a more efficient form of counting. Children can best work with tally charts when they have learnt to count in fives.

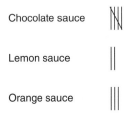

Chocolate sauce

Lemon sauce

Orange sauce

Figure 15.9 *Tally chart showing children's choices of toppings for pancakes*

The bar chart (see Figure 15.10) is the next stage in the progression. Here the data is represented as a continuous bar. Each individual piece of information is no longer identifiable. The measurement of the height of the bar tells us the amount for that particular category. Thus, the labelling of the vertical axis should allow the reading of the measurement of the top of each bar. In this way, the labelling of this axis resembles a number line (see Chapter 9). The numbers need to label the points on the axis, normally starting with zero.

Pictograms, block graphs and bar charts can be displayed vertically or horizontally. ICT packages enable children to compare representations quickly to decide which is most effective in displaying the data.

Data can be represented in more complex ways in which one-to-one correspondence is abandoned. Pictograms can be constructed where a key shows clearly that each picture might be worth two, five or ten pieces of data. The scale on the vertical

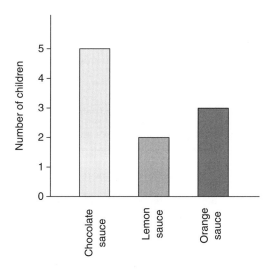

Figure 15.10 *Bar chart showing children's choice of toppings for pancakes*

axes of a bar chart might increase in twos, fives, tens or any other number rather than ones. This matches the development in children's counting from counting in ones, to counting in multiples.

Children also engage in different types of data as they progress in their understanding of data handling. Most of the data which children are asked to represent up to the age of 8 is what is termed as discrete. This is defined as information which can be sorted into separate and distinct categories (Haylock, 2010). It is usually gathered by counting. Children might collect discrete data such as their favourite playground game or their choice of packed lunch or school dinner. In these examples, there is no inherent order in the data and it would not be important to consider the order of each category. Sometimes the discrete data categories have an inherent order and it is normal to represent these categories in order, such as the birthday months of the children in the class or children's bedtimes.

Recording and representing data can be done in a number of ways. We might use a pictogram, a block graph or a bar chart to show the same information. Part of children's learning of data handling involves their evaluation of different ways of recording the same information (Barmby et al., 2009). ICT is a valuable tool here as it immediately forms graphs and charts which can easily be interchanged. Children can begin to say why one form of recording, say as a pictogram, might be clearer than another.

Line graphs, scattergrams and pie charts will also be introduced to children at a later stage as well as specific measures of average such as mean, mode and median.

Progression in interpreting data

Finally, we can also trace a progression in the questions children can answer in their interpretation of data.

- Questions which ask for one piece of information:
  - ○ Which is the most popular choice of pancake topping?
  - ○ How many children prefer orange on their pancakes?

- Questions which ask for interpretation of more than one piece of information:
  - ○ How many more children prefer lemon than orange on their pancake?
  - ○ How many people like orange or lemon on their pancake?

- Questions requiring reasoning:
  - ○ What would our findings look like if we asked the staff too?
  - ○ Why might more children prefer chocolate topping?
  - ○ If we asked the class next door would we get the same outcome?

Children's difficulties in data handling

Ryan and Williams (2007) analysed children's responses to a range of tasks where they were required to extract information from tables, charts and graphs. The authors discuss children's common errors to these questions. When young children are asked to interpret data to find one piece of information, they tend to answer with the most popular item, perhaps because this is the prototype question, the question they have been most usually asked in the past. This shows the importance of asking a range of questions, and encouraging children to ask their own questions about data. When interpreting more complex graphs, Ryan and Williams report that children often ignore the labelling of the vertical axis, assuming a unitary scale, increasing in ones. Children also need to experience representing and recording information using different scales so that considering the scale of the vertical axis is a natural part of interpreting a graph.

Summary

In this chapter we have argued that data handling is a key skill for adult life. As adults, we use data to solve problems, make judgements and to communicate ideas. We become aware that data can be used to persuade and mislead us. Children's use of data therefore needs to be purposeful. It should help them to solve meaningful problems and communicate information which matters to them. It is best considered as part of a cycle involving the asking and answering of a question. The use of ICT to draw graphs and charts can allow children to spend more time on interpreting data to solve problems. ICT also allows children to quickly move between representations of the same data in order to develop their skills of evaluating different ways in which data can be presented.

Children's understanding of data handling can be traced from their earliest experiences of handling items and exploring their properties. Sorting everyday items according to one criterion is the basis of more complex data handling. Children represent information in increasingly abstract ways. They answer more complex questions as their understanding develops.

Children will generate their own questions for data handling, if they are allowed the time to do so, and if the process of asking and answering a question using data is modelled for them. In this way, data handling is a natural way of solving meaningful problems.

Further reading

Haylock, D. (2010) *Mathematics Explained for Primary Teachers*, 4th edn. London: Sage.
This book provides a discussion of the subject knowledge required to teach data handling well and also refers to research which analyses the progression of children's understanding of each part of the data-handling process.
Sutherland, R. (2007) *Teaching for Learning Mathematics*. Maidenhead: Open University Press.
This book offers an analysis of data handling as a form of introducing children to mathematical thinking.
Barmby, P., Bilsborough, L., Harries, T. and Higgins, S. (2009) *Primary Mathematics: Teaching for Understanding*. Maidenhead: Open University Press.
This book has a chapter on data handling, tracing progression and discussing how best to teach children to understand the key ideas.

Glossary

Accountability	Being answerable to others and taking responsibility for decisions and actions for children's learning.
Agency	Having a sense of control over actions and choices.
Algorithm	A procedure for performing a calculation.
Analogue clock	A clock with a dial where the position of the hands indicates the time.
Associative Law	The associative law holds for addition and for multiplication only. It states that the outcome of an addition or multiplication is unchanged when operations are performed in a different order, for example, (3 + 4) + 5 = 3 + (4 + 5) and (2 × 5) × 4 = 2 × (5 × 4).
Axes	Vertical and horizontal lines used to frame graphs and charts.
Bar chart	A graphical data representation in which the length of bars is used to indicate the frequency of discrete data categories.
Base	The number of different digits used for representing numbers within a counting system.
Block graph	A data representation showing the frequency of discrete data categories by using blocks arranged in rows or columns. One block is shown for each piece of data.
Capacity	A measure of the space within a container or of the liquid or material poured into it.
Cardinal number	Using a number as a descriptor of the number of items in a set.
Cardinality	Knowing the last number in a count indicates the cardinal value of the set.
Carroll diagram	A sorting diagram with rectangular areas labelled with relevant criteria and their corresponding negations (for example, 'red' and 'not red').
Commutative law	The commutative law holds for addition and for multiplication only. It states that the answer to an addition or multiplication is unchanged when the numbers on either side of the operation sign are interchanged, for example 4 + 2 = 2 + 4 and 5 x 7 = 7 × 5.
Common denominators	Fractions with the same denominator, for example $4/5$, $7/5$, $1/5$.

Concept	An abstract, generalised idea.
Conjecture	A proposed general statement about a pattern which has yet to be verified.
Consecutive numbers	Whole numbers which follow one another in the counting sequence.
Conservation (of number or measures)	Knowing that a quantity is still the same (without recounting or re-measuring) regardless of its arrangement.
Continuous data	Data which can take any value on a continuum, usually collected by measuring.
Criterion	An attribute used to decide whether an item is included in, or excluded from, a set when sorting.
Data (plural), datum (singular)	Pieces of information, often displayed in graphs, lists or tables.
Decimal	A fractional number expressed using the base 10 place value system extended to include tenths, hundredths, thousandths, and so on.
Denominator	The bottom number in a written fraction, representing the number of parts into which a whole has been divided.
Diagnostic assessment	Assessment designed to diagnose the cause of a difficulty experienced by a child.
Digits	The set of ten symbols (0–9) used to write whole numbers (for example, in the number 25 the digits are 2 and 5).
Digital clock	A clock which uses digits to display the number of hours and minutes in either 12-hour or 24-hour format.
Discrete data	Data which belong to one of a number of distinct categories and are normally collected by counting.
Distributive law	The distribution of one operation over another. The distributive law for multiplication over addition or subtraction states that partitioning a number and multiplying its component parts separately has the same outcome as multiplying the number, for example we could calculate 3×25 using $3 \times (20 + 5) = (3 \times 20) + (3 \times 5)$ and 4×19 using $4 \times (20 - 1) = (4 \times 20) - (4 \times 1)$. The distributive law also holds for division over addition and subtraction (provided the division is to the right of the addition or subtraction), for example for $36 \div 2$ we can calculate $(30 + 6) \div 2 = (30 \div 2) + (6 \div 2)$ and for $56 \div 2$ we can calculate $(60 - 4) \div 2 = (60 \div 2) - (4 \div 2)$.
Equivalent	Equal in value but may be represented differently, for example $1/2 = 2/4 = 0.5$.
Evaluative assessment	Assessment to judge the quality of teaching and learning.
Factor	A number that divides exactly into another number.
Factorise	Writing a number as a multiplication of its factors.

Formative assessment	Assessment at the time of teaching which enables an adult to identify the next steps in learning.
Fractions	A way of representing part of a whole, or part of a set.
Free-flow play	Play in which children select activities and resources.
Frequency table	A table showing how many times each data category occurs.
Generalising	Forming a general idea, conclusion or concept by recognising common properties of instances.
Idiosyncratic	Peculiar, or particular, to the individual.
Improper fractions	Fractions where the numerator is greater than the denominator (sometimes called 'top-heavy' fractions), such as $3/_2$.
Inverse operation	A mathematical operation which reverses the effect of another operation.
Line graph	A representation of continuous data shown by a continuous line.
Mass	The measure of the quantity of matter in an object.
Mean	The average of a set of data found by adding all the data values and dividing by the number of data values.
Median	The middle data value in an ordered set of data. If there are two middle values, the median is the mean of the two.
Misconception	Partial, faulty or alternative conceptions based on incomplete or immature reasoning or under- or over-generalisations.
Mixed numbers	A fraction between two whole numbers which is expressed as a whole number and a fractional part, for example $4\ 1/_2$.
Mode	The most frequent data value.
Motif	The repeating unit within a pattern.
Multiple	A number that can be made by multiplying a given number by another, for example 10, 15 and 20 are multiples of 5.
Natural numbers	The positive whole numbers 1, 2, 3 …
Net	A flat shape which can be folded up into a three-dimensional solid.
Nominal number	The use of a number as a label.
Numerals	The symbols (1, 2, 3 …) used to represent numbers.
Numerator	The top part of a written fraction, representing the number of equal parts taken from a whole.
One-to-one correspondence	Matching or pairing the contents of two sets (a set may be a set of items, symbols, or counting numbers) such that every element of one set is paired with a corresponding element of the second set and no elements of either set are left unpaired.

Operation	A mathematical function which produces an output value from one or more input values (for example addition, subtraction, multiplication and division).
Ordinal number	Using numbers to indicate position or order.
Ordinality	Knowing the order of the numbers.
Partitioning	Splitting a number into parts, for example hundreds, tens and ones.
Pictogram	A data representation using pictures or icons displayed in vertical or horizontal lines.
Pie chart	A data representation showing data categories proportionally as sectors of a circle.
Polygon	A two-dimensional closed shape with only straight sides.
Regular polygon	A polygon in which all the sides are equal in length and all the angles are the same size.
Rich task	Non-routine tasks that promote mathematical thinking and talk.
Role-play	Playful imitation of the roles of others (for example teacher, dog, policeman).
Scattergram	A data representation for two variables showing a set of data plotted as points to explore possible relationships.
Schemas	Repeated behaviours that characterise children's exploration of particular ideas and concepts (for example enclosing, rotating or transforming).
Small world play	Using toys such as trains, farm animals or people to symbolise characters or objects.
Subitising	Instant recognition of small quantities without explicitly counting.
Summative assessment	Assessment designed to make a judgement about what children know, understand or are able to do at a certain point in time.
Tally	A counting record in which vertical marks are made for each item, with every fifth mark made diagonally.
Taxonomy	A classification into categories, based on similarities.
Tessellation	Covering a flat surface using repeated shapes without overlaps or gaps between them.
Topology	The study of properties that are preserved when objects are deformed, twisted, and stretched. For example, in topology a square and a circle are said to be equivalent because one can be stretched or squeezed to look like the other.
Transformation	Changing a shape by applying the same process to each point in the shape, for example, through:
	Translation: sliding a shape in a straight line from one position to another, without turning

Rotation: turning a shape through an angle about a point (known as the centre of rotation)

Reflection: reflecting a shape in a mirror line

Enlargement: enlarging a shape by a scale factor.

Venn diagram A sorting diagram, with the whole or universal set enclosed by a rectangle and, within this, subsets, usually shown as circles, each labelled by the relevant criterion.

Volume The amount of space occupied by an object.

Weight The force exerted on an object by gravity.

Zero as a placeholder The use of zero digits to mark empty places within numbers and so 'hold' the place of the other (non-zero) digits.

References

Advisory Committee on Mathematics Education (ACME) (2008) *Mathematics in Primary Years: A Discussion Paper for the Rose Review of the Primary Curriculum.* Available at: http://www.acme-uk.org/media/1769/rose%20review%20maths%20paper%20final%20sept%2008.pdf (accessed 3 January 2013).

Allen, R.E. (1990) *The Concise Oxford Dictionary of Current English.* Oxford: Oxford University Press.

Alexander, R. (2004) *Towards Dialogic Teaching: Rethinking Classroom Talk.* York: Dialogos.

Alloway, T.P. (2006) 'How does working memory work in the classroom?' *Educational Research and Reviews,* 1(4): 134–9.

Anghileri, J. (2001) 'Development of division strategies for Year 5 pupils in ten English schools'. *British Educational Research Journal,* 27(1): 85–103.

Anghileri, J. (2006) *Teaching Number Sense,* 2nd edn. London: Continuum.

Anghileri, J. (2008) 'Uses of counting in multiplication and division', in I. Thompson (ed.) *Teaching and Learning Early Number.* Maidenhead: Open University Press.

Anning, A., Cullen, J. and Fleer, M. (2004) *Early Childhood Education: Society and Culture.* London: Sage.

Askew, M. (2012) *Transforming Primary Mathematics.* Abingdon: Routledge.

Askew, M., Bibby, T. and Brown, M. (2001) *Raising Attainment in Primary Number Sense: from Counting to Strategy.* London: Beam Education.

Askew, M., Brown, M., Rhodes, V., Wiliam, D. and Johnson, D. (1997) *Effective Teachers of Numeracy: Report of a Study Carried Out for the Teacher Training Agency.* London: King's College, University of London.

Atherton, J.S. (2011) *Learning and Teaching; Constructivism in Learning.* Available at: http://www.learningandteaching.info/learning/constructivism.htm#Vygotsky (accessed 5 February 2013).

Athey, C. (1990) *Extending Thought in Young Children: A Parent–Teacher Partnership.* London: Paul Chapman.

Atkinson, S. (1992) *Mathematics with Reason: The Emergent Approach to Primary Maths.* London: Hodder and Stoughton.

Barmby, P., Bilsborough, L., Harries, T. and Higgins, S. (2009) *Primary Mathematics: Teaching for Understanding.* Maidenhead: Open University Press.

Barmby, P., Harries, T. and Higgins, S. (2010) 'Teaching for Understanding/Understanding for Teaching', in I. Thompson (ed.) *Issues in Teaching Numeracy in Primary Schools.* 2nd edn. Maidenhead: Open University Press.

Baroody, A.J. (1987) *Children's Mathematical Thinking.* New York: Teachers College Press.

Baroody, A., Bajwa, N. and Eiland, M. (2009) 'Why can't Johnny remember the basic facts?' *Developmental Disabilities Research Reviews*, 15(1): 69–79.

Beckett, C., Maughan, B., Rutter, M., Castle, J., Colvert, E., Groothues, C., Kreppner, J., Stevens, S., O'Connor, T.G. and Sonuga-Barke, E.J.S. (2006) 'Do the effects of early severe deprivation on cognition persist into early adolescence? Findings from the English and Romanian Adoptees Study', *Child Development*, 77(3): 696–711.

Beckley, P. (2011) *Learning in Early Childhood*. London: Sage.

Bell, A.W. (1993) 'Some experiments in diagnostic teaching', *Educational Studies in Mathematics*, 24(1): 115–37.

Bermejo, V. (1996) 'Cardinality development and counting', *Developmental Psychology*, 32(2): 263–68.

Bermejo, V., Morales, S. and deOsuna, J.G. (2004) 'Supporting children's development of cardinality understanding', *Learning and Instruction*, 14(4): 381–98.

Bilton, H. (2002) *Outdoor Play in the Early Years: Management and Innovation*, 2nd edn. London: David Fulton.

Black, P. and Wiliam, D. (1998) *Inside the Black Box: Raising Standards through Classroom Assessment*. London: King's College.

Blake, Q. (2010) *Mr Magnolia*. London: Random House Children's Books.

Blinko, J. (2000) *Shape, Space and Measure*. London: A and C Black.

Bloom, B.S. (Ed.), Engelhart, M.D., Furst, E.J., Hill, W.H., & Krathwohl, D.R. (1956) *Taxonomy of Educational Objectives: The Classification of Educational Goals. Handbook 1: Cognitive Domain*. New York: David McKay.

Boaler, J. (2009) *The Elephant in the Classroom*. London: Souvenir Press.

Bottle, G. (1999) 'A study of children's mathematical experiences in the home', *Early Years: An International Journal of Research and Development*, 20(1): 53–64.

Bottle, G., Donaldson, G., Birrell, D., Harris, A., Taylor, H., Lawrence, C. and Wild, J. (2005) *Teaching Mathematics in the Primary School*. London: Continuum.

Boulet, G. (1998) 'Didactical implications of children's difficulties in learning the fraction concept', *Focus on Learning Problems in Mathematics*, 20(4): 19–34.

Boulton-Lewis, G. (1987) 'Recent cognitive theories applied to sequential length measuring knowledge in young children', *British Journal of Educational Psychology*, 57(3): 330–42.

Briggs, M. and Davis, S. (2008) *Creative Teaching: Mathematics in the Early Years and Primary Classroom*. Abingdon: Routledge.

Briggs, M. and Hansen, A. (2012) *Play-based Learning in the Primary School*. London: Sage.

Brown, T. and Leibling, H. (2007) *The Really Useful Maths Book: A Guide to Interactive Teaching*, 2nd edn. Abingdon: Routledge.

Bruce, R.A. (2000) 'Factors within pre-school educational establishments that affect the number attainment of the young child', unpublished EdD thesis. University of Leeds.

Bruce, R.A. and Threlfall, J. (2004) 'One, two, three and counting', *Educational Studies in Mathematics*, 55(1–3): 3–26.

Bruce, T. (1991) *Time to Play: In Early Childhood Education*. Abingdon: Hodder and Stoughton.

Bruce, T. (2001) *Learning Through Play: Babies, Toddlers and the Foundation Years*. London: Hodder and Stoughton.

Bruce, T. (2004) *Developing Learning in Early Childhood*. London: Sage.

Bruce, T. (2005) *Early Childhood Education*, 3rd edn. London: Hodder and Stoughton.

Bruner, J.S. (1966) *Toward a Theory of Instruction*. Cambridge, MA: Belknap Press.

Bruner, J.S. (1983) *Child's Talk*. New York: Norton.

Bruner, J. (1986) *Actual Minds, Possible Worlds*. Cambridge, MA and London: Harvard University Press.

Bruner, J. (1990) *Acts of Meaning*. Cambridge, MA: Harvard University Press.

Bruner, J.S. and Kenney, H.J. (1974) 'Representation and Mathematics Learning'. In J.S. Bruner *Beyond the Information Given: Studies in the Psychology of Knowing*. London: Allen and Unwin.

Bryant, P. (2009) *Key Understandings in Mathematics Learning: Paper 5: Understanding Space and its Representation in Mathematics*. London: Nuffield Foundation.

Carle, E. (1969) *The Very Hungry Caterpillar*. London: Penguin Books.

Carpenter, T.P. and Moser, J.M. (1983) 'The acquisition of addition and subtraction concepts', in Lesh, R. and Landau, M. (eds) *Acquisition of Mathematical Concepts and Processes*. New York: Academic Press.

Carpenter, T.P. and Moser, J.M. (1984) 'The acquisition of addition and subtraction concepts in grades one through three', *Journal for Research into Mathematics Education*, 15(3): 179–202.

Carraher, T.N., Carraher, D.W. and Schliemann, A.D. (1985) 'Mathematics in the streets and in schools', *British Journal of Developmental Psychology*, 3(1): 21–9.

Carruthers, E. (2007) 'Children's outdoor experiences: A sense of adventure?', in J. Moyles (ed.) *Early Years Foundations: Meeting the Challenge*. Maidenhead: Open University Press.

Carruthers, E. and Worthington, M. (2006) *Children's Mathematics: Making Marks, Making Meaning*, 2nd edn. London: Sage.

Carruthers, E. and Worthington, M. (2008) 'Children's mathematical graphics: Young children calculating for meaning', in I. Thompson (ed.) *Teaching and Learning Early Number*, 2nd edn. Maidenhead: Open University Press.

Carruthers, E. and Worthington, M. (2011) *Children's Mathematics Network*. Available at: http://www.childrens-mathematics.net/ (accessed 16 January 2013).

Castle, K. and Needham, J. (2007) 'First graders' understanding of measurement', *Early Childhood Education Journal*, 35(3): 215–21.

Catterall, R. (2008) 'Doing time', *Mathematics Teaching*, 209: 37–39.

Central Advisory Council for Education (England) (CACE) (1967) *The Plowden Report: Children and their Primary Schools*. London: Her Majesty's Stationery Office.

Clark, A. and Moss, P. (2011) *Listening to Young Children: The Mosaic Approach*, 2nd edn. London: National Children's Bureau and Joseph Rowntree Foundation.

Clausen-May, T. (2005) *Teaching Maths to Pupils with Different Learning Styles*. London: Paul Chapman.

Clemson, D. and Clemson, W. (1994) *Mathematics in the Early Years*. London: Routledge.

Cockburn, A.D. and Littler, G. (2008) *Mathematical Misconceptions: A Guide for Primary Teachers*. London: Sage.

Copley, J.V. (2000) *The Young Child and Mathematics*. Washington, DC: NAEYC.

Cowan, R., Dowker, A., Christakis, A. and Bailey, S. (1996) 'Even more precisely assessing children's understanding of the order-irrelevance principle', *Journal of Experimental Child Psychology*, 62(1): 84–101.

Cox, T. and Sanders, S. (1994) *The Impact of the National Curriculum on the Teaching of Five Year Olds*. London: Falmer Press.

Cunningham, K. (2007) 'The environment and the outdoor classroom as a mathematical resource', in D. Drews and A. Hansen (eds) *Using Resources to Support Mathematical Thinking*. Exeter: Learning Matters.

Dabell, J. (2008) 'Using concept cartoons', *Mathematics Teaching*, 209: 34–6.

DCSF (2007) *The Children's Plan: Building Brighter Futures*. Norwich: Her Majesty's Stationery Office.

DCSF (2008) *Independent Review of Mathematics Teaching in Early Years Settings and Primary Schools*. Nottingham: DCSF.

De Abreu, G. and Cline, T. (2005) 'Parents' representations of their children's mathematics learning in multi-ethnic primary schools', *British Educational Research Journal*, 31(6): 697–722.

Dehaene, S. (1997) *The Number Sense*. Harmondsworth: Penguin Press.

Delaney, K. (2010) 'Making connections: Teachers and children using resources effectively', in I. Thompson (ed.) *Issues in Teaching Numeracy in Primary Schools*, 2nd edn. Maidenhead: Open University Press.

De Moor, E. (2005) 'Domain description geometry', in M. van den Heuvel-Panhuizen and K. Buys (eds) *Young Children Learn Measurement and Geometry: A Learning-Teaching Trajectory with Intermediate Attainment Targets for the Lower Grades in Primary School*. Utrecht: Freudenthal Institute, Utrecht University.

DES (1982) *Mathematics Counts*. London: HMSO.

DES (1988) *National Curriculum Task Group on Assessment and Testing: A Report*. London: DES.

Desforges, C. and Abouchaar, A. (2003) *The Impact of Parental Involvement, Parental Support and Family Education on Pupil Achievement and Adjustment: A Literature Review* (Research Report 433). London: DfES.

DfE (2012a) *Statutory Framework for the Early Years Foundation Stage*. Available at: https://www.education.gov.uk/publications/standard/publicationDetail/Page1/DFE-00023-2012 (accessed 6 February 2013).

DfE (2012b) *Teachers' Standards*. Available at: https://www.education.gov.uk/publications/standard/SchoolsSO/Page1/DFE-00066-2011 (accessed 6 February 2013).

DfEE (1999a) *The National Curriculum: Handbook for Primary Teachers in England*. London: DfEE and QCA.

DfEE (1999b) *The National Numeracy Strategy: Framework for Teaching Mathematics from Reception to Year 6*. Sudbury: DfEE.

DfES (2006) *Primary National Strategy: Primary Framework for Literacy and Mathematics*. Norwich: DfES.

DfES (2007a) *Every Parent Matters*. Available at: https://www.education.gov.uk/publications/eOrderingDownload/Every%20Parent%20Matters.pdf (accessed 6 February 2013).

DfES (2007b) *The Early Years Foundation Stage: Setting the Standards for Learning, Development and Care for Children from Birth to Five*. Nottingham: DfES.

Dickson, L., Brown, M. and Gibson, O. (1984) *Children Learning Mathematics: A Teacher's Guide to Recent Research*. London: Cassell.

Dockett, S. and Fleer, M. (1999) *Play and Pedagogy in Early Childhood*. Marrickville, NSW: Harcourt Brace.

Docking, J. (1990) *Primary Schools and Parents, Rights, Responsibilities and Relationships*. London: Hodder and Stoughton.

Donaldson, G. (2007) 'Inner city spaces', in R. Austin (ed.) *Letting the Outside In: Developing Teaching and Learning beyond the Early Years Classroom*. Stoke-on-Trent: Trentham Books.

Donaldson, M. (1978) *Children's Minds*. London: Fontana.

Dowker, A. (2008) 'Individual differences in numerical abilities in pre-schoolers', *Developmental Science*, 11(5): 650–54.

Downton, A. (2010) 'Challenging multiplicative problems can elicit sophisticated strategies', in L. Sparrow, B. Kissane and C. Hurst (eds) *Shaping the Future of Mathematics Education*

(Proceedings of the 33rd Annual Conference of the Mathematics Education Research Group of Australasia), 169–76. Fremantle: MERGA.

Drews, D. (2011) 'Errors and misconceptions: The teachers' role', in A. Hansen (ed.) *Children's Errors in* Mathematics, 2nd edn. Exeter: Learning Matters.

Drews, D. and Hansen, A. (eds) (2007) *Using Resources to Support Mathematical Thinking: Primary and Early Years.* Exeter: Learning Matters.

Dudgeon, J. and Hansen, A. (2011) 'Measures', in A. Hansen (ed.) *Children's Errors in Mathematics*, 2nd edn. Exeter: Learning Matters.

Dunhill, A., Elliott, B. and Shaw, A. (2009) *Effective Communication and Engagement with Children and Young People, their Families and Carers.* Exeter: Learning Matters.

Ell, F., Irwin, K., and McNaughton, S. (2004) 'Two pathways to multiplicative thinking', in I. Putt, R. Faragher and M. McLean (eds) *Mathematics Education for the Third Millennium, Towards 2010* (Proceedings of the 27th Annual Conference of the Mathematics Education Research Group of Australasia, Townsville), 199–206. Sydney: MERGA.

ESTYN (2009) *Best Practice in Mathematics for Pupils Aged 3 to 7 Years.* Available at: http://www.estyn.gov.uk/english/docViewer/177531.9/best-practice-in-mathematics-for-pupils-aged-3-to-7-years-june-2009/?navmap=30,163 (accessed 6 February 2013).

ESTYN (2011) *Literacy and the Foundation Stage.* Available at: http://www.estyn.gov.uk/english/docViewer/228910.5/literacy-and-the-foundation-phase-september-2011/?navmap=30,163 (accessed 6 February 2013).

Field, F. (2010) *The Foundation Years: Preventing Poor Children Becoming Poor Adults: The Report of the Independent Review on Poverty and Life Chances.* London: HM Government. Available at: http://www.nfm.org.uk/component/jdownloads/finish/74/333 (accessed 6 February 2013).

Fischbein, E., Deri, M., Nello, M.S. and Marino, M.S. (1985) 'The role of implicit models in solving verbal problems in multiplication and division', *Journal for Research in Mathematics Education*, 16(1): 3–17.

Foxman, D. and Beishuizen, M. (2002) 'Mental calculation methods used by 11 year olds in different attainment bands: A reanalysis of data from the 1987 APU survey in the UK', *Educational Studies in Mathematics*, 51(1/2): 41–69.

Freudenthal, H. (1973) *Mathematics as an Educational Task.* Dordrecht: D. Reidel.

Frobisher, L., Monaghan, J., Orton, A., Orton, J., Roper, T. and Threlfall, J. (1999) *Learning to Teach Number: A Handbook for Students and Teachers in the Primary School.* Cheltenham: Stanley Thornes.

Frobisher, L., Frobisher, A., Orton, A. and Orton, J. (2007) *Learning to Teach Shape and Space: A Handbook for Students and Teachers in the Primary School.* Cheltenham: Nelson Thornes.

Fry, S. (2012) *Grandpa's Garden.* Oxford: Barefoot Books.

Fuson, K. (1988) *Children's Counting and Concepts of Number.* New York: Springer-Verlag.

Gelman, R. and Gallistel, C. (1978) *The Child's Understanding of Number.* Cambridge: Harvard University Press.

Gifford, S. (2005) *Teaching Mathematics 3–5: Developing Learning in the Foundation Stage.* Maidenhead: Open University Press.

Gifford, S. (2008) '"How do you teach nursery children mathematics?" In search of a mathematics pedagogy in the early years', in I. Thompson (ed.) *Teaching and Learning Early Number*, 2nd edn. Maidenhead: Open University Press.

Glazzard, J., Chadwick, D., Webster, A. and Percival, J. (2010) *Assessment for Learning in the Early Years Foundation Stage.* London: Sage.

Greer, B. (1992) 'Multiplication and Division as Models of Situations', in D. Grouws (ed.) *Handbook of Research on Mathematics Teaching and Learning.* New York: Macmillan.

Hansen, A. (ed.) (2011) *Children's Errors in Mathematics*, 2nd edn. Exeter: Learning Matters.

Hansen, A. and Vaukins, D. (2012) *Primary Mathematics across the Curriculum*, 2nd edn. London: Sage.

Haylock, D. (2010) *Mathematics Explained for Primary Teachers*, 4th edn. London: Sage.

Haylock, D. and Cockburn, A. (2013) *Understanding Mathematics for Young Children*, 4th edn. London: Sage.

Headington, R. (2011) 'Assessment and accountability', in J. Moyles, J. Georgesen and J. Payler (eds) *Beginning Teaching: Beginning Learning in Early Years and Primary* Education, 4th edn. Maidenhead: Open University Press.

Hegarty, P. (1996) 'Quality on display: Tasks, learning and the classroom', in H. Cooper, P. Hegarty, P. Hegarty and N. Simco (eds) (1996) *Display in the Classroom*. London: David Fulton.

Heirdsfield, A.M., Cooper, T.J., Mulligan, J. and Irons, C.J. (1999) 'Children's multiplication and division strategies', in O. Zaslavsky (ed.) *Proceedings of the 23rd Psychology of Mathematics Education Conference*, 3: 89–96. Haifa, Israel: PME.

Higgins, S. (2008) 'Mathematical learning and the use of information and communications technology in the early years', in I. Thompson. (ed.) *Teaching and Learning Early Number*, 2nd edn. Maidenhead: Open University Press.

Hobart, C. and Frankel, J. (2009) *A Practical Guide to Child Observation and Assessment*, 4th edn. Cheltenham: Nelson Thornes.

Hodgen, J. and Askew, M. (2010) 'Assessment for learning: What is all the fuss about?', in I. Thompson (ed.) *Issues in Teaching Numeracy in Primary Schools*, 2nd edn. Maidenhead: Open University Press.

Hopkins, C., Pope, S. and Pepperell, S. (2004) *Understanding Primary Mathematics*. London: David Fulton.

Hughes, B. (2012) *Evolutionary Playwork*, 2nd edn. Abingdon: Routledge.

Hughes, M. (1975) 'Egocentrism in preschool children', unpublished doctoral dissertation, Edinburgh University.

Hughes, M. (1986) *Children and Number: Difficulties in Learning Mathematics*. Oxford: Basil Blackwell.

Hughes, M. and Pollard, A. (2006) 'Home–school knowledge exchange in context', *Educational Review*, 58(4): 385–95.

Husbands, C. (2012) 'What we need to learn from the tiger mothers', *Times Educational Supplement*, 27 January 2012. Available at: http://www.tes.co.uk/article.aspx?storycode=6169467 (accessed 6 February 2013).

Johnston-Wilder, S. and Mason, J. (2005) *Developing Thinking in Geometry*. London: Paul Chapman.

Joyce, R. (2012) *Outdoor Learning: Past and Present*. Maidenhead: Open University Press.

Keijzer, R. and Terwel, J. (2004) 'A low-achiever's learning process in mathematics: Shirley's fraction learning', *Journal of Classroom Instruction*, 39(2): 10–23.

Kershner, R. and Pointon, P. (2000) 'Children's views of the primary classroom as an environment for work and learning', *Research in Education*, 64(1): 64–77.

Knight, S. (2009) *Forest Schools and Outdoor Learning in the Early Years*. London: Sage.

Koshy, V., Ernest, P. and Casey, R. (2000) *Mathematics for Primary Teachers*. London: Routledge.

Kouba, V.L. (1989) 'Children's solution strategies for equivalent set multiplication and division word problems', *Journal for Research in Mathematics Education*, 20(2): 147–58.

Krathwohl, D.R. (2002) 'A revision of Bloom's taxonomy: An overview', *Theory into Practice*, 41(4): 212–18.

Laevers, F. (1994) *The Innovative Project: Experiential Education 1976–1995*. Leuven: Research Centre for Early Childhood and Primary Education.

Lawton, F. and Hansen, A. (2011) 'Numbers and the number system', in A. Hansen (ed.) *Children's Errors in Mathematics*, 2nd edn. Exeter: Learning Matters.

Learning Outside the Classroom. Available at: http://www.lotc.org.uk/why/early-years/ (accessed 15 February 2013).

Lee, C. (2006) *Language for Learning Mathematics: Assessment for Learning in Practice*. Maidenhead: Open University Press.

LeFevre, J., Smith-Chant, B., Fast, L., Skwarchuk, S., Sargla, E., Arnup, J., Penner-Wigler, M., Bisanz, J. and Kamawar, D. (2006) 'What counts as knowing? The development of conceptual and procedural knowledge of counting from kindergarten through Grade 2', *Journal of Experimental Child Psychology*, 93(4): 285–303.

Liebeck, P. (1984) *How Children Learn Mathematics*. London: Penguin.

Littler, G. and Jirotkova, D. (2008) 'Highlighting the learning process', in A.D. Cockburn and G. Littler (eds) *Mathematical Misconceptions: A Guide for Primary Teachers*. London: Sage.

MacGregor, H. (1998) *Tom Thumb's Musical Maths*. London: A and C Black.

Maclellan, E. (2008) 'Counting: What it is and why it matters', in I. Thompson (ed.) *Teaching and Learning Early Number*, 2nd edn. Maidenhead: Open University Press.

Maclellan, E. (2012) 'Number sense: The underpinning understanding for early quantitative literacy', *Numeracy*, 5(2) Article 3. Available at: http://dx.doi.org/10.5038/1936-4660.5.2.3 (accessed 6 February 2013).

MaLT (2005) *Mathematics Assessment for Learning and Teaching*. London: Hodder and Stoughton.

Mansergh, J. (2009) *Tables with a Number Stick*. Derby: Association of Teachers of Mathematics. Available at: http://www.youtube.com/watch?v=yXdHGBfoqfw (accessed 6 February 2013).

Mason, J., Burton, L. and Stacey, K. (2010) *Thinking Mathematically*, 2nd edn. Harlow: Pearson.

Matthews, J. (2003) *Drawing and Painting – Children and Visual Representation*, 2nd edn. London: Sage.

Maynard, T. (2007) 'Making the best of what you've got: Adopting and adapting the forest school approach', in R. Austin (ed.) *Letting the Outside in: Developing Teaching and Learning beyond the Early Years Classroom*. Stoke-on-Trent: Trentham Books.

McGrath, C. (2010) *Supporting Early Mathematical Development*. Abingdon: Routledge.

McIntosh, A., Reys, B. and Reys, R. (1992) 'A proposed framework for examining number sense', *For the Learning of Mathematics*, 12(3): 25–31.

Milbourne, A. (2007) *How Big is a Million?* London: Usbourne.

Moll, L., Amanti, C., Neff, D. and Gonzalez, N. (1992) 'Funds of knowledge for teaching: Using a qualitative approach to connect homes and classrooms', *Theory Into Practice*, 31(2), 132–41.

Montague-Smith, A. (1997) *Mathematics in Nursery Education*. London: David Fulton.

Montague-Smith, A. and Price, A. (2012) *Mathematics in Early Years Education,* 3rd edn. London: Routledge.

Mooney, C., Briggs, M., Fletcher, M., Hansen, A. and McCullouch, J. (2012a) *Primary Mathematics: Teaching Theory and Practice*, 6th edn. London: Sage.

Mooney, C., Ferrie, L., Fox, S., Hansen, A. and Wrathmell R. (2012b) *Primary Mathematics Knowledge and Understanding*, 6th edn. London: Sage.

Moseley, C. (2010) 'Stories for primary mathematics', *Mathematics Teaching*, 219: 16–17.

Moss, G. (2001) 'Seeing with the camera: Analysing children's photographs of literacy in the home', *Journal of Research in Reading*, 24(3): 266–78.

Moyles, J. (2005) *The Excellence of Play*. Maidenhead: Open University Press.

Moyles, J. (ed.) (2010) *Thinking About Play: Developing a Reflective Approach*. Maidenhead: Open University Press.

Muijs, D. and Reynolds, D. (2005) *Effective Teaching*, 2nd edn. London: Sage.

Mulligan, J. and Mitchelmore, M. (1997) 'Young children's intuitive models of multiplication and division', *Journal for Research in Mathematics Education*, 28(3): 309–30.

Mulligan, J. and Mitchelmore, M. (2009) 'Awareness of pattern and structure in early mathematical development', *Mathematics Education Research Journal*, 21(2): 33–49.

Munn, P. (2008) 'Children's beliefs about counting', in I. Thompson (ed.) *Teaching and Learning Early Number*, 2nd edn. Maidenhead: Open University Press.

Murphy, S. (2001) *Captain Invincible and the Space Shapes*. New York: Harper Collins.

National Centre for Excellence in Teaching Mathematics. Available at: https://www.ncetm.org.uk/resources/9268 (accessed 15 February 2013).

Nicholson, S. (1972) 'The theory of loose parts: An important principle for design', *Studies in Design Education Craft and Technology*, 4(2): 5–14. Available at: http://ojs.lboro.ac.uk/ojs/index.php/SDEC/article/view/1204/1171 (accessed 6 February 2013).

Nunes, T., Bryant, P., Hurry, J. and Pretzlik, U. (2006) *Fractions: Difficult but Crucial in Mathematics Learning*. London: Teaching and Learning Research Programme. Available at: http://www.tlrp.org/pub/documents/no13_nunes.pdf (accessed 6 February 2013).

Nunes, T., Bryant, P., Sylva, K. and Barros, R. (2009a) *Development of Maths Capabilities and Confidence in Primary School. Research Brief DCSF-RB118* London: DSCF.

Nunes, T., Bryant, P. and Watson, A. (2009b) *Key Understandings in Mathematics Learning: A Review Commissioned by the Nuffield Foundation*. London: Nuffield Foundation.

Nunes, T., Light, P. and Mason, J. (1993) 'Tools for thought: The measurement of length and area', *Learning and Instruction*, 3(1): 39–54.

Nutbrown, C. (2011) *Threads of Thinking*, 4th edn. London: Sage.

OECD (2010) *PISA 2009 Results: What Students Know and Can Do – Student Performance in Reading, Mathematics and Science (Volume I)*. OECD. Available at: http://dx.doi.org/10.1787/9789264091450-en (accessed 25 May 2012).

OfSTED (2008) *Mathematics: Understanding the Score*. London: OfSTED.

Orton, A. (ed.) (2005) *Pattern in the Teaching and Learning of Mathematics*. London: Cassell.

Osana, H.P. and Rayner, V. (2010) 'Developing numeracy: Promoting a rich learning environment for young children', *Encyclopedia of Language and Literacy Development* (pp. 1–12). London, ON: Canadian Language and Literacy Research Network. Available at: http://www.literacyencyclopedia.ca/pdfs/topic.php?topId=286 (accessed 6 February 2013).

O'Sullivan, L., Harris, A., Sangster, M., Donaldson, G., Wild, J. and Bottle, G. (2005) *Reflective Reader: Primary Mathematics*. Exeter: Learning Matters.

Ouvry, M. (2003) *Exercising Muscles and Minds*. London: National Children's Bureau.

Pagni, D. (2004) 'Fractions and decimals', *Australian Mathematics Teacher*, 60(4): 28–30.

Palaiologou, I. (2008) *Childhood Observation*. Exeter: Learning Matters.

Papatheodorou, T. and Luff, P. with Gill, J. (2012) *Child Observation for Learning and Research*. Harlow: Pearson.

Parker-Rees, R., Leeson, C., Willan, J. and Savage, J. (2010) *Early Childhood Studies*, 3rd edn. Exeter: Learning Matters.

Pepperell, S., Hopkins, C., Gifford, S. and Tallant, P. (2009) *Mathematics in the Primary School: A Sense of Progression*, 3rd edn. Abingdon: Routledge.

Piaget, J. (1953) *Logic and Psychology*. Manchester: Manchester University Press.

Piaget, J. (1962) *Play, Dreams and Imitation in Childhood*. New York: Norton.

Piaget, J. (1965) *The Child's Conception of Number.* New York: Norton.

Piaget, J. and Inhelder, B. (1956) *The Child's Conception of Space.* London: Routledge and Kegan Paul.

Piaget, J., Inhelder, B. and Szeminska, A. (1960) *The Child's Conception of Geometry.* London: Routledge and Kegan Paul.

Polya, G. (2004) *How to Solve It: A New Aspect of Mathematical Method.* Expanded Princeton Science Library Edition. Princeton, NJ: Princeton University Press.

Pound, L. (2006) *Supporting Mathematical Development in the Early Years*, 2nd edn. Maidenhead: Open University Press.

Pound, L. and Lee, T. (2011) *Teaching Mathematics Creatively.* London: Routledge.

Pratt, N. (2006) *Interactive Maths Teaching in the Primary School.* London: Paul Chapman.

Pugh, G. and De'Ath, E. (1989) *Working Towards Partnership in the Early Years.* London: National Children's Bureau.

Pulley-Sayre, A. and Sayre, J. (2003) *One is a Snail, Ten is a Crab.* London: Walker Books.

Resnick, L.B., Nesher, P., Leonard, F., Magone, M., Omanson, S. and Peled, I. (1989) 'Conceptual bases or arithmetic errors: The case of decimal fractions', *Journal for Research in Mathematics Education*, 20(1): 8–27.

Riley, J. (2007) *Learning in the Early Years*, 2nd edn. Los Angeles: Sage.

Rittle-Johnson, B. and Star, J.R. (2007) 'Does comparing solution methods facilitate conceptual and procedural knowledge? An experimental study on learning to solve equations', *Journal of Educational Psychology*, 99(3): 561–74.

Ross, S. (2002) 'Place value: Problem solving and written assessment', *Teaching Children Mathematics*, 8(7): 419–23.

Roulston, S., Law, J., Rush, R., Clegg, J. and Peters, T. (2010) *Investigating the Role of Language in Children's Early Educational Outcomes.* Research Report DFE-RR134. London: DfE. Available at: https://www.education.gov.uk/publications/eOrderingDownload/DFE-RR134.pdf (accessed: 29 May 2013).

Ryan, J. and Williams, J. (2007) *Children's Mathematics 4–15: Learning from Errors and Misconceptions.* Maidenhead: Open University Press.

Ryan, J. and Williams, J. (2010) 'Children's mathematical understanding as a work in progress: Learning from errors and misconceptions', in I. Thompson (ed.) *Issues in Teaching Numeracy in Primary Schools*, 2nd edn. Maidenhead: Open University Press.

Scanlan, M. (2011) 'Reaching out: Fostering partnership with parents', in J. Moyles, J. Georgeson and J. Payler (eds) *Beginning Teaching, Beginning Learning in Early Years and Primary Education.* Maidenhead: Open University Press.

Schaffer, H.R. (1996) *Social Development.* Oxford: Basil Blackwell.

Schaffer, H.R. (1997) *Mothering.* London: Fontana.

Schneider, M., Heine, A., Thaler, V., Torbeyns, J., De Smedt, B. and Verschaffel, L. (2008) 'A validation of eye movements as a measure of elementary school children's developing number sense', *Cognitive Development*, 23(3): 424–37.

Sinclair, J. and Coulthard, M. (1975) *Towards an Analysis of Discourse.* Oxford: Oxford University Press.

Siraj-Blatchford, I., Sylva, K., Muttock, S., Gilden, R. and Bell, D. (2002) *Researching Effective Pedagogy in the Early Years (REPEY) (Research Report 356).* London: DfES.

Skemp, R. (1971) *The Psychology of Learning Mathematics.* Harmondsworth: Penguin.

Smidt, S. (2011) *Playing to Learn: The Role of Play in the Early Years.* London: Routledge.

Sophian, C. (1995) *Children's Numbers.* Madison, WI: Brown and Benchmark.

Sophian, C. (1998) 'A developmental perspective on children's counting', in C. Donlan (ed.) *The Development of Mathematical Skills.* Hove: Psychology Press.

Spooner, M. (2002) *Errors and Misconceptions in Maths at Key Stage 2: Working Towards Success in SATs*. London: David Fulton.

Stafylidou, S. and Vosiadou, S. (2004) 'The development of students' understanding of the numerical value of fractions', *Learning and Instruction*, 14(5): 503–18.

Stephan, M. and Clements, D.H. (2003) 'Linear and area measurement in prekindergarten to Grade 2', in D.H. Clements (ed.) *Learning and Teaching Measurement*. Reston, VA: National Council of Teachers of Mathematics.

Stevens, J. and Scott, K. (2002) 'Developing mathematics out-of-doors', *Mathematics Teaching*, 180: 20–22.

Stone, P., Fisher, L. and Marshall, E. (2012) 'The benefits of engaging in research informed practice', in *Mathematics Teaching*, 227: 31–33.

Suggate, J., Davies, A. and Goulding, M. (2010) *Mathematical Knowledge for Primary Teachers*, 4th edn. Abingdon: Routledge.

Sutherland, R. (2007) *Teaching for Learning Mathematics*. Maidenhead: Open University Press.

Swan, M. (2001) 'Dealing with misconceptions in mathematics', in P. Gates (ed.) *Issues in Mathematics Teaching*. London: RoutledgeFalmer.

Swan, M. (2003) 'Making sense of mathematics', in I. Thompson (ed.) *Enhancing Primary Mathematics Teaching*. Maidenhead: Open University Press.

Tarr, P. (2004) 'Consider the walls', *Young Children*, 59(3): 88–92. Available at: http://journal.naeyc.org/btj/200405/ConsidertheWalls.pdf (accessed 10 February 2013).

Taylor, R. (2011) 'A research study of outdoor learning: An evaluation of the impact that a forest school experience has on the development of children in the Foundation Stage', unpublished MA dissertation, Canterbury Christ Church University.

Thompson, I. (2000) 'Mental calculation strategies for addition and subtraction – part 2', *Mathematics in School*, 29(1): 24–26.

Thompson, I. (2008a) 'Addressing errors and misconceptions with young children', in I. Thompson (ed.) *Teaching and Learning Early Number*, 2nd edn. Maidenhead: Open University Press.

Thompson, I. (2008b) 'From counting to deriving number facts', in I. Thompson (ed.) *Teaching and Learning Early Number*, 2nd edn. Maidenhead: Open University Press.

Thompson, I. (2008c) 'What do young children's mathematical graphics tell us about the teaching of written calculation?' in I. Thompson (ed.) *Teaching and Learning Early Number*, 2nd edn. Maidenhead: Open University Press.

Thompson, I. (2010) 'Getting your head around mental calculation', in I. Thompson (ed.) *Issues in Teaching Numeracy in Primary Schools*, 2nd edn. Maidenhead: Open University Press.

Thompson, I. and Bramald, R. (2002) *An Investigation of the Relationship between Young Children's Understanding of the Concept of Place Value and their Competence at Mental Addition* (Report for the Nuffield Foundation). Newcastle upon Tyne: University of Newcastle upon Tyne.

Threlfall, J. (2002) 'Flexible mental calculation', *Educational Studies in Mathematics*, 50(1): 29–42.

Threlfall, J. (2008) 'Development in oral counting, enumeration and counting for cardinality', in I. Thompson (ed.) *Teaching and Learning Early Number*, 2nd edn. Maidenhead: Open University Press.

Tizard, B. and Hughes, M. (1984) *Young Children Learning: Talking and Thinking at Home and at School*. London: Fontana.

Torbeyns, J., Verschaffel, L. and Ghesquière, P. (2005) 'Simple addition strategies in a first-grade class with multiple strategy instruction', *Cognition and Instruction*, 23(1): 1–21.

Tovey, H. (2007) *Playing Outdoors: Spaces and Places, Risk and Challenge*. Maidenhead: Open University Press.

Tucker, K. (2008) 'Mathematics through play', in I. Thompson (ed.) *Teaching and Learning Early Number*, 2nd edn. Maidenhead: Open University Press.

Tucker, K. (2010) *Mathematics Through Play in the Early Years*, 2nd edn. London: Sage.

Turner, S. and McCullough, J. (2004) *Making Connections in Primary Mathematics*. London: David Fulton.

Van den Heuvel-Panhuizen, M. (2001) 'Realistic mathematics education', in J. Anghileri (ed.) *Principles and Practice in Arithmetic Teaching*. Buckingham: Open University Press.

Van den Heuvel-Panhuizen, M. and Buys, K. (eds) (2005) *Young Children Learn Measurement and Geometry: A Learning-Teaching Trajectory with Intermediate Attainment Targets for the Lower Grades in Primary School*. Utrecht: Freudenthal Institute, Utrecht University.

Van Hiele, P.M. (1986) *Structure and Insight: A Theory of Mathematics Education*. Orlando: Academic Press.

Vygotsky, L.S. (1978) *Mind in Society*. Cambridge, MA: Harvard University Press.

Vygotsky, L.S. (1986) *Thought and Language*. Ed. and trans. A. Kozulin. London: MIT Press.

Warden, C. (2005) *The Potential of a Puddle*. Auchterarder: Mindstretchers.

Warden, C. (2007) *Nurture through Nature*. Auchterarder: Mindstretchers.

Wells, G. (2009) *The Meaning Makers*, 2nd edn. Bristol: Multilingual Matters.

Wheeldon, I. (2006) 'Peer talk', *Mathematics Teaching*, 199: 39–41.

White, J. (2008) *Playing and Learning Outdoors: Making Provision for High-Quality Experiences in the Outdoor Environment*. Abingdon: Routledge.

Williams, H. and Thompson, I. (2003) 'Calculators for all?', in I. Thompson (ed.) *Enhancing Primary Mathematics*. Maidenhead: Open University Press.

Williams-Siegfredsen, J. (2007) 'Developing pedagogically appropriate practice', in R. Austin (ed.) *Letting the Outside In: Developing Teaching and Learning Beyond the Early Years Classroom*. Stoke-on-Trent: Trentham Books.

Winter, J. (2010) 'Home–school knowledge exchange', in I. Thompson (ed.) *Issues in Teaching Numeracy in Primary Schools*, 2nd edn. Maidenhead: Open University Press.

Winter, J., Andrews, J., Greenhough, P., Hughes, M., Salway, L. and Yee, W.C. (2009) *Improving Primary Mathematics: Linking Home and School*. Abingdon: Routledge.

Winter, J., Salway, L., Yee, W.C. and Hughes, M. (2004) 'Linking home and school mathematics: The home–school knowledge exchange project', *Research in Mathematics Education*, 6(1): 59–75.

Wood, D. (1998) *How Children Think and Learn*, 2nd edn. Oxford: Basil Blackwell.

Wood, J. and Attfield, A. (1996) *Play, Learning and the Early Childhood Curriculum*. London: Paul Chapman.

Index